Mary Millhollon
Internet expert, Web designer, and writer

with Jeff Castrina
Web designer
and consultant

Faster Smarter

Web Page Creation

Take charge of Web design and production
faster, smarter, *better!*

PUBLISHED BY
Microsoft Press
A Division of Microsoft Corporation
One Microsoft Way
Redmond, Washington 98052-6399

Library of Congress Cataloging-in-Publication Data
Millhollon, Mary.
    Faster Smarter Web Page Creation / Mary Millhollon, with Jeff Castrina.--[2nd ed.]
       p. cm.
    Includes index.
    ISBN 0-7356-1860-7
    1. Web sites--Design.   I. Castrina, Jeff. II. Millhollon, Mary. Easy Web Page Creation.
III. Title.

TK5105.888 .M557 2002
005.7'2--dc21   2002028893

Printed and bound in the United States of America.

2 3 4 5 6 7 8 9   QWE   8 7 6 5 4 3

Distributed in Canada by H.B. Fenn and Company Ltd.

A CIP catalogue record for this book is available from the British Library.

Microsoft Press books are available through booksellers and distributors worldwide. For further informa-
tion about international editions, contact your local Microsoft Corporation office or contact Microsoft
Press International directly at fax (425) 936-7329. Visit our Web site at www.microsoft.com/mspress.
Send comments to *mspinput@microsoft.com*.

Encarta, FrontPage, Microsoft, Microsoft Press, MS-DOS, MSN, PowerPoint, and Windows are either
registered trademarks or trademarks of Microsoft Corporation in the United States and/or other countries.
Other product and company names mentioned herein may be the trademarks of their respective owners.

The example companies, organizations, products, domain names, e-mail addresses, logos, people, places,
and events depicted herein are fictitious. No association with any real company, organization, product,
domain name, e-mail address, logo, person, place, or event is intended or should be inferred.

Acquisitions Editor: Alex Blanton
Project Editor: Kristen Weatherby
Series Editor: Kristen Weatherby

Body Part No. X08-95128

Table of Contents

Part I: The Talk: Web Page Basics

In Part One, you'll learn about Web page creation and design, quell lingering feelings of doubt (yes—you *can* create Web pages), and acquire knowledge you can use to move forward with confidence. In these early chapters, you'll find all sorts of tips, tricks, and theory along with a wealth of online links to resources and examples. By the time you've finished reading Part One, you'll be ready to create the four Web sites described in Part Two.

Part II: The Walk: Creating Web Pages

In Part Two, you'll find four project chapters designed to help you acquire some well-rounded, hands-on experience as you walk through the Web site creation process. As we're sure you've heard, never underestimate the value of hands-on experience! The chapters in this part are arranged progressively, from simplest to hardest, so you can ease your way into more advanced Web page creation tasks.

Part III: The Rest: Going Live and Moving On

After you post your Web site, you should count on providing at least a small dose of continuing attention to it. Sure, you could slap any old Web page onto the Web and leave it there unattended, but your site would quickly grow dusty and probably wouldn't be revisited very often. To have a truly successful site, you need to tend to your Web pages every so often. The purpose of the Part Three chapters is to show you how to *go live* (get your pages online) and stay alive.

This book is dedicated to our readers—who time and again prove to be some of the most friendly, interesting, and eclectic people online—along with all the other creative people who keep the Internet dynamic by adding (and updating) their "two cents worth" on the Web.

Acknowledgments

First and foremost, thanks to Debbie McKenna, our agent at the Moore Literary Agency (thanks Debbie!). Next, we thank Alex Blanton, acquisitions editor at Microsoft Press, and Kristen Weatherby, an amazing editor at Microsoft Press who must've been a professional juggler in a past life, for bringing the new Faster Smarter series to fruition. We're also very appreciative of all the hard work and attention to detail exerted by the editorial and design team, including Joe Gustaitis, the principal copy editor, Ron Miller, principal tech editor, and the project team at nSight. It certainly takes a good team to create a good book.

Closer to home, we thank each other (Mary thanks Jeff, and Jeff thanks Mary)—you know you've found a good collaboration when "working" hardly feels like work at all. Finally, a special thanks to Ellen, Tim, Tori, and Mark Millhollon for visiting for three weeks during the end of this book's production cycle and keeping life outside of work highly enjoyable (you guys are *always* great to vacation with!) and, of course, thanks to Vivi, Young Link, and the Keeper of the Buried Treasure (a.k.a. Robert, Matthew, and JD) for distracting and inspiring us with their nicely offbeat and active imaginations

Introduction

Beware! If you read our earlier book *Easy Web Page Creation*, we want you to know—*Faster Smarter Web Page Creation* is an *update* of our highly acclaimed *Easy Web Page Creation* book. Many readers of *Easy Web Page Creation* are waiting for the "next installment" book—this isn't it. Instead, *Faster Smarter Web Page Creation* is the same great book (!) updated with current information and Microsoft Office XP projects (so if you're using Microsoft Office 2000, we recommend that you check out *Easy Web Page Creation*). In *Faster Smarter Web Page Creation*, the Chapter 7 MSN and Chapter 9 Word 2002 projects are completely new, and we've updated and added text, graphics, and resources throughout the entire book. Furthermore, we're continuing to offer *www.creationguide.com* as a dynamic resource for readers and the Web design community. Please visit us online anytime, regardless of whether you read *Easy Web Page Creation*, *Faster Smarter Web Page Creation*, or both. Now, on to introducing you to this book—*Faster Smarter Web Page Creation*.

Where We're Coming From

A couple years ago, while co-teaching a course on graphics and the Web, a nagging suspicion solidified into crystal clarity—people from all walks of life want to build a home page but they don't have the foggiest idea where to begin.

With that thought in mind, we visited a few bookstores to scope out some Web site creation books so that we could drop a couple book names whenever we heard the increasingly familiar "I want to make a Web site, but…" line. While rooting around bookstores, we found lots of pretty good Web design and HTML books; surprisingly, though, none wholly met our needs. We were specifically looking for a book or two that kept Web page creation simple yet comprehensive. We wanted an information-packed, easy-to-understand book for everyone that contained theory and hands-on practice—a book for our friends and acquaintances who find computers interesting but don't necessarily want to earn full-fledged geek status anytime soon. When we didn't find what we were looking for, we wrote *Easy Web Page Creation*. Now, a little over a year later, we're providing *Faster Smarter Web Page Creation* to ensure that you have the most current information in these quick-paced computer-driven days.

This Book Could Be for You

Faster Smarter Web Page Creation focuses on the great number of people who want to create a Web presence but don't have the resources or desire to hire a Webmaster. This book is for you if you have basic computing skills (such as the ability to use a mouse, open folders, run desktop programs, and so forth) and are actively contemplating building a Web site. In *Faster Smarter Web Page Creation*, we've consolidated all the facts and tips you need to know to successfully build a Web site.

As you'll soon see, the knowledge we impart in this book is designed to build on the knowledge you already have. For example, you might have an inkling that certain applications, such as Microsoft Word and Microsoft FrontPage, can dramatically shorten the Web-page-creation learning curve for most people. Furthermore, you might be aware that your Internet service provider (ISP) grants a certain amount of free server space along with your Internet connectivity—and server space certainly *sounds* like a good resource. But most would-be Web developers find that the catch lies in the details. Sure, applications and server space are readily available, but how can you combine these resources to create a Web site? In *Faster Smarter Web Page Creation*, we address this very issue, using a friendly, step-by-step (and concept-by-concept) approach to creating, posting, and maintaining Web sites on the Internet. Specifically, the book is divided into three parts and one Web site (*www.creationguide.com*), with each part (and each chapter within) building on information presented in prior sections and chapters.

- ■ **Part One—The Talk: Web Page Basics**   Part One provides the necessary background for Web page and Web site creation. In these chapters, we cover fundamental mechanics as well as design issues associated with Web sites. They are packed with information and tips about Web page text, graphics, page components, and site-creation techniques and utilities. Furthermore, we discuss key planning processes and recommend tools that come in handy during Web site creation. By the end of Part One, you'll be ready to tackle creating Web sites, which we explain how to do in detail in Part Two.

- ■ **Part Two—The Walk: Creating Web Pages**   Part Two provides you with practical, hands-on experience by walking you through the process of creating four Web sites—one per chapter. In this part of the book, we dedicate a separate chapter to creating a Web page using four different utilities—MSN, Notepad, Word, and FrontPage. Each chapter introduces the utility, presents a planning scenario, provides easy-to-follow procedures for hands-on practice, and lists additional resources.

■ **Part Three—The Rest: Going Live and Moving On**   In Part Three, you'll learn how to upload, archive, and maintain Web pages after you've created them. This part also provides information about future directions you can take in your Web development efforts—both by updating your pages and advancing your skills as a Web developer.

Faster Smarter Web Page Creation is written in an easy-going style and is packed with all the information necessary to enable you to create, post, and maintain Web sites. Each chapter begins with introductory text and concludes with a "Key Points" section that summarizes the chapter with a brief bulleted list. Every chapter includes tips, notes, sidebars, "lingo" notes to explain specialized vocabulary, and "Try This!" elements that provide you with hands-on experiences directly related to the concepts presented in the text.

Finally, for maximum assistance and convenience (and because we like to create Web sites), we've created a dynamic online resource, which we call the Creation Guide Web site (located at *www.creationguide.com*), especially for the *Faster Smarter Web Page Creation* and *Easy Web Page Creation* books. We opted to put the Internet to work instead of including a CD-ROM with our books because CD-ROMs quickly become outdated (especially when you're talking about the Web). On the companion Web site, you'll find numerous samples, resources, exercise files, links to reader pages, and reader comments. Many of the figures in the book are also featured on the Creation Guide site, and additional chapter resources can be found only online. We strongly encourage you to visit the companion site while you're reading the book (we've liberally sprinkled references to the site throughout the text) as well as any time after you've finished the book and are searching for additional resources. Plus, we'll be happy to post a link to your page on the Creation Guide site if you create a Web site you'd like to share after reading this book.

System Particulars

At this point, we need to take a couple of technical moments to discuss system requirements—nothing too complicated, though, we assure you. Fortunately, you'll find that for the most part we wrote this book for all computer platforms. The theory and Web creation basics described in Parts One and Three are almost completely universal, which means that the text applies to most computer systems and platforms. In Part Two, we do use several specific applications to show you how to create Web sites. Namely, we used Microsoft Word 2002 in

Chapter 9 and Microsoft FrontPage 2002 in Chapter 10. Otherwise, the bulk of the book's text is nonspecific to application or operating system. You might notice, though, that we captured all the screens shots on computers running Windows XP. Screen shots of online content are displayed primarily in Microsoft Internet Explorer 5, unless otherwise indicated in the text. That's about as technical as we need to get at this point. (See—that wasn't so bad.)

Most of All...

Now that we've spent a couple pages summarizing the book's approach and structure, let's put that "practical" information aside. You see, beyond this book, our sincere underlying goal is to get you started—to get you over the hump of thinking that you can't create a Web site and into the realm of realizing that you *can* build a Web site, and pretty easily, too. We designed this book to give you a strong foundation in Web development—a foundation that will serve you well now, while you create an immediate Web presence, as well as in the future, when you work on more advanced Web development endeavors. Most of all, we wrote this book so that you can experience first-hand the enjoyment of building Web pages and the value you can gain from owning your own Web site.

Support

Every effort has been made to ensure the accuracy of this book. Microsoft Press provides corrections for books at the following address:

> *http://mspress.microsoft.com/support/*

If you have comments, questions, or ideas regarding this book, please send them to Microsoft Press via e-mail to:

> *mspinput@microsoft.com*

or via postal mail to:

> Microsoft Press
> Attn: *Faster Smarter Web Page Creation* Editor
> One Microsoft Way
> Redmond, WA 98052-6399

You can also contact the authors directly at *mm@creationguide.com* or *jc@creationguide.com* with any comments or suggestions or send feedback via *www.creationguide.com/feedback.html*.

Please note that product support is not offered through the above addresses.

Part I

The Talk: Web Page Basics

The other day we went hiking with some friends. But we didn't simply wake up, stretch, walk out the front door, and start climbing. Instead, the event sort of evolved:

"Hey, want to go for a hike on Friday?"

"Sounds good. Where do you want to go?"

And without realizing it, the planning process had begun—we were *talking* about taking a hike. We were calling friends, checking online databases for nearby trails, selecting a time to meet, thinking about supplies—all this, and we hadn't even taken a single step.

Web design follows a similar path. Before you build a Web site, you need to mull it over, talk about it, learn some Web site design principles, plan how to best create your site, and gather your supplies—basically, you need to treat this like any other undertaking. You need to plan. Fortunately, *planning* doesn't have to be synonymous with *boring*.

The goal of Part One is to serve as the "Where do you want to go, and who's going to drive?" portion of the book. In this part, you'll learn about Web page creation and design, quell lingering feelings of doubt (you'll see that you *can* create Web pages), and acquire the knowledge you need to move forward with confidence. By the time you finish Part One, you'll be the proud owner of a wealth of Web design knowledge, you'll be fully prepared to start planning your own Web sites, and you'll be ready to create the four Web sites described in Part Two's project chapters. So, let's get the show on the road (and the pages on the Web)—let's talk!

Chapter 1

Demystifying Your (Future) Home Page

Most likely, you're fairly familiar with the not-so-newfangled invention called the *Internet*. Further, we're willing to bet that if you're contemplating the idea of creating a Web presence, then you know how to use a computer on some level. We're also assuming that you've surfed the Web, you can use basic applications (such as word-processing packages), and you can click a mouse with the best of 'em. Fortunately, your basic computing knowledge is all you need to be able to create Web pages—well, your basic computing knowledge along with this book, of course!

Lingo   The *Internet* is the hardware that's connected together to create a massive worldwide network.

Your first job on the road to becoming a Web page developer entails building on what you already know. For instance, in addition to moderate computing capabilities, you should have an inkling of how the Internet, the Web, and Web pages relate to one another. Therefore, in the spirit of our goal of clarity and simplicity, we'll cut to the chase in this chapter and briefly describe the main elements of the world's largest network—the Internet, the Web, and Web pages.

After we get the fundamentals out of the way, we'll spend the remainder of this book talking about planning and building your Web pages.

The Internet—Just a Bunch of Hardware

To put it simply, the Internet, or the Net, is hardware—lots of hardware—connected together to create a massive worldwide network. The Internet's hardware encompasses all the components a person can physically touch, including computers, *routers*, cables, telephone lines, high-speed data circuits, and other physical network pieces.

Lingo   *Routers* are relay components between networks.

For now, that's really all you need to know about the Internet—it's the hardware. No need to regale you with a long diatribe about how the U.S. government's Cold War paranoia spurred the development of a noncentralized computer network. If you're curious about the history of the Internet, you can find information online and at your local bookstore or library. (Also, see the resource section on this book's companion Web page at *www.creationguide.com/resources* for some history-of-the-Internet resources.) Now that we've clearly identified that the Internet is the hardware, let's take the next logical step. Like all computer hardware (think of your desktop or laptop computer), the Internet needs software—otherwise, the Internet's hardware components would simply sit and gather dust (for the most part) on a worldwide basis. Enter the World Wide Web.

Lingo   The *Web* consists of software that enables information sharing on the Internet.

The Web—Some Software for the Hardware

The World Wide Web (also known as WWW or just "the Web") is a little more esoteric than the Internet. That's because the Web consists of software (including programs, documents, and files) that enables information to travel along the Internet's hardware. To help illustrate the Web's role relative to the Internet, here's a short story we first told a few years ago when explaining the role of the Web to Internet newbies:

> Long ago (back when insects and arachnids could talk), there lived a spider of unusually bright intellect named Tim. After watching the ants work all day, Tim met up with the lead ant at the time, Bill. The ants, as usual, were incredibly successful at gathering and storing food, but Tim thought the spiders could team up with the ants to make life easier for both groups. Tim approached Bill with this plan, and Bill saw the logic in it. In fact, Bill suggested that they

incorporate other creatures into the workgroups as well. Soon, Tim and Bill recruited grasshoppers, flies, and earthworms to become partners in the food-gathering venture. The creatures thought it was a splendid idea, so they got together and created an elaborate labyrinth of anthills, spiderwebs, burrows, and tunnels to assist in the food-gathering venture. The system was in place; it looked perfect; it was time for the work to begin. But, much to the creatures' disappointment, chaos ensued. Even though all the paths and connections were in place, flies had a hard time navigating the tunnels, grasshoppers had difficulty staying in line, earthworms were just too heavy to walk across the spiderwebs, and, of course, the ants' expectations were much too high for any of the other groups to meet. What the creatures had was a network. What they needed was something or someone who could cross all mediums of the network safely. They needed a universal creature.

This short story provides a good analogy of the Internet–Web relationship. As we said earlier in this chapter, the Internet is the infrastructure for transmitting information—an infrastructure made up of computers, routers, cables, telephone lines, high-speed data circuits, and information bases called *servers* (rather than anthills, spiderwebs, and tunnels). Unfortunately, just as spiderwebs can't support earthworms, not all computers can support all computer file formats. To include every available method (or *protocol*) for understanding the various document formats on all computers would be impractical. So, the Internet community devised its own universal creature, more commonly known as the World Wide Web.

Lingo *Servers* are powerful high-capacity network-linked computers that store files and respond to users' requests to view and access the stored files. A *protocol* is a set of rules that describe how data should be transmitted. The Web uses Hypertext Transfer Protocol (HTTP) to transmit Hypertext Markup Language (HTML) documents.

Initially, Tim Berners-Lee conceived and developed the Web at the CERN laboratory in Switzerland for the high-energy physics community. (By the way, although Tim is considered to be of extremely high intellect, he is not a spider!) The Web quickly attracted a great deal of attention and spread beyond the physics arena. As with the history of the Internet, you can find reams of information about the history of the Web online and in numerous computer books.

For our purposes, you only need to know that the Internet is the hardware and the Web is the software. Simple enough. Now, we're ready to move to the next level—the files the Web software supports on the Internet hardware.

Web Pages—A Few Files on the Net

Now we come face-to-face with the heart of the matter—Web pages. Basically, when you strip away all the highfalutin technobabble, Web pages are files. To be specific, Web pages are HTML files. No need for your eyes to glaze over at the sight of "HTML"; in Part Two of this book, we clear up the mysteries of HTML. At this point, all you need to know is that Web pages are simply files that the Web supports, just like document (.doc) files are files that Microsoft Word supports.

Because Web pages are files, you don't have to stretch your imagination too far to realize that creating a Web page is simply the act of creating a specific type of file on your computer. Word documents, spreadsheets, databases, Web pages—they're all types of files. Clearly, you can see that Web pages aren't mysterious entities. They can't overwhelm you—they're computer files, and you've worked with computer files numerous times.

So, don't let Web pages intimidate you. Of course, this isn't to say that Web pages don't have a few idiosyncrasies that set them apart from other files. Namely, Web pages almost always incorporate multiple files and hyperlinks, and they are frequently rounded up into groups called *Web sites*.

Lingo   A *Web site* is a collection of related Web pages, usually including a home page and related subpages.

The Multifile Nature of Web Pages

Granted, we just said Web pages are simply files, and we stand by that. But we should clarify a bit regarding the kinds of files we're referring to. While you read the next couple paragraphs, you might think we're providing a little too much information at this point—but we're really not. You should have at least an inkling (not necessarily a firm grasp, just yet) of Web page components and interactions before we get too far along. Enough of the disclaimer; on to the information.

First, at the most basic level, every Web page is a *text document*. A text document is a file that contains words, letters, and numbers without any formatting. For instance, opening Notepad or WordPad in Microsoft Windows (click Start, point to Programs or All Programs, click Accessories, and then select Notepad or WordPad) and typing your name, a catchy phrase, miscellaneous letters, a few numbers, or anything, really, creates a text document—not a Web page, mind you, just a text document. Figure 1-1 shows a simple example of a text document open in Notepad.

Lingo   A *text document* is a file that contains words, letters, and numbers without any formatting.

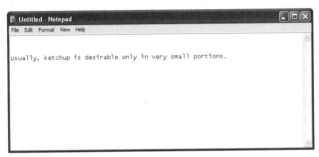

Figure 1-1   A text document contains just that—text!

To upgrade your text document to a potential Web page, you simply add specific HTML commands, as shown in Figure 1-2.

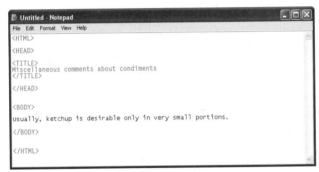

Figure 1-2   This text document contains fundamental HTML commands along with title text and one line of body text.

Web Pages and Browsers   To view Web pages, you use a browser (such as Microsoft Internet Explorer). In most cases, a browser application resides on the local computer (the computer you're working on). You can delete, install, upgrade, and customize your browser just as you delete, install, upgrade, and customize other software applications on your computer (including Microsoft Office programs, such as Word and Microsoft Excel). One slight confusion occasionally crops up regarding where the Internet ends and your computer begins. Clarifying comes easily—when you view a Web page in your browser, the toolbars, menu bars, status bars, and so forth surrounding a Web page are part of the browser application, which resides on your computer; the content within the browser's main window reflects the Internet content.

After you add HTML commands, you save the text document with an .html or .htm extension in place of .txt or .doc. (Don't sweat the specifics at this point.) Then, you can open the document in a browser application, such as Internet Explorer.

Figure 1-3 shows how the text document with the HTML commands shown in Figure 1-2 appears in a browser (to see the page online, visit *www.creationguide.com/ketchup*). Notice that only the body text and the title bar text, and not the HTML commands, appear in Figure 1-3. Just the body text and title bar text show because HTML commands merely provide instructions to browsers regarding *how* to display information, not *what* to display.

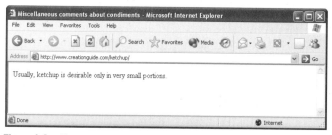

Figure 1-3   You can view a properly configured basic text document containing HTML commands in a browser.

Don't worry if this HTML explanation seems a little vague at the moment. We walk you through the process of creating a Web site using HTML in Notepad or WordPad later in this book (in Chapter 8). You'll see then that HTML is fairly clear-cut if you take it one step at a time. (And if you want some added inspiration, in other Part Two chapters you'll find that you can create Web pages without knowing HTML at all.) At this point, you mainly need to recognize the following basic premise: *Web pages are text documents.*

You might've noticed that a paradox seems to be emerging here because we've adamantly stated that Web pages are text documents. But, if Web pages are text documents, why does the Web overflow with graphics? Fortunately, you can use HTML text documents in conjunction with specific graphics file types on the Web. (Namely, the Web supports graphics files with .gif, .jpeg, and .png extensions—but let's save the graphics file format discussion for Chapter 3.)

Here's the scoop. To show a graphic on a Web page, an HTML (text) document includes commands that tell a browser where to find a particular graphic and how to display it on the page (including position, size, and so forth). Thus, the multifile nature of Web pages is unveiled. Generally, when you look at a Web page online, you're looking at a few files—an HTML (text) file and some graphics files.

Try This! You can see for yourself how HTML works. First, ensure that Windows is configured to show file extensions:

1   Open your Control Panel (in Windows XP, choose Control Panel from the Start menu; in earlier versions of Windows, click Start, point to Settings, and then click Control Panel).

2   In the Control Panel, double-click Folder Options, and then click the View tab.

3   Clear the Hide File Extensions For Known File Types check box, and then click OK.

After you've configured Windows to display file extensions, type the HTML text shown in Figure 1-2 into a Notepad document. Save the Notepad document to your desktop (so you can easily delete it later) as a text (.txt) file by selecting Text Document from the Save As Type box, and close Notepad.

Next, display your desktop, right-click the text file you just created, and select Rename. Replace the .txt extension with an .html extension. When Windows displays a message box asking if you're sure you want to change the file type (and warning you of potential "dangers"), click Yes—you're not wreaking any sort of havoc in this instance.

Now, you're ready to view the document in your browser. To do so, you can:

■   Double-click the HTML file you just created.

■   Open your browser, and drag the HTML file's icon into the browser window.

■   Open your browser, and type the path to the HTML file in the browser's Address bar.

If your file doesn't look similar to the file shown in Figure 1-3, visit *www.creationguide.com/ ketchup*, choose Source from the View menu to display the page's HTML source code (for more information about source code, see the "A Little More HTML" sidebar later in this chapter), and compare the online source code with the document you created. Keep in mind that after you change a TXT file to an HTML file, you'll need to open the document from within Notepad if you want to edit the file's text.

To illustrate the multifile concept, take a look at a past version of the Arizona Film Society's home page shown in Figure 1-4. As you can see, the Arizona Film Society's home page consists of three files—an HTML document (index.html) and two graphics files (afs_title.gif and 4members.jpg). Figure 1-5 depicts a Windows folder view of the files used to create the home page illustrated in Figure 1-4. (Notice that the Windows folder contains the same HTML file and graphics files.)

Note   As you probably know, one of the Web's major draws is its dynamic nature. Many Web pages are frequently updated and modified. To aid our discussion, we've frozen a copy of one of the Arizona Film Society's past home pages on the companion Web site, *www.creationguide.com/afs*. To see Web flux in action, visit the Arizona Film Society's current home page at *www.azfilmsociety.com* and notice that the page has been modified. (In fact, the page has been modified a number of times since we froze the sample home page we use in this chapter.)

A Little More HTML   The text and HTML commands used to create a Web page are collectively called the Web page's *source code*. (*Source code* refers to the text and HTML commands used to create a Web page.) Most browsers enable you to display a Web page's source code. For example, to display source code using Internet Explorer, you choose Source from the View menu, as shown here:

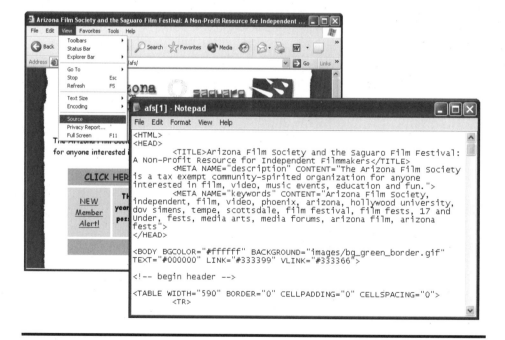

Index.html (Home Page)

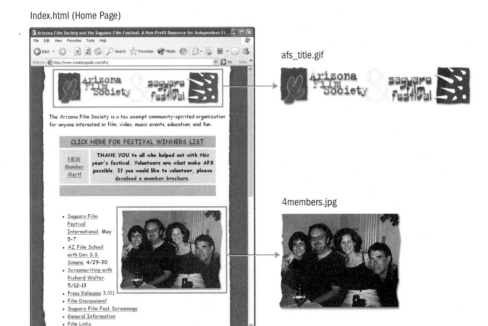

Figure 1-4   An HTML text file and two graphics files combining to create the Arizona Film Society's home page (*www.creationguide.com/afs*).

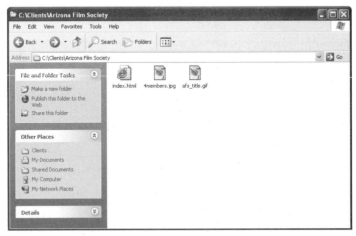

Figure 1-5   The folder view of the Arizona Film Society's home page shows that three files combine to display the page online.

After reviewing Figures 1-4 and 1-5, you're ready for another "bottom line" blanket statement. Basically, you need to walk away from this discussion with the following information: *When you view a Web page in your Internet browser, you're usually viewing a number of files working together to create a single page.*

Having safely tucked away the knowledge that a Web page consists of multiple files, you should now consciously consider that a Web page isn't a solo form of communiqué, like a flyer on your windshield. Instead, a Web page almost always uses hyperlinks to link to other Web pages.

Lingo *Hyperlinks* are clickable text or graphics that enable you to access additional Internet resources, such as another location on the current Web page, another Web page, or a file for downloading.

Hyperlinks and Web sites

As we stated at the beginning of this chapter, we assume that if you want to create a Web page, you've surfed the Web. Thus, you've most likely clicked numerous *hyperlinks.* As you probably know, hyperlinks are clickable text or graphics that enable you to access additional Internet resources and Web pages. More technically speaking, hyperlinks are elements included in HTML documents that point to other Web pages or Internet documents (similar to how some HTML commands point to graphics files) or other areas on the same page. Figure 1-6 shows how a couple hyperlinks on the Arizona Film Society's home page point to other Web pages. Clicking a hyperlink displays another area on the current page or another Web page—which can be any page on the Internet (not just a Web page you've created), located anywhere in the world.

As a Web page developer, using hyperlinks naturally progresses to using multiple Web pages. Generally speaking, you usually won't want to place all your information on one big, long home page. Instead, you'll probably want to create a series of smaller Web pages that relate and link to one another. This collection of related pages forms your Web site.

Index.html (Home Page)   winners.html

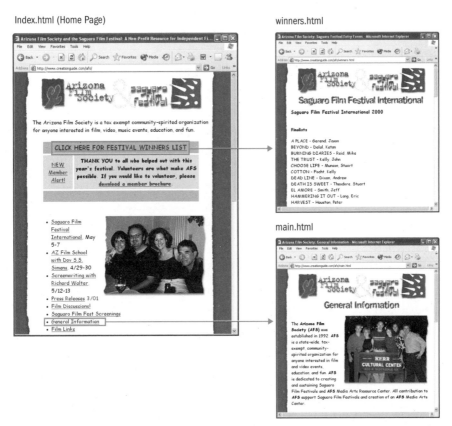

main.html

Figure 1-6   Hyperlinks take viewers to other Web pages, other areas on the same page, or other Internet resources.

From Your Head to the Web (and Back Again)

At this point in the chapter, the components are laid on the table: the Internet, the Web, browsers, Web pages, hyperlinks, and Web sites. This roll call of components is a good start, but we face the small detail of how a text file and a few graphics files that you've created on your computer are turned into a Web page on the Internet. Before we wade too deeply into the muck and mire of Web page transmissions, let's debunk a surprisingly popular myth: *People who view your Web pages have access to your desktop computer.* The preceding statement is *not* true! Rest assured, Web pages are not stored on personal computers. Instead, Web page files are stored on *servers.*

The Client/Server Nature of the Web

Servers are simply powerful computers that store Internet files and run special software designed to respond to *client requests*. Of course, now we've introduced the term *client*. Let's stop this circuitous approach and briefly indulge in some geekspeak.

Basically, Web files are transmitted using what is known as the *client/server model*. In the client/server model, one system (a server) connected to a network serves the request of another system (the client). For the purposes of Web design, a *client* is a fancy name for a browser (such as Internet Explorer) running on a user's computer, and a *server* is the combination of a powerful computer that stores Web pages and the software that responds to requests to display Web pages stored on that powerful computer. Therefore, when you access a Web page, the following process takes place:

1   You connect your computer to the Internet and open your browser. Then you enter a Web address (URL) in the Address bar and press Enter, or you click a hyperlink on your browser's start page.

> **Lingo**   URL (pronounced "you-are-ell") stands for *Uniform Resource Locator*. A URL refers to an Internet address that tells your Web browser where to look on the Internet to find a specific Web page.

2   The client (your browser) sends the typed URL or the URL associated with a hyperlink across phone lines, cables, and maybe routers to your Internet service provider (ISP). Your ISP is the company you pay to provide you with access to the Internet.

3   Your ISP then sends your URL request across the Internet through more cables, routers, and other high-speed data circuits to the system (the server) maintaining the requested Web page.

4   The server sends the Web page information across the Internet to your ISP, and, finally, your ISP forwards the information to your computer.

> **Note**   Please keep in mind that this chapter presents a simplified (albeit accurate) explanation of the basic Web page retrieval process.

From a Web page developer's perspective, after you create a Web page, you copy your Web page's files to a server that will be hosting your Web page—similar to how you can copy a file from your hard disk onto a floppy disk (except that you copy your Web page's files across Internet lines, as described later in this book in Chapter 11). Using current File Transfer Protocol (FTP) applications, Web Folders (and My Network Places), or Web publishing wizards, the process of copying your Web page files to a server can be as simple as dragging files from your local folder into a folder on the server you're using to host your Web site. Therefore, when others view your published Web page, they access the server that stores copies of your files, not your computer.

That's a wrap on our fundamentals review. At this point, you're ready to forge ahead with the design and implementation of your Web pages, as described in the upcoming pages of this book. But before closing this chapter, we'd like to brief you on what's coming in the next few chapters.

Progressing at a Steady Clip

As you might suspect, much of the work of creating a Web page entails planning your Web page (and Web site) before you sit down at your computer. You need to spend at least a little time thinking about content—including text and graphics—as well as devising your page's layout. Although designing Web pages is a creative process, it's not a black art devoid of structure. In the course of this book, we pass along a few basic tenets that will help make the process of creating your Web page easier. Our expertise comes not only from our own years of online experience but also from numerous usability studies that many other designers, engineers, and information specialists have performed. From these sources, we have drawn some basic conclusions about text, graphics, and colors on the Web that we have proven in practice. Therefore, the remaining chapters in Part One—Chapters 2 through 6—address the information you should know about Web page design, including issues surrounding text, graphics, colors, helpful software programs, and Web page planning. You'll find the next few chapters packed with pertinent Web page creation information that will make your future Web design endeavors more successful. Therefore, we highly recommend that you read (or at least scan) Part One before diving into Part Two.

Of course, we also know that you might be champing at the bit to create a Web presence *now*. We know the feeling. Thus, if you simply can't wait, go ahead and skip to Chapter 7 to get your feet wet by creating your first Web page on MSN's free server space. Similar to some other online services, MSN offers free server space to users who want to create Web pages by using an online wizard. You can create an MSN Group Web site within an hour or two and have your first Web page with your very own URL posted today. If you do decide to jump ahead to Chapter 7, be sure to return to Chapters 2 through 6 to brush up on the basics of creating Web pages before you go any further. Then you'll be fully prepared to create the more advanced Web pages presented in Chapters 8 through 10.

Finally, regardless of how you wind your way through this book and onto the Web, when all's said and done, remember to review Chapters 11 and 12. Chapter 11 describes how to go "live" (if you're using any method of Web page publishing other than MSN or another free hosting service), and Chapter 12 addresses updating and archiving your information. Although updating and archiving might sound fairly dull, these processes are critical. After all, if you spend time and effort to create a Web page, you probably won't want it to shrivel and die from neglect within a few weeks.

All in all, by the time you complete this book, you'll have mastered the basics of creating Web pages in a number of ways. You'll no longer cringe when you see expressions like *HTML* and *domain name*, and your skills will serve as a strong foundation that you can build on to create a wide variety of more advanced Web pages.

Key Points

- The Internet is hardware.

- The Web is software (including programs and documents).

- Browsers are applications that enable you to view Web pages.

- Most basic Web pages consist of multiple files—an HTML (text) file and graphics files.

- A Web site is a group of related Web pages.

- Hyperlinks provide access to other Web pages, other locations on the same page, and other Internet resources.

- The Internet uses the client/server model, in which a server responds to client requests for information.

- Internet users access Web pages that are stored on servers.

- If you can use a computer, you can create a Web page!

Chapter 2

Creating and Shaping Web Text

When people contemplate building Web pages, they usually think of design first—that is, how the page will look rather than what it should say. And that's understandable as well as desirable. In fact, quite a bit of this book is devoted to Web page design. But at the heart of every Web page is *content*. After all, most people build Web pages because they have a message they want to share—even if that message simply proclaims, "Look what I've been up to lately!"

To be successful, your Web page must provide information that quickly captures viewers' attention; otherwise, viewers won't stay more than a couple of seconds and probably won't return. Therefore, you should start to think about your Web page's content before you get too far into its design.

If you follow along with this text, you'll be well on your way to having your Web pages' content fully spelled out and formulated by the end of this chapter. But even if you don't progress that far in creating content for a particular Web site, you'll be able to identify and create good Web text in general. Furthermore, you'll know how you can maximize the use of text on your future Web pages.

With this know-how in mind, you'll be able to ease into blending content and design when you start to build your Web pages.

Now, back to the matter at hand—online text. Reasonably enough, you might be thinking that you're quite capable of using words so you don't really need to read about Web page text. But rest assured, even if you're a full-time writer, you can benefit from the tips in this chapter. Although good online text has a lot in common with good printed text, it also varies from printed text in a number of key ways. You'll see as you progress through this chapter that creating effective online text involves mastering and blending the arts of clarity, marketing, visual appeal, technological limitations, and a little reader psychology.

Readers' Approach to Online Pages

The first concept you need to address is that readers respond to Web pages differently from the way they respond to printed pages. In early studies, Web experts found that reading a block of text online took approximately 25 percent longer than reading the same text on a printed page. In other words, in the amount of time you spend reading 75 words online, you could read 100 words on a printed page. Experts now debate whether online reading speeds are on the rise due to improved monitors, use of color, or general increased familiarity of reading online text. Regardless of exact percentages, the majority of experts agree—people's reading speeds slow down significantly when they read online text (as compared to hard copy text), even though many people are getting better at reading online. One way people have adapted to the slowness of online text reading is that they frequently *scan* Web page text instead of reading every word that flashes across the monitor.

Basically, a user scans a Web page to find an item of interest that encourages the user to click a link or back up and read the content in more depth. If a Web page doesn't grab a user quickly—within 10 seconds (according to most usability studies)—the user will very likely move on to another page (or another site altogether). Creating easily scanned pages also increases your Web page's credibility as well as improves the page's chance of being ranked higher by search engines (because your Web page's main ideas are easier to identify). Therefore, whenever you create content for a Web page, keep the scanning concept in the forefront of your thought processes. In this chapter, we describe a variety of methods you can employ to improve your Web pages' scannability.

Note   On average, most visitors determine within 10 seconds if a Web page contains the information they want or need. If the Web page seems to fulfill their need, most users will still spend less than 30 seconds viewing the Web page.

To illustrate the scanning concept, compare Figures 2-1 and 2-2. (You can view the Web pages shown in these figures online at *www.creationguide.com/ants/bulletant-bad.html* and *www.creationguide.com/ants/bulletant-good.html*.) Figure 2-1 shows a Web page that doesn't adhere to good online-text practices, whereas Figure 2-2 follows the textual advice presented in this chapter. Notice how much faster you can identify the text's main points in Figure 2-2 than in Figure 2-1. The upcoming text explains why and provides pointers for you to use when creating your own online text.

Figure 2-1   An ineffective presentation of Web page text can send readers off packing before they read a word of your content.

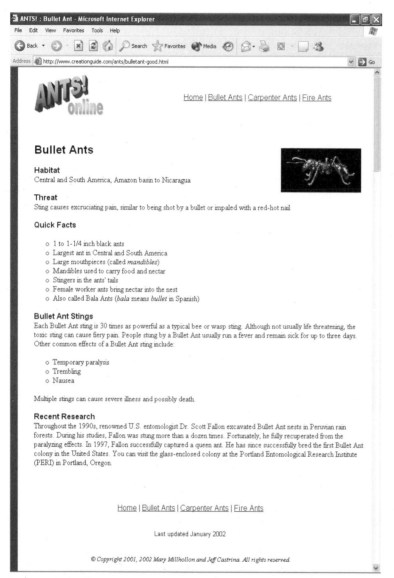

Figure 2-2   An effective presentation of Web page text provides a high level of scannability, making it easy for readers to find the information they need.

Now that we've made a case for thinking about your text and recognizing how readers approach Web pages, let's briefly look at the fundamental roles text plays on a Web page. Then we'll discuss the details involved in shaping and streamlining online text.

Textual Elements of a Web Page

Most Web pages use a variety of textual components, as illustrated in Figure 2-3. As you can see in the figure (as well as on most Web pages), the textual elements described in the following subsections appear on Web pages.

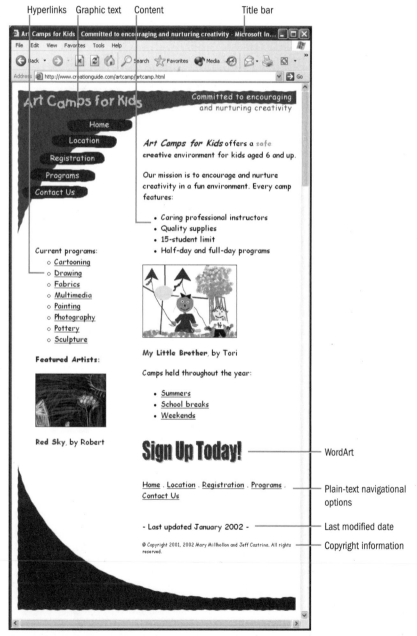

Figure 2-3   Effective Web pages contain a number of common textual elements.

Title Bar

When you create a Web page, you create the text that appears in a browser window's title bar. The key to title text is to make it concise, clear, and useful. Notice that when you open a Web page, the Web page's title text also appears in your Microsoft Windows taskbar. Taskbar text simplifies a user's job when switching among a number of open windows. Therefore, although you can insert clever or witty title text if you want to, you should generally lean toward useful and clear instead. Notice the lame vs. helpful title bar text shown earlier in Figures 2-1 and 2-2.

> **Tip**   For added clarity (on taskbar buttons especially), skip leading articles (*the, a, an*) in a Web page's title bar text. Using snappy, descriptive titles helps your pages stand out within users' workspaces as well as stand out in search engine results that organize Web pages by title.

Content

A Web page's content refers to its substance—the reason people are visiting the site. As described in the next few sections, a Web page's content should be clear, brief, easy to scan, informative, timely, and grammatically correct (among other qualities). Keep in mind that no matter how beautiful a Web site, the Internet's most engaging feature is text. After all, in addition to Web sites, a few hundred million people regularly rely on online text to send e-mail messages, chat using instant messaging, and post to discussion groups.

> **Tip**   One way to obtain content for your Web pages is to take advantage of Web content providers. A number of news bureaus, media centers, special interest groups, private contractors, and other information specialists provide Web content to Web sites on a regular basis, usually for a fee. To find a content provider, visit your favorite search engine (we like *www.google.com*) and search for Web content providers.

Hyperlinks

Hyperlinks provide form and clarity to a group of Web pages (or one long Web page) by linking your home page (as well as ancillary pages) to areas that contain specific related information. In other words, hyperlinks help you to organize your information, and they enable others to access your information quickly and easily. Textual hyperlinks should be clear, consistent, and appropriately placed, as we discuss later in this chapter and in Chapter 4.

> **Note**   You'll notice that we use the words *link* and *hyperlink* interchangeably.

Logos, Graphical Text, and WordArt

You can use logos, graphical text, and WordArt to add a professional look to your Web pages. As we explain in Chapter 3, you can use graphical text to add a consistent look and feel to a group of related Web pages. Having all the parts of your Web site appear interrelated clearly indicates to users that they are still within the realm of your Web site even as they click from page to page. Furthermore, logos, graphical text, and WordArt are frequently used to provide a consistent graphical link to a site's home page. You might have discovered while surfing the Web that you can usually click a company's logo to return to the site's home page. (If you haven't discovered this secret, you should test it out during your next Web surfing session.) Whenever possible, take advantage of this practice by linking your logo to your home page throughout your Web site.

Lingo   *Graphical text* is a general term that refers to text used to create graphical elements on your Web pages, including stylized buttons, banners, titles, and so forth. *WordArt* is a Microsoft Word feature that enables you to create stylized text-based graphics, such as custom headings and logos. For example, in Figures 2-1 and 2-2, we created the "Ants! Online" logo element using Word's WordArt feature, and in Figure 2-3 the "Sign Up Today!" graphical text is a WordArt element.

Try This!   If you're viewing the "good" Ants! Online page (Figure 2-2) online, you can click the *Ants! Online* WordArt logo in the page's upper-left corner to display the fictitious site's home page.

Forms and Menu Items

Although not illustrated in this chapter's figures, some Web pages use text for forms and menu items. We imagine you've run across online forms (especially if you've purchased a book or CD from Amazon.com or viewed an online map in Microsoft Encarta). The key to forms and menus is clarity—users must clearly know what to select, how to enter text in a form's text boxes, and which action they should perform next. We won't be working with forms and menu items until much later in this book (Chapter 10) because forms and menus are fairly advanced techniques for Web pages. In the meantime, if you're interested in reading up on the role that text plays in creating forms and menus, thumb through some graphical user interface (GUI, pronounced "gooey") books, which you can find in bookstores and libraries. Be careful before you invest in a GUI book, though; many GUI books target programmers and software developers and the text might present more information than you need.

Plain-Text Navigational Options

Many Web designers opt to format their menu bar and navigation elements (buttons) only as graphics (in Figure 2-3, the buttons in the top-left area essentially serve as the home page's navigation bar). Using graphic navigation elements is fine, but we recommend that you also display your navigation hyperlinks as plain text in conjunction with your graphic elements. If your Web page's design uses a graphical menu bar or buttons, you can avoid disrupting the layout of your Web pages by showing textual hyperlinks along the bottom of your page. Offering an alternative to graphics-based links is useful because some viewers turn off their browser's graphics capabilities to expedite Web page downloads. If you don't provide text-based navigation components, some users might not discover how to get to your site's ancillary pages.

> **Tip**   As an added bonus, adding text-based navigation links to the bottom of your Web pages helps users move to other pages in your Web site without having to scroll to the top of the current page to access the main navigation links.

Date or "Last Modified" Information

Generally, you should include a date element on your Web pages. The date can be as nondescript as a small line of text located near the bottom of your page. If regularly updated content is one of your page's main selling points, however, you might want to make the date much more noticeable by placing it higher on your page and nearer the "prime" upper-left area. On the other hand, if you don't plan to update your site regularly, you might opt to omit publishing a last-modified date. (Frankly, we don't recommend that you plan on *not* updating your site, but in some circumstances you might be able to get away with a static page or two within your site.)

> **See Also**   You'll hear more about the importance of Web pages' upper-left corner in Chapter 4.

Copyright Information

You own the copyright to all original text and graphics you create. Therefore, to protect your property, you should add a copyright notice to your Web pages. Keep in mind that if you use freeware (such as copyright-free graphics that you've downloaded from another Web site) on your Web page, the freeware is free for anyone else to use as well.

When you add copyright text, the information can be as simple as
© Copyright 2002 Your Name or Company Name. All rights reserved. Furthermore,

the copyright information should be placed near the bottom of the page and in a font size that's noticeably smaller than the Web page's body text.

Tip   To create © in Microsoft Word, press Ctrl+Alt+C.

Now that we've touched on the basic textual elements of Web pages, you're ready to shape and write Web page content.

Writing for the Web

As mentioned earlier in this chapter, good Web writing shares some basic similarities with well-written printed text. For example, Web text should be clear, grammatical, and well formulated, and it should be written for a specific audience. But Web text requires some unique considerations that don't crop up when you're writing for another medium. One reason Web text requires this unique approach is that Web pages are *nonlinear*. Users don't often methodically read through a Web page or Web site as they would a novel; nor do they "watch" a Web site in the way they would a scripted TV show. Instead, Web surfers scan a page, read a couple snippets of text that interest them, click a link (you hope), possibly read a paragraph or two in depth, check out a picture or other multimedia element, and then click again to access another page or site. Therefore, you need to form and mold your text (and page design) to cater to the desires and habits of Web surfers.

Web Text Attracts Users' Attention Before Graphics   Here's yet another reason to take your Web page's text seriously. According to Jakob Nielsen, author of *Designing Web Usability* (New Riders, 2000) and a leading expert on Web page usability, Web text frequently grabs a reader's attention before graphics do. As Nielsen reports, "It is almost twice as common for users to fixate on the text as on the images upon their initial visit to a page. In general, users were first drawn to headlines, article summaries, and captions. They often did not look at the images at all until the second or third visit to a page."

Organizing Web Text

Writing Web text requires you to take a new approach to wordsmithing—specifically, when writing for the Web, you need to think *topic*, not *document*. Fortunately, you can effectively shape your Web text by using a combination of methods. Namely, you should adhere to the inverted pyramid methodology (described next) whenever possible, use headings and hyperlinks effectively, and streamline your paragraphs and body text.

Inverted Pyramid Methodology

Most Web professionals liken Web content to newspaper text. And to an extent, the analogy works. Like news text, Web text should fundamentally take the classic *inverted pyramid* form. An inverted pyramid approach places the most important information at the beginning of a story, including stating the conclusion up front (usually in the heading). In traditional news writing, a good story answers the questions *Who? What? Where? When? Why?* and *How?* as rapidly and succinctly as possible in order of importance. For example, a news report on a freeway car fire would probably first answer the question *What?*—a car fire—and then quickly answer the questions *Where?*—on the freeway—*When?*—during rush hour—and *Why?*—overheated engine. Of course, if the burning car belonged to the president, the story's *Who?* element would jump to the top of the pyramid. After the key points are stated in an inverted pyramid story, the remainder of the article serves to fill in the details and wind down to the least important information at the end.

As we said, you should also generally take an inverted pyramid approach when you're writing Web pages, especially if your page contains substantial textual content. A number of online news sites effectively use a modified approach to the inverted pyramid setup. For example, *www.iwon.com*, one of our favorite news sites, uses a clear-cut variation of the inverted pyramid. On *www.iwon.com*, the home page shows links similar to the following hierarchy under a "Today's Headlines" heading:

Top News
    Headline
    Headline
    . . .

Sports News
    Headline
    Headline
    . . .

Business News
    Headline
    Headline
    . . .

Entertainment News
    Headline
    Headline
    . . .

Using the preceding setup, users can click a main heading (such as Top News, Sports News, Business News, or Entertainment News in the preceding example) to view the first few lines of each headline's story. For example, let's say you click the Top News link. You would then see the following layout:

Top story
    A few lines of text providing the main gist of the story
More Headlines
Headline
    A few lines of text providing the main gist of the story
Headline
    A few lines of text providing the main gist of the story

At this point, you could click a headline to read the full version of the story. Notice the trickle-down effect of the information—main headline, short synopsis, and full story. Imagine if the home page contained every full news story of the day—readers would flee from the text-packed site quicker than the page could download.

Note   To help speed up the trickle-down informational process, you can also click a headline on the *www.iwon.com* home page to display the full story of any headline that immediately captures your interest.

Try This!   To see a large collection of examples of manipulating text online, visit the Headwaters News site at *www.headwatersnews.org*. This site provides links to numerous online newspapers covering the Rockies and is a project of the Center for the Rocky Mountain West at the University of Montana. Click links to stories on the site to see a wide variety of examples of how different news sites display text. Compare how the text is treated on the various sites—notice the font faces, font sizes, alignment techniques, column widths, white spaces, and so forth—and determine what you believe works and doesn't work. Then, you can apply your findings to your own Web pages.

Although the news-site setup described here is highly effective, it's probably much more complex than your Web pages need to be. (We're pretty sure you're relieved to hear that!) The setup of *www.iwon.com* provides a good example of the inverted pyramid methodology. On your pages, you'll be more concerned with ensuring that your most important points (the key points in an inverted pyramid) display quickly and "jump out" at readers. You can achieve this effect by employing a few key techniques, including using headings and hyperlinks wisely and streamlining your text for Web use.

Brainstorms, Headings, and Hyperlinks

Now that the theory of serving the best information first is firmly in place, you're ready to start thinking about actual content. When it comes to creating text, some people have a hard time getting started. Therefore, we suggest a popular, free-form approach to creating your Web text—brainstorming with a pencil, pen, or keyboard. To effectively brainstorm, follow these steps:

1 Sit down with a pad of paper (or your laptop, if you're lucky), and jot down every concept you want to include in your Web site or Web page. Don't worry about organization or wording. The goal here is to get your ideas out of your head and onto paper (or screen).

2 After you have all the topics that you want to include on your Web page in front of you in hard-copy form (print your electronic notes, if necessary), write a *keyword* next to each topic. You might find that multiple topics can be associated with the same keyword. That's fine— in fact, that will help you group your information later. Again, don't overanalyze the details; you're working on big umbrella concepts at this point.

> **Lingo**   A *keyword* is a word or phrase that succinctly summarizes the overall essence of a concept or topic. Frequently, a keyword also serves as a main idea that encompasses a group of related concepts.

3 Review each keyword, and determine which keywords deserve to be headings and which should be hyperlinks. A heading calls attention to a brief amount of information on an existing page; in contrast, a hyperlink indicates that you have enough related text to create a separate Web page from existing information or that you've organized chunks of information on the current page into logical sections.

Figures 2-1 and 2-2 shown earlier in this chapter provide an ideal example of effective brainstorming. As you can see, Figure 2-1 displays a large block of text—essentially an information brain dump; Figure 2-2 shows where keywords (formatted as headings) come into play to point out the main facts included in the text. If you were brainstorming about bullet ants, you might come up with the paragraph in Figure 2-1. Then when you reviewed your paragraph, you would come up with the heading topics shown in Figure 2-2. Remember—clearly calling attention to key points for users is critical. Not only is reading online more arduous than reading printed text, but millions of Web pages are also vying for users' time and attention.

> **Tip**   To determine whether key topics should be hyperlinks on your home page, visualize your home page as a fancy table of contents that summarizes the Web site's main ideas and points users to each area of the site. (See the home page shown in Figure 2-3.)

To illustrate how brainstorming can organize a Web *site* as well as a Web *page*, let's view the Ants! Online menu bar shown in Figure 2-4. By looking at the menu bar's hyperlinks, you can instantaneously see that the Ants! Online site includes a home page and three ant species pages. You can almost visualize exactly how the site's brainstorming session might've progressed—the types of ants emerged as the big ideas (thereby necessitating hyperlinks and separate Web pages), and the main facts about each type of ant served to create headings (such as Habitat, Threat, Quick Facts, and so forth, as shown in Figure 2-2). Brainstorming—which is the first step before outlining or flowcharting a Web site—helps you visualize your approach to your Web pages and Web site, which in turn helps you write clear, topic-driven text.

Figure 2-4   The Ants! Online menu bar clearly defines the site's organization.

The Shape of Body Text

At this point, you should have a fair idea of the information you want to include on your home page, as well as the logical headings. You should also have a feel for possible ancillary (linked) pages. You're now ready to begin molding the ideas you freely jotted down into user-friendly text. In other words, it's time to write.

Copyrights and Web Text   Because you'll be creating and publishing text on the Web, you should know a little about copyright laws. Copyright laws protect intellectual property. Among other countries, most of Europe, Canada, Japan, and the United States are members of the Berne Union, and they adhere to the rulings of the Berne Convention, which initially laid the groundwork for copyright issues in 1886 and has since passed through a number of revisions.

According to current Berne Convention guidelines, a writer of an original work automatically holds the work's copyright (unless the writer specifically waives that right) for life plus 50 years at a minimum. Some countries guarantee a longer copyright; for example, the United States grants a copyright for life plus 70 years after death. Furthermore, the Berne Convention rulings stipulate that a copyright is granted automatically, without any paperwork or other required formalities.

Keep in mind that the copyright laws protect the actual words used to express an idea—not the idea itself. Therefore, you shouldn't copy text off the Web and paste it into your site. Instead, if you want to include information you found on another site, you should paraphrase relevant text and reference the original source or provide a link to the original source's Web page.

Fortunately, you don't need to stall yourself at this time by fixating on finding the perfect words (which don't exist!) or devising precise sentence structures. Right now, simply formulate your message in rough-draft form. Use the inverted pyramid style to organize your brainstormed ideas. Cut to the chase and display your main topics first. Then convert your brainstormed ideas into readable sentences and clear headings. Most of all, keep in mind that readers will scan your page before they ever read your paragraphs, so begin to implement or at least think about visual cues—such as headings, sidebars, and formatted typography. (In Chapter 4, we describe how to use page-layout elements that can add to your page's scannability as well.) That's a lot to keep in mind. To help simplify this stage, here's a checklist of considerations you can refer to as you write Web text:

❑   Introduce one idea per paragraph.

> **Note**   In the next section, we describe how to streamline your Web text, so if your paragraphs run a little long at this stage, don't sweat it.

❑   Keep sentences short without dumbing down.

❑   Use simple sentence structures. Avoid compound sentences and unnecessary subordinate clauses.

❑   Think about how you can highlight keywords later during the design phase (such as by inserting hyperlinks or using color or typeface variations, as shown in Figure 2-3).

❑   Aim to limit paragraphs to approximately 75 words or fewer, if possible. In Figure 2-2, the "Recent Research" paragraph shows the approximate maximum length of an online paragraph.

❑   Use bulleted lists whenever possible.

❑   Use numbered lists only when you're presenting a series of steps.

❑   Insert informative headings and subheadings to break up text and highlight key points.

❑   Keep headlines simple and direct, use active verbs, and choose meaningful over clever wording—a reader who scans only a Web page's headlines should leave the page with at least some valuable information.

❑   Ensure that the hierarchy of the headings is clear, both editorially and visually. In other words, make sure your main headings follow a logical system of subordination and are displayed uniquely, such as by formatting main headings larger than subheadings or differentiating them by color or typeface. On Web pages, using two or three levels of headings is plenty.

❑   Separate paragraphs within a section by using *white space* (space without any content, either textual or graphical). As you'll see in Chapters 3 and 4 (and beyond), white space is your friend!

❑   Avoid having too many hyperlinks in body text. Don't embed hyperlinks within paragraphs unless the hyperlinks add extremely pertinent information to your content and you're sure readers will return to your page after clicking the embedded link. Embedding hyperlinks within paragraphs frequently leads readers astray. Generally, hyperlinks should be used to aid navigation.

Writing Effectively for an Online Audience

You've organized your information by topic, written paragraphs, added bulleted lists, inserted headings, and indicated which key points will serve as hyperlinks. Your Web text should be shaping up nicely by now, but the actual wording probably still needs some attention. As with all good writing, you're not finished with the process until you've polished and streamlined your text (as well as read and revised it at least a million times!). One way to fine-tune your text is by looking for and avoiding specific types of writing weaknesses. The number-one way to streamline Web text entails strengthening your sentences.

Strong Sentences

Never fear—you won't need steroids or garlic to create strong sentences. Strengthening your sentences merely involves packing as much meaning into each word or clause as possible. As we discussed earlier in this chapter, because you want to limit the number of words you use to convey your Web page's information, you need to make the most of the words that make the cut.

On Web pages, conciseness is the key (so if you're a Dickensian writer, you'll face a greater challenge than the minimalists out there). To strengthen your text, go through your copy word by word and line by line to ensure that the text implements the following techniques as much as possible:

Tip   When writing precise Web text, be cautious when using terms that have alternate online significance, such as *home, back, forward, browse*, and so forth.

■ **Precise words**   Your text should use clear, easily understood words. If you mean *Haight & Ashbury*, don't write *The intersection in which Haight Street crosses across Ashbury Street*.

In addition, opt for shorter words over longer words. For instance, choose *use* instead of *utilize*, or choose *lie* instead of *prevarication*.

■ **Strong verbs**   Whenever possible, your sentences should use short, solid verbs. For example, instead of writing *This page serves to explain* ... simply write *This page explains* ...

Also, replace *to be* verbs (*is, are, was, were*—you get the idea) with more specific action verbs whenever possible. For example, instead of writing *The TV is on in the background, and it's loud.* replace both instances of *is* with one strong verb: *The TV blares in the background.*

When you use strong verbs, you add life to your text and frequently reduce sentence lengths.

Tip   To practice reworking sentences, surf the Web for a while. When you see passive text or weak verbs, stop and consider how you could modify the text to be more concise, precise, and active.

■ **Active voice**   When you use active voice, your sentences clearly show who or what performs the action. Using active voice works hand in hand with implementing strong verbs. To illustrate, here's a passive-voice sentence: *Many homes were destroyed by the tornado.*

Notice that the tornado performed the action (destroyed), yet the word *tornado* appears dead last in the sentence. To make the preceding sentence active, move the word that's performing the action closer to the beginning of the sentence and change the verb, as follows: *The tornado destroyed many homes.*

■ **Clear antecedents** Frequently, writers insert pronouns—such as *it, he, she, they,* and so forth—and readers are left wondering just what the pronoun refers to. You can easily eliminate antecedent problems by replacing all unclear pronouns with specific text. (Hint: When in doubt, replace the pronoun; better to be overly clear than even slightly vague.) A key antecedent tip is to limit the use of the word *it,* and especially avoid starting sentences with weak "crutch" constructs, such as *It is*. For example, the following sentence is grammatically correct but not as strong as it could be: *It is common for cats to sleep all day while you work to put food in their bowls.*

You can strengthen this sentence simply by eliminating *It is*, as follows: *Commonly, cats sleep all day while you work to put food in their bowls.*

You should also avoid starting your sentences with *There is* and *There are*. Both constructs are weak and almost as commonly overused as *It is*.

Something You Can Do to Keep Things Clear Watch out for all variations of the word *thing*—the term frequently weakens otherwise strong sentences and headings. To quickly eliminate this vagary from your text, use your word processor's Search feature to find each instance of *thing*. (Some writers might be surprised to see how often the term pops up.) Replace the word with more specific terminology whenever you can.

Spelling and Grammar

After you streamline your text, the final stage of writing involves checking your spelling and grammar. This step has few gray areas, so we'll put it simply: *Always, always, always run your spelling checker on your Web page's copy (yet be vigilantly aware of its limitations). Then print out your text and read it from the hard-copy version—out loud!*

Reading your copy out loud slows down your perception of the text so that you can see misspellings as well as hear when your grammar takes a nosedive. If you change your text significantly during your hard-copy read-through, make the changes to your Web text, save the changed text, print it out, and read it aloud again. At this point, you might even consider having a friend or professional read over your text to gain the benefit of a "second pair of eyes." Finally, when you think you have your text just right, put it down for a couple hours (or longer). Then return to the hard copy with fresh eyes and ears, and read it aloud one last time.

Our recommended polishing process might sound time-consuming and possibly annoying to anyone sitting in your general vicinity, but it's well worth it. (And if you're concerned about wasting paper by repeatedly printing your modified Web text, cross out the old text and print the revised edition on the page's flip side.) Almost no other Web site design error erodes your credibility faster than misspellings and incorrect grammar on your Web pages.

Tip   If you need to brush up on your grammar skills, we highly recommend that you snag a copy of *When Words Collide: A Media Writer's Guide to Grammar and Style* (Wadsworth, 1999, now in its fifth edition) by Lauren Kessler and Duncan McDonald. Because the guide targets media writers, you'll also find tips regarding how to streamline your text (including creating active sentence structures, avoiding compound sentences, applying proper punctuation, and more).

Tricks to Proofreading Online Text   Because misspellings, bad grammar, and typographical errors steal your online credibility, you should take polishing your Web text seriously. Here's a quick list of sure-fire techniques that you can use when you proofread your online text:

- Set aside time for proofreading and *only* proofreading. Don't try to proofread while you reformat headings, adjust table settings, or complete some other task.

- Go through your text multiple times and check different elements during each pass. For example, on one pass, check just the spelling and capitalization of headings. In subsequent passes you can check figure captions, acronyms, side bars, formatting, punctuation, and body text. (That might sound like a lot of passes, but you'll most likely be surprised at what you'll find even after you've made four or five trips through your text.)

- Have a second or third pair of eyes review your text.

- Print and read hard copy versions of your Web pages at various stages throughout the development process.

Treating Text as a Design Element

As you know, text on a Web page informs as well as adds to a page's overall design. (Refer to Figure 2-3.) In Chapter 4, we delve into how to combine Web text with Web art to create attractive and effective layouts, but you should start to mull over basic text-design issues while you're pulling your text together. Therefore, while you create your content and read Chapters 3 and 4, keep the following text-design issues in mind (don't worry if you're not particularly clear about how to implement the following techniques; in Chapter 4, we revisit these issues when we discuss Web page layouts in more detail):

- Create graphical titles and headings for added artistic effect.

- Display pull-quotes and sidebars to lighten text-heavy pages.

- Add WordArt, logos, graphical text, and banners to create a consistent look and feel throughout your site. (In Chapter 9, we describe how to use Microsoft Word to create WordArt.)

- Use easy-to-understand icons in place of words, similar to the "new," "hot," and "home" icons that are sprinkled throughout the Web.

- Judiciously apply color or other typographical formatting (such as boldface or italic) to draw attention to important words and concepts.

- Use drop caps or hung initials (larger first letters in a paragraph) to indicate the beginning of a section.

- Ensure that backgrounds don't interfere with the text's readability.

- Include important data (such as contact information, company name, and so forth) as text, even if the information appears in graphical form elsewhere on the page. Some people turn off their graphics to speed up surfing, which means they'll miss graphical information provided on your page.

- Avoid tiny print—if in doubt, let the users define the text's size through their default browser settings.

- Use easy-to-read, cross-platform compatible fonts. Currently, the fonts most compatible with Windows-based and Apple Macintosh machines include Arial, Arial Narrow, Comic Sans, Courier New, Times New Roman, and Verdana.

Finally, as a parting text tip after all the dos and don'ts outlined in this chapter, we want to suggest that you have fun with your Web page's content. The Web grants you the freedom to quickly and creatively impart information in new ways. Think about exactly what you want to say, and then write your message as clearly and actively as possible. Once you start to write strong concise sentences, you'll be hooked.

Key Points

- Users scan Web pages instead of reading them linearly.

- Titles, contents, hyperlinks, logos, WordArt creations, graphical text elements, forms, menus, navigation options, last-modified dates, and copyright information represent typical uses of Web page text.

- The text on a Web page attracts users' attention before the graphics do.

- Web page information should loosely emulate the traditional inverted pyramid news-style writing methodology.

- Brainstorm to clarify your Web page's main points, headings, and links.

- Write clear, active sentences and well-formed, concise paragraphs.

- Keep headings and hyperlinks clear and descriptive.

- Use bulleted lists and a heading hierarchy to help readers quickly identify key points.

- Include important information as text to cater to users who opt not to download Web graphics.

- Spell-check, spell-check, and then spell-check again (and don't forget to print and read the text aloud).

- Check your grammar.

- Start to think about text design elements, including typographical formatting, color, and graphical text elements.

- Most of all, after taking into account the strengths and limitations of Web writing, allow the writing experience to be an enjoyable and creative process.

Chapter 3

Creating and Using Art on the Web

In this chapter, we simplify the topic of Web graphics. In a perfect world, we'd dedicate pages and pages to the nuances of using graphics on the Web (mostly because we like graphics), but then you'd never get to the rest of the book. We also don't want you to feel overwhelmed when it comes to using Web graphics. As you might have discovered, you can easily find an overabundance of information about advanced graphics by looking on the Internet and in bookstores everywhere. Fortunately, you can use Web graphics effectively without immersing yourself in gamma theory and rasterizing. Therefore, we've opted to take the practical approach of presenting what we deem to be the most significant and fundamental information about Web page graphics. Think of this chapter as your personal crash course in Web art. By the time you reach the "Key Points" section at the end of the chapter, you'll have plenty to think about, a few tricks up your sleeve, a cocktail party quip or two, and a number of places to turn to during your search, acquisition, creation, and preparation of Web art.

Mechanics of Web Graphics

Before you start flipping through this chapter to check out the pictures and
unearth the addresses to our online examples, you really need to read this section to make sure you understand a few key Web graphics issues. As you know,
Web graphics look fairly similar to printed graphics, but some Web-specific factors come into play when you're creating and using graphics on the Web. Specifically, online graphics require you to consider color limitations, file formats,
and file sizes as well as possible transparency, downloading, and animation
issues. Acquiring an awareness of three main factors—colors, file types, and file
sizes—enables you to begin using graphics on your Web pages and provides a
jumping-off point for further graphics study. Therefore, the overall plan of attack
here is to tuck some Web graphics fundamentals into a cranial corner or two
before opening your mind to the more creative (and fun) prospects of using,
gathering, and creating Web graphics. Let's get started by looking at how graphics display color.

Pixels, Palettes, and Colors

First and foremost, every online graphic consists of a bunch of tiny colored
squares working together to form an image. In a way, online graphics emulate
a painting technique called *pointillism*. Pointillism, introduced by French painter
Georges Seurat (1859–1891), is the art of painting pictures one dot (or tiny brush
stroke) at a time. Through pointillism, Seurat broke each image on his canvas
down into tiny dots of color. When you look closely at a pointillist painting, you
can see each dot. As you move away from the painting, the dots blend together
to create a picture. Computers display pictures using a technique similar to
pointillism, except that instead of painted dots, computers divide pictures into
colored squares, called *pixels*. For example, take a look at the cherries in Figure
3-1. (For a full-color visual representation, display the graphic online by visiting
www.creationguide.com/cherries.) Figure 3-1 could be any graphic displayed on
your screen. As you can see, the graphic looks like most other pictures online
(or in printed material, for that matter), and there are no blatant signs of dots,
squares, or pixels.

Lingo   A *pixel* is one square on a grid of thousands of squares that are individually colored to
create an image.

Figure 3-1   A couple cherries stand in as a typical graphic.

Now let's look at the graphic a little more closely. If you open the cherries picture in a graphics editing application (for quickest results, drag the image from *www.creationguide.com/cherries* into a graphics editing program, such as Jasc Paint Shop Pro, Adobe Photoshop, or Microsoft Paint) and then dramatically magnify the image, you'll be able to see the actual squares (pixels) that make up the picture, as shown in Figure 3-2. If you magnify the cherries on your monitor, you'll see that the picture's colors and shades vary from pixel to pixel, or square to square.

Tip   If you don't have a graphics editing application on your system or if you want to test-drive a popular "full-service" graphics editing application, visit *www.jasc.com* and download a free trial version of Paint Shop Pro. We have more to say about graphics editing applications later in this chapter, as well as in Chapter 5.

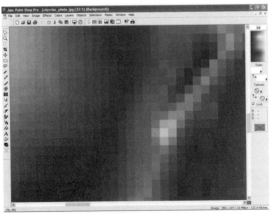

Figure 3-2   When you magnify an online image, you can see the image's pixels.

Try This! To illustrate this section's pixels discussion firsthand, display *www.creationguide.com/ cherries* in your browser. Right-click the cherries graphic and select Save Picture As or Save Image As (the command varies by browser).

Save the picture to your computer's hard disk, and be sure to remember *where* you save the figure. For this exercise, we recommend that you save the picture to your desktop for easy access as well as quick deletion later. Next, open your graphics program—such as Jasc Paint Shop Pro, Microsoft Paint, or Adobe Photoshop—and then open the file in the application. (You can also import an online picture into your graphics program by dragging the image from your browser into a graphics program, or by right-clicking the picture and choosing Copy and then opening your graphics program and pasting the image into your graphics application.)

To view the image's pixels, enlarge the picture by using your graphics program's Zoom Tool or Magnifying Glass. To further illustrate how pixels work, incrementally decrease the image's view (or "zoom out") to a slightly more viewable size, as shown here:

If you zoom out slowly, you can see how the pixels start to blend to create a clear image.

Now that you know about pixels, we can talk a little about *palettes*. A palette is simply the table of colors used in a graphic. Some Web graphics (namely, graphics saved using the GIF file format, as described in the next section) use a limited collection of colors. You can assign a palette to an image, or you can let your graphics program generate a palette automatically as you create and edit an image. A GIF palette can hold up to 256 colors, but many images use fewer colors than that. For example, looking at Figure 3-3 (and online at *www.creationguide.com/palettes/samples.html*), the cherries graphic uses 8 colors and the hot pepper graphic uses 128 colors. Notice the pictures' sizes—the cherries graphic is 3 KB (very small), and the hot pepper graphic is 7 KB (almost as small as the cherry GIF graphic).

Lingo   A *palette* holds the set of colors used in a graphic.

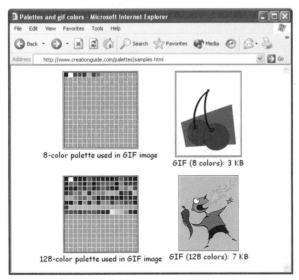

Figure 3-3   The cherries graphic's palette contains 8 colors, and the hot pepper graphic's palette contains 128 colors.

Generally, most graphics applications enable you to view the colors included in a GIF graphic's palette. Furthermore, you can reduce the size of a GIF image by reducing or limiting the number of colors in the picture's palette. And, as you probably know, smaller file sizes equate to quicker download times on the Web.

Lingo   In some Web graphics applications and documentation, a palette is also referred to as a *color look-up table* (CLUT) or simply a *color table*.

Try This!   To view a color palette, display *www.creationguide.com/palettes/samples.html* and then right-click and save either the cherries or hot pepper GIF image to your computer's hard disk. Next, open the GIF image in your graphics editor. To display the image's palette in Paint Shop Pro, select Edit Palette from the Colors menu. In Photoshop, select Mode from the Image menu, and then select Color Table. (We realize that every graphics package has its own menu options; we provide the preceding two commands to give you an idea of the type of command you should look for in your graphics application.)

As we just mentioned, palettes come into play when you use GIF images. We realize we haven't defined GIFs yet—or any Web-friendly image formats for that matter. Now that you have a feel for the nature of pixels and palettes, however, let's move on and discuss graphics file formats that you can use on the

Web. We'll talk more about palettes when we discuss GIFs later in this chapter. We also cover palettes in Chapter 4, when we talk about choosing colors for your Web site.

Graphics File Formats

As you might recall, in Chapter 1 we said that every graphic on a Web page is stored as a separate file. As a refresher, turn again to Figure 1-4 in Chapter 1. Notice the names of the two image files used in Figure 1-4.

The title bar figure's file name ends with a .gif file extension (*afs_title.gif*), and the other figure's file name ends with a .jpg file extension (*4members.jpg*). Graphics file extensions work on the same principles as other file formats. For example, if you see a file on your desktop named *holiday_gift_list.doc*, you know by the .doc extension that the file is probably a Microsoft Word document, and you'll want to open the document in Word (especially if you suspect that you're one of the people listed on the holiday gift list!). Similarly, if you see a file on your desktop named *bills.xls*, you know the .xls indicates a Microsoft Excel document, so you could open the file in Excel (although you might want to avoid files named *bills*). In relation to Web graphics, your Web pages can include graphics images that use the .gif and .jpeg (or .jpg) file extensions because most popular Web browsers can display GIF and JPEG (pronounced "jay-peg") files.

GIFs

GIFs are the most widely supported graphics type on the Web (which means that almost all browsers—old, new, and in-between—can display GIF images). GIF stands for *Graphics Interchange Format*. CompuServe created this format in the 1980s as an efficient means to transmit images across data networks. The GIF format's main strength is that GIF images are usually small, which means that they download and display quickly.

Lingo   *GIF* (Graphics Interchange Format) is a graphics file format used to create images for use on the Internet. GIF images can contain up to 256 colors.

As we mentioned earlier in this chapter, GIF images use palettes and support up to 256 colors (which makes them 8-bit graphics). Because GIFs support a limited number of colors, you should use GIFs for flat color areas (such as the blue and green areas in the Art Camps for Kids Web page shown at *www.creationguide.com/artcamp* and in Chapter 2) logos, line art, icons, cartoonlike illustrations, buttons, horizontal rules, bullets, backgrounds, and other graphical elements that require few colors. Figure 3-4 shows some examples of typical uses of GIF images (to see the images online, visit *www.creationguide.com/gifs*).

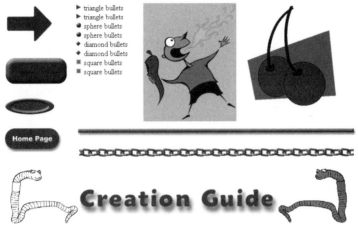

Figure 3-4   Line art, horizontal rules, buttons, bullets, and graphical text are typical uses of GIF files.

In addition to being palette-reliant, small, and efficient, GIFs perform three special tricks—interlacing, transparency, and animation.

■ **Interlaced GIFs**   Normally, a GIF image appears on screen row by row, from top to bottom of the image, like pulling down a window shade. If you want to, you (as a Web page designer) can change how a GIF downloads onto viewers' monitors by saving your GIF file as an interlaced GIF file. An interlaced GIF graphic displays on users' screens as blurred or jagged at first and then gradually becomes clearer. Figure 3-5 shows an interlaced GIF in the midst of downloading. The figure on the left shows the image before it's fully downloaded, and the figure on the right shows the fully downloaded image. To view the interlaced GIF online, visit *www.creationguide.com/interlaced*.

Note   If you're using a fast Internet connection, such as a cable modem, you probably won't see the effects of interlacing.

Figure 3-5   On slower Internet connections, you can see how an interlaced GIF displays blurred before downloading completes.

Interlaced GIFs are good to use when you want to transmit an image's main idea to readers while they wait for the complete download. The drawback of interlaced GIFs is that they have slightly larger file sizes than conventional (noninterlaced) GIF images. Therefore, for buttons, icons, and small graphics, you're better off sticking to the conventional GIF file format.

- **Transparent GIFs**   Transparent GIFs (GIFs that use the GIF89a format) enable you to design icons, logos, and other elements that appear to be cut out, thereby allowing the Web page's background to show through areas of the image. For example, as you can see in the right side of Figure 3-6 (and online at *www.creationguide.com/transparent*), the background shows through in the transparent GIF to create the illusion of a nonrectangular image.

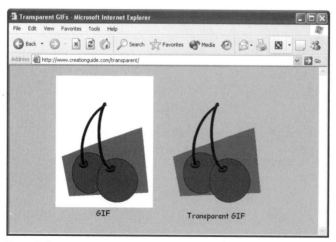

Figure 3-6   Comparing a standard GIF with a transparent GIF shows how transparency allows a Web page's background color (or pattern) to show through.

When you create a transparent GIF, you essentially specify a unique color in your image to serve as your transparent color. For example, you could color the background of your picture hot pink and then assign hot pink to be the picture's transparent color—just make sure hot pink doesn't show up elsewhere in your image or you'll create unwanted transparent spots. When a browser encounters the transparent color, the browser doesn't show any graphics information in the color's area, which enables the Web page's background to show through.

Note If a GIF's background color matches your Web page's background color—such as an image with a white background on a Web page with a white background—you automatically achieve the illusion of transparency.

■ **Animated GIFs**   The last GIF "trick" involves animation. Using GIF animation tools and graphics editing programs, you can layer GIFs and save the layers in a "stack" to create simple animations. When a browser displays the stacked GIF images, it displays each image one after the other. This technique is similar to the old flip-card "movies" that were popular long before most of us came into existence. Moving icons, rollover buttons, and some banner ads are prime examples of animated GIFs. Figure 3-7 illustrates the theory behind animated GIFs. To see the smiley animation and an animated button in action, visit *www.creationguide.com/animated_gifs*. As you'll see later in this chapter, you can download free animated GIFs and GIF animation tools from the Web.

Animated GIF: Uses layers of GIF images to achieve animation.

frame 01 frame 02 frame 03 frame 04 frame 05 frame 06 frame 07 frame 08 frame 09 frame 10

Figure 3-7   A series of GIF images can display in succession to create animations.

Tip   The Clip Art in Microsoft Office XP includes animated GIFs as well as transparent GIFs that you can use on your Web pages. To identify a Clip Art item that's an animated GIF, look for a gold star in the lower-right corner of the thumbnail image in the Clip Organizer. To identify a Clip Art item that has a transparent background, look for items that appear to be "cut out" in the Clip Organizer. You can test an image's transparency by inserting the image into a Word document that has a color background. Later in this chapter, in "Adding Transparency to an Image," we show you how to apply transparency to a GIF image.

"Safe" Colors for the Web   As you know, all computer systems are not created equal. Many people have a heck of a time keeping up with the computer industry's rapid pace of hardware development. Therefore, when you design Web pages, you should keep in mind that not all people will be able to access your pages if your pages require the latest and greatest display hardware. In fact, approximately 10 percent of all Web surfers are restricted to viewing Web pages in 256 colors (although most new systems display millions of colors, so the 256-color design issue will probably soon be a design consideration of the past). Therefore, for the next couple years, when you design your Web pages and create GIF images, you might consider relying on colors that 256-color monitors can display without a hitch. The universal colors are referred to as the *Web-safe* or *browser-safe* colors. If your Web page uses colors other than Web-safe colors, systems that support only 256 colors will resort to *dithering* the nonstandard colors.

> **Lingo**   *Dither* refers to the random dot pattern that results when colors are approximated by mixing similar and available colors from a limited palette.

To avoid dither, stick to the 216 Web-safe colors. (The other 40 colors out of the 256 are reserved for the computer system's use.) To see the Web-safe color palette, visit *www.creationguide.com/palettes*, and, to see the colors in color chart format, visit *www.creationguide.com/colorchart*. Graphics editing programs usually provide a Web-safe palette that you can load when working with GIF images, or you can copy the palette shown on *www.creationguide.com/palettes* and create your own Web-safe color palette based on the Web image. For example, open the color palette image in Paint Shop Pro and choose Save Palette from the Colors menu.

JPEGs

In addition to GIF graphics, your Web pages will probably include JPEG images. The JPEG image file format was created by and named after the *Joint Photographic Experts Group*. This image format supports millions of colors, and JPEGs are almost universally supported by browsers. (Technically speaking, JPEGs support 24-bit color, which is also referred to as *full color* or *true color*.) Because JPEGs can contain millions of colors, JPEG graphics frequently display photographic images online.

> **Lingo**   *JPEG* (Joint Photographic Experts Group) is a graphics file format used to display photographic-quality and other high-color images on the Internet. The JPEG file format can support millions of colors.

When you're working with JPEGs for your Web pages, you can specify whether you want to save your JPEGs as standard or progressive:

- ◾ **Standard** When you save an image as a standard JPEG file, the image loads line by line from the top of the screen down, similar to how GIFs download by default.

- ◾ **Progressive** When you save an image as a progressive JPEG file, the image first appears blurry and then becomes more focused as the image data is downloaded (similar to interlaced GIFs). With fast Internet connection speeds, the progressive rendering might not be readily apparent to viewers; instead, after a delay, the image will seem to "pop up" onto the page. In our experience, progressive JPEGs seem to create smaller file sizes and download slightly quicker than standard JPEG files.

Note   When a JPEG image displays on a system that supports only 8-bit color (256 colors), the browser reduces the colors in the image to the Web palette and some dithering will occur.

Another JPEG configuration parameter that you can use to your advantage is *compression*. Compression is a process that reduces an image's file size by throwing out some color information. JPEG compression is called a "lossy" compression scheme because once you compress an image the deleted information is lost. Fortunately, if you're careful, people viewing the image online can't easily discern the information loss.

Tip   When increasing a JPEG image's compression, always save a copy of the original image first. Then, use the Save As command whenever you further compress the file to create a new file. Once an image is compressed using JPEG's compression scheme, the information that's removed is lost.

Keep in mind that the more you compress an image, the smaller the image's file size becomes, but the resulting image won't be as sharp as a less compressed image. Therefore, you should experiment with various compression settings when configuring JPEG images for your Web pages. To view online images using standard and progressive rendering as well as to compare compressed images, visit *www.creationguide.com/jpegs*.

At this point, you should be comfortable with the idea of progressive and compressed JPEG files, but we haven't yet explained how to configure these types of settings for a JPEG image. Fortunately, most image editing programs make specifying JPEG file parameters fairly easy. To access JPEG file settings in Paint Shop Pro, follow these steps:

1   Open your JPEG image in Paint Shop Pro. (Feel free to practice with any of the fruit.jpg images shown on *www.creationguide.com/jpegs.*)

2   Choose Save As from the File menu to display the Save As dialog box.

3   Enter a new filename, and then click Options to access the Save Options dialog box, shown in Figure 3-8.

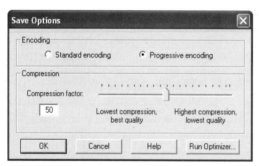

Figure 3-8   The Save Options dialog box enables you to configure JPEG compression and render settings in Paint Shop Pro.

4   Specify an encoding option (Standard or Progressive), select a compression setting, click OK, and then click Save.

To configure JPEG settings in Photoshop, follow these steps:

1   Open your JPEG image in Photoshop. (Feel free to practice with any of the fruit.jpg images shown on *www.creationguide.com/jpegs.*)

2   Choose Save from the File menu.

3   Enter a file name, and click Save. The JPEG Options dialog box opens. Specify compression settings by moving the Quality slider in the JPEG Options dialog box, and then click OK.

PNG

The third (and final) graphic type we address in this chapter is the *PNG* file format. PNG (pronounced "ping") stands for *Portable Network Graphics*. Similar to GIFs, PNG files are small, they load quickly, and they support transparency. PNG files transmit faster than GIFs, but only the newer browsers support them.

Lingo   *PNG (Portable Network Graphics)* is a graphics file format designed to replace GIF images on the Internet.

Initially, the PNG file format was devised because Unisys, the makers of the GIF compression algorithm, decided to enforce the patents for that algorithm—meaning that software vendors had to pay to use it. But you really don't need to know the details about the PNG vs. GIF debate. Just know that newer major browsers (including Microsoft Internet Explorer 5 and later) can display PNG images, but most Web designers don't use PNGs in deference to users who surf the Web with older or less technologically advanced browsers. At this point, your Web pages probably shouldn't use PNGs either.

Note Internet Explorer for Microsoft Windows began to incorporate some PNG support in 1997 and began providing PNG support in Macintosh versions of Internet Explorer in 2000. Therefore, the PNG file format is slowly starting to catch on as developers watch the percentage of users who have access to the most up-to-date or most technologically advanced browsers. From a developer's perspective, there's currently no reason to risk losing viewers by using a PNG file format when the GIF file format is readily available, just as easy to use, and widely recognized in almost all browsers (regardless of version).

Size Matters

The last major "technical" Web graphics consideration that we cover in this chapter is file size, which is directly related to download speeds. As a Web surfer, you've probably caught yourself drumming your mouse impatiently while waiting for pages that take longer than 10 seconds to display (or, even more likely, clicking away before the slow page ever fully displays). As a Web designer, you need to hold on to that impatient feeling. When you design Web pages and use Web art, you should always keep one eye on your design and another eye on the user's perspective. (That almost sounds painful!)

When you use Web art, you can take advantage of a few techniques that will help keep your file sizes manageable. We already covered a few key topics earlier in this chapter that can help to reduce file sizes and speed download times, including these:

- Avoid dither in GIF images by using Web-safe colors whenever possible, especially in large, flat color areas. (Just think—before reading this chapter, that sentence wouldn't have made a bit of sense to you.)

- Configure JPEG images to render progressively.

- Compress JPEG images to reduce file sizes.

In addition to using the three preceding graphics file techniques, you can control download speeds by resizing your images, cropping images, and using thumbnails. We briefly describe each technique in the following sections. Please keep in mind that the actual mechanics of accomplishing certain tasks vary among graphics editing tools.

Resizing Graphics

One of the best ways to conserve download time is to physically resize your images in a graphics editor. Note that we're talking about resizing the image, not simply changing your view. Zooming in and out changes your view of an image, but it doesn't affect the file's actual size or dimensions. Try to size your images to the approximate size you want to display them on your Web page. Figure 3-9 shows the Resize dialog box you use in Paint Shop Pro to resize an image. To access the Resize dialog box, open the image and then select Resize from the Image menu.

Keep in mind that smaller images result in smaller file sizes, which result in quicker download times.

Tip   Usually, you'll want to ensure that the Maintain Aspect Ratio option (or its equivalent in your graphics program) is selected when you resize graphics; otherwise, you could distort your images.

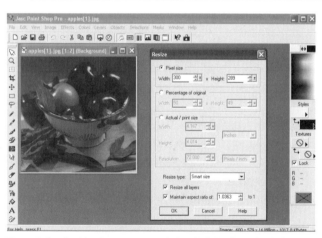

Figure 3-9   Resizing images to actual sizes in Paint Shop Pro helps to minimize download times.

Try This!   To experiment with resizing images, open a JPEG image in your graphics editor and then change the image's width or height setting. You can use the apples image stored at *www.creationguide.com/sizing/apples.jpg*. Save the JPEG image, and then repeat the process a number of times using various measurements, renaming each version with a unique, meaningful name (such as apples400w.jpg for a picture that's resized to 400 pixels wide). After you've created a few variously sized images, view the images locally in your browser window—that is, either navigate to the figures by using your browser's Address toolbar or drag the JPEG images' file name icons into your browser window.

Sizing Images Just Right—A Quick Trick When you first start to design Web pages, you might not know what sizes your graphics should be. To help you resize a graphic to the size you want it to appear on your Web page, you can use a Web editing program, such as Microsoft FrontPage.

To determine the optimal size for a Web graphic, follow these steps:

1 Insert the graphic into a blank Web page in FrontPage (for example) and resize the picture by dragging the image's selection handles.

2 After the image is sized to your liking, display the image's properties (in FrontPage, right-click the graphic and select Picture Properties on the pop-up menu), and note (and then write down) the image's height and width parameters.

3 Reopen the image in your graphic's editing program and then resize the graphic by entering the numbers you copied from FrontPage (or other Web editing program) into the appropriate dialog box. For instance, in Paint Shop Pro, you open the Resize dialog box by choosing Resize on the Image menu, and, in MS Paint, you open the Attributes dialog box by choosing Attributes on the Image menu.

Cropping Images

In addition to resizing an image, you can *crop* an image to reduce its size. When you crop an image, you cut out the portion of the image that you don't want to use. *Cropping* is frequently used to remove any unwanted or unneeded portions of your photograph. For example, you might want to crop the apples.jpg image shown in Figure 3-9 to show a closeup of the green apple amidst the red apples in the colander. Figure 3-10 shows crop lines (the dashed lines that surround the portion of the image you want to retain) in the apples.jpg image, which is 50 KB, and the result of cropping apples.jpg. The cropped version is only 6 KB.

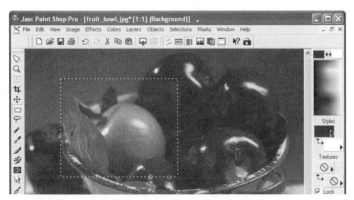

Figure 3-10   The crop marks indicate the portion of an image that will be used as a Web graphic. The cropped image contains only the information you bounded by the crop marks.

Lingo   *Cropping* refers to cutting off a part of an image, such as unnecessary portions of a graphic.

Try This! To crop an image, follow these steps:

1   Open an image in your graphics editor.

2   Click the selection tool (which usually looks like a dashed rectangle or square in the application's toolbar).

3   Click and drag in your image to outline the area of the image you want to retain. (If you outline the wrong area, press Esc and try again.)

4   After you have an area selected, choose Crop To Selection (in Paint Shop Pro) or Crop (in Photoshop) from the Image menu, or select a similar command in your graphics editing program.

Using Thumbnails

After you master the art of resizing and cropping images, you're ready to use *thumbnails*. A thumbnail is a small picture that links to a larger image. (The larger image is usually the same as the thumbnail, but we've seen some creative uses of thumbnails in our day.) When you use thumbnails, viewers can choose to view the small image and be done with it or they can click the thumbnail to view the larger image. In other words, when you use thumbnails, you grant viewers the option to download large images if they're willing to endure the longer download times.

Lingo   A *thumbnail* is a miniature version or small portion of a graphic. Frequently, on Web pages, thumbnail graphics are hyperlinked to larger versions of the graphic.

The trick to using thumbnails is to create two graphics with different names. Usually, you use the same image for both graphics, and you make one image small with a quick download time and the other image (while optimized to the best of your ability, of course) larger with a longer download time. Then you display the small image on your Web page, and you link the small image to the larger image. (We'll show you how to link images in Part Two of this book.) Figure 3-11 shows two thumbnails. The left thumbnail displays the entire linked image, and the right thumbnail shows a cropped portion of the linked graphic. Figure 3-11 also shows the larger graphic that's linked to the thumbnails. By clicking either thumbnail shown in Figure 3-11, you can open a window displaying a large view of the apples.jpg image.

Figure 3-11 Both thumbnails of the apples link to a sizable rendition of the apples.jpg image.

Try This! To view thumbnails in action, click them at *www.creationguide.com/sizing*.

The Art of Using Web Graphics

Now that we've gotten the technical aspects of graphics out of the way, let's talk briefly about graphic design. The overriding premise of Web graphics is that your Web page's graphics should serve two masters—aesthetics and utility. Ideally, every piece of art on your Web page should contribute to both causes by looking good and serving a purpose. Therefore, this chapter helps you to brush up on the various types of aesthetically appealing and useful graphics that you should start to consider for your Web pages, including these:

- Photographs and illustrations
- Buttons and logos
- Icons, bullets, and horizontal rules
- Graphical text
- Backgrounds

In the next few sections, we take a quick look at each of the preceding graphical elements.

Photographs and Illustrations

We won't dwell too long on photographs and illustrations given our extended discussion of image formats earlier in this chapter. As we've mentioned numerous times, the key to using photographs and illustrations is to keep the file sizes as small as possible so that they download quickly. Furthermore, you should ensure that your photographs and illustrations add to your page's content instead of detract from your message. Imagine waiting patiently for a movie review Web page to download only to find that the page contains a couple links to reviews and a large picture of the Web designer's dog wearing sunglasses. Without a second thought, you'd probably dash off to find a faster, more useful movie review site for future reference.

Lingo   An *image map* is a graphic that's formatted so that various areas of the graphic serve as hyperlinks to related Web pages. For example, in Chapter 10, we show you how to create an image map out of a solar system graphic, in which viewers can click a planet to access a related Web page that contains details about the selected planet.

One use of photographs and illustrations that we haven't mentioned yet is *image maps*. Images maps are graphics that have clickable areas that enable you to visit various Web pages. Quite possibly, you've clicked your state or country on an online map to get local information. If done properly, image maps represent a good mix of aesthetics and utility, but they should be used judiciously. Image maps involve mildly complex HTML coding; plus you need to ensure that you don't create an image map with a graphic that takes forever to download. In Chapter 10, we show you how you can create an image map using FrontPage.

Buttons and Logos

Buttons and logos are a Web page's bread-and-butter graphics. No doubt you've clicked a countless number of buttons and caught sight of more than a few logos. Thus, you're well aware that buttons help you to navigate around a site and logos brand a Web page as well as provide a quick link to a site's home page. The MSN logo, online at *www.msn.com*, is easy to spot, appears consistently on every page, and serves as a reliable hyperlink to the MSN home page.

On your Web pages, the key to successfully using graphic buttons and logos is consistency. If you're using a logo, ensure that the logo is instantly identifiable and easily visible on every page. For example, your logo should use the same colors throughout your site and appear in the same area on every page.

(We'll talk more about page setup in later chapters.) Your logo should also link to your site's home page in every instance. If you're using custom buttons, use the same buttons on every page in your site and position them in the same location on each page, if possible.

See Also   *Later in this chapter, we show you a quick way to create simple custom buttons using Word.*

Consistently displaying buttons and logos adds an overall feeling of unity to your site and speeds up the downloading process. Once a viewer downloads your home page, your button and logo graphics will be stored in the temporary cache of the user's machine. If the same button and logo images appear on your Web site's ancillary pages and are referenced with the same file names, the user's browser won't have to redownload the button graphics because the graphics will already be stored on the user's computer. In turn, less downloading means quicker page displays. Kind of a sneaky design tactic, but it's great for reducing download times.

Lingo   The *temporary cache* is a portion of your hard drive that's set aside in accordance with your browser's settings, and its main job is to temporarily store copies of the Web pages and images you view. To view your temporary cache settings in Internet Explorer, click Internet Options on the Tools menu, and click the Settings button in the Temporary Internet Files section.

Icons, Bullets, and Horizontal Rules

Icons, bullets, and horizontal rules help draw attention to elements on your Web pages as well as quickly communicate information in place of text. But tread lightly when you're using these elements. A fine line exists between clarifying and cluttering. When used sparingly and with discretion, icons, bullets, and rules can add a professional look to a page. When overused, these elements can make your page look amateurish and bury your message in visual mayhem.

Tip   You can combine icons and button features to create picture buttons. For example, you might use a small picture of a house to serve as your Home button.

Icons are small graphics used to call attention to a particular feature or to communicate a brief message. For example, you might use a graphic icon that looks like an envelope on your Web page to quickly identify a link to an e-mail form that viewers can use to send feedback to you. To get a feel for the effective use of icons, surf around a few online auction sites (such as Amazon and eBay), and you'll see all sorts of icons. Notice how each icon is a simple graphic that clearly denotes a particular message.

Bullets are small graphics added at the beginning of entries in a list or series. When you add graphical bullets to your Web pages, make sure that the graphics you use draw attention to your list and not to the bullets themselves. For example, any of the small bullets shown in Figure 3-12 (and online at *www.creationguide.com/bullets*) are effective bullet graphics; in contrast, spinning rainbow-colored bouncing bullets will drive most users away from your page before they even attempt to read your content.

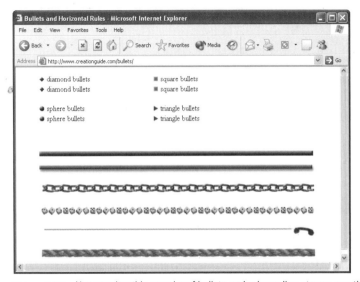

Figure 3-12   You can view this sampler of bullets and rules online at *www.creationguide.com/bullets*.

Horizontal rules denote sections in your Web pages. You can insert a graphical rule (as shown in Figure 3-12), or you can create a standard horizontal rule by using HTML code, as described in the following Try This! feature. In our opinion, you should limit your use of horizontal rules. Horizontal rules tend to chop up pages (thereby making them harder to read), and, 9 times out of 10, a little white space or a heading might serve your needs better than adding a horizontal rule. Used appropriately, horizontal rules can be useful, especially in long, text-heavy pages. For instance, to see judicious use of a horizontal rule to separate heading information from the main body of the Web page, visit *www.bughouseproductions.com/bhp*.

Try This! You can add bullets and rules to your Web pages without creating a graphic. To create a bulleted list in HTML (without adding custom graphical bullets), you use the following tags:

`<UL>`	(identifies the beginning of the list)
`<LI>`	(marks the beginning of each list item)
`</LI>`	(marks the end of each list item)
`</UL>`	(identifies the end of the list)

To create a horizontal rule, you use the `<HR>` tag, in which you can specify the following properties for a horizontal rule:

`SIZE`	(the height of the rule line in pixels)
`WIDTH`	(either in percentage of page width or in absolute pixels)
`ALIGN`	(center, left, or right justified)
`NOSHADE`	(by default, HTML horizontal rules display with a shadow)

To see HTML bullets and rules in action, open a blank Notepad document, and type the following:

```
<HTML>
<HEAD>
<TITLE>
Bulleted Lists and Horizontal Rules
</TITLE>
</HEAD>
<BODY>
<H1> Fruit </H1>
<UL>
      <LI> Grapes </LI>
      <LI> Kiwis </LI>
      <LI> Watermelon </LI>
</UL>
<HR SIZE="8" WIDTH="80%" ALIGN="CENTER" NOSHADE>
</BODY>
</HTML>
```

Save the file as test.html, and then open the document in your browser. Your bulleted list and horizontal rule should look similar to those shown here in Microsoft Internet Explorer (and on *www.creationguide.com/list*):

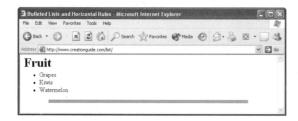

By the way, as you might've noticed, we snuck in the `<H1>` heading tag just for fun.

Graphical Text

As you may or may not know, browsers display text differently based on the browser's make, model, and year. But sticking with standard text when designing a Web page is rarely exciting or desirable. Fortunately, graphics provide a livable workaround. Basically, *graphical text* refers to text elements that have been created and then saved as a GIF or JPEG image that you can insert into your Web page as a picture. Graphical text includes titles, headings, and page banners. (A *banner* is generally a rectangular graphic that blends art and text and usually runs across the top or side of a Web page.) Using graphical text, you can customize text without relying on fonts that might or might not be installed on users' computers. Figure 3-13 (and online at *www.creationguide.com/ graphicaltext*) shows some text that can be imported into a graphics editing program, cropped, and used as graphical text on a Web page. Notice the bottom entry in Figure 3-13.

Note   In Chapter 9, we show you how to create WordArt in Microsoft Word.

Figure 3-13   Graphical text comes in a variety of styles and forms.

Backgrounds

You can modify your Web page's background in two ways: by coloring the background or by displaying a graphic beneath your Web page's contents. The key to using backgrounds is to ensure that together your content and the background create a striking contrast. Above all else, your content must be easy to read. If your background makes your page hard to read, lose the background (no matter how cool the color or pattern).

Adding background color to a Web page simply entails adding to your Web page an instruction that tells browsers which color to display. When you add a background image to your Web page, the image displays repeatedly across and down a user's screen (in a pattern called *tiling*) to create the illusion of a large graphical background. We'll cover background commands, colors, and images throughout Part Two of this book. In the meantime, Figure 3-14 shows some sample background images. You can visit the background samples online at *www.creationguide.com/backgrounds*. Click any sample to see a Web page filled with the background image.

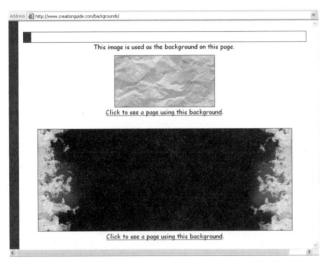

Figure 3-14   You test the sample background images online by visiting *www.creationguide.com/ backgrounds*.

Tip   You can find lots of free background patterns on the Web (for starters, visit our online resources page at *www.creationguide.com/resources*). Some Web page editor programs, such as FrontPage, also provide a selection of background patterns.

Acquiring Art

Now that you're on top of some of the *what* and *how* of graphics, you're ready for the *where*—as in, *where* are you going to find graphics for your Web page? Years ago, when we first started designing Web pages, we asked ourselves the same question. Today, we're more interested in where we can store all the graphics we've collected! Fortunately for you, acquiring graphics nowadays is pretty easy. Therefore, in this section, we briefly describe where you can find graphics as well as introduce you to the art of creating your own. Specifically, we talk about acquiring prepared art, custom art (that you create), and photographs.

> **Tip**   As you acquire and create images for your Web site, keep the files stored together in a folder on your desktop and give each graphic a unique, clearly identifiable name. You'll thank yourself later if you keep your images somewhat organized now.

Prepared Art

Prepared art is plentiful—you just need to know where to look. You can obtain Web graphics from a number of resources, including these:

- **Clip art**   You can buy clip art CD-ROMs wherever software is sold, or you can use the clip art that comes with applications such as Word.

- **Free online art**   Many Web sites provide art free (making the art freeware) from their Web sites. You simply use the "right-click and save" method to copy the images to your disk.

  > **Note**   When you save Web graphics from the Internet for your own use, make sure the artwork is truly freeware; otherwise, you might violate copyright laws. If you're unsure about whether a graphic is free for use, send an e-mail message to the site's Webmaster and ask permission to use the artwork.

- **Online art vendors**   A number of major vendors sell artwork online.

- **Graphic designers**   If you have a specific need and want a professional product, you can hire computer artists and graphic designers to create custom art for you.

  > **Tip**   You can find a few links to free art and art vendor Web sites by visiting our resources page at *www.creationguide.com/resources*.

Custom Art

Sometimes, Web pages beg for custom art. You can pay a designer to create the custom art (as mentioned in the preceding section), or you can try your hand at creating your own art (which we recommend in most cases). Creating custom art isn't as difficult as some people believe. Like any endeavor, the more you work at it, the better your results. But we're not here to give you a pep talk, so instead let's focus on how you can create your own custom art.

At this point, the most useful types of custom art that you can create are graphical text elements (such as title text and banners) and buttons. Fortunately, you can create custom art in almost any graphics editor as well as desktop applications, such as Word. Therefore, to ease any drawing anxiety issues you might be facing, we'll start right off with a brief exercise in creating a button in Word. After that, and just for good measure, we'll give you a quick lesson in adding transparency to an image using Word as well.

Creating a Button in Word

We provide this exercise simply to prove to you that you can create custom art, but if you like the buttons you create, you should save them for later. (In Part Two, we show you how to insert and link buttons as well as show you how to create and link WordArt components.) Here's how to create a button in Word:

1 Open a new document in Word.

2 Display your Drawing toolbar (if necessary) by pointing to Toolbars on the View menu and choosing Drawing from the submenu. Figure 3-15 shows the Drawing toolbar in Word.

Figure 3-15 The Drawing toolbar in Word contains all the tools you need to design a Web page button.

3 In the Drawing toolbar, click AutoShapes, point to Basic Shapes, and click Rounded Rectangle, as shown in Figure 3-16.

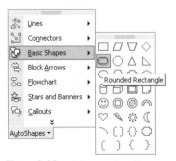

Figure 3-16 Select an AutoShape to begin creating your button.

Tip You can hold your mouse arrow over a button or graphical menu option to see the name of the button or option. For instance, to see the names of the AutoShapes, hold your mouse arrow over the small illustration of the AutoShape on the menu.

4   Click on the blank Word document, and then drag to create the button's outline, as shown in Figure 3-17. The button shown in Figure 3-17 is approximately .5 inches tall and 1 inch wide. If you want to set the AutoShape's size to exact measurements, you can configure the Height and Width settings in the Format AutoShape dialog box (right-click the AutoShape, choose Format AutoShape, and click the Size tab).

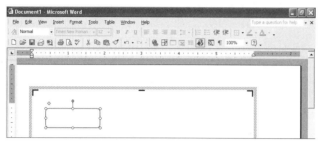

Figure 3-17   Click and drag to draw a button directly in a Word document.

5   In the Drawing toolbar, click the Text Box icon, click inside the AutoShape, and type **Home**.

6   Select the *Home* text, click the Font drop-down arrow in the Formatting toolbar, select Arial (or any other font, if you prefer), click the Bold button in the Formatting toolbar, click the Font Size drop-down arrow in the Formatting toolbar, select 18, and, finally, click the Center button in the Formatting toolbar. Click in an area inside the button, but off your text. Your button should now look similar to the one shown in Figure 3-18.

Tip   If necessary, you can resize your button by clicking and dragging the small squares (known as *handles*) that display around the edge of your selected button.

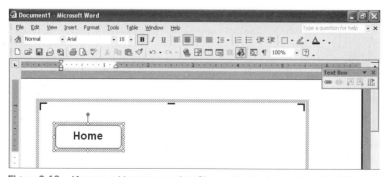

Figure 3-18   After you add text to your AutoShape, the drawing begins to look like a button.

7 On the Drawing toolbar, click the Fill Color (the paint can icon) arrow and then click a color. The button's background color displays. You can change the button's fill color by selecting another color with the Fill Color tool.

8 In the Drawing toolbar, click the Shadow Style button and then click Shadow Style 6. Click anywhere in the Word document outside of the Drawing Canvas to deselect the button. Your button should look similar to the one shown in Figure 3-19.

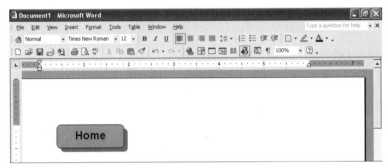

Figure 3-19 The formatted AutoShape is ready to be copied into a graphics program.

The next step involves saving your button as a GIF image for your Web page. You can convert your image to a GIF file in a number of ways in Word, but for now, we'll show you a quick and easy way to use Paint Shop Pro to make the conversion.

> **Tip** If you're creating your entire Web page in Word, you don't need to export the AutoShape button into a graphics program. Instead, you can add hyperlink properties directly to the button in Word, as described in Chapter 9, to make the button "clickable."

9 With your newly designed button displaying, press the Print Scrn button on your keyboard to create a copy of your screen display.

10 Open Paint Shop Pro, and choose Paste As New Image from the Edit menu. Your Word document view should be pasted into Paint Shop Pro, as shown in Figure 3-20.

> **Tip** You can also copy and paste the AutoShape button by right-clicking the edge of the button in Word and choosing Copy. Then, in Paint Shop Pro, right-click in the window, and choose Paste As New Image.

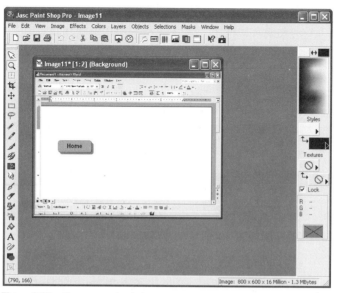

Figure 3-20   To create a simple button image, you can paste a copy of your desktop into a paint program, such as Paint Shop Pro.

11 In Paint Shop Pro, click the Selection tool (the dotted rectangle on the Tool Palette), outline the button, and then choose Crop To Selection from the Image menu to cut out the button.

12 Choose Save As from the File menu to open the Save As dialog box. Save the button as a GIF file.

Tip   After you create one button in Word, you can use the existing button as a template to create similar buttons with different text.

Now that your button is saved as a GIF, the image is ready to be used as an image button in your Web pages. We show you how to insert buttons into Web pages and add hyperlink properties to buttons later in this book, in Part Two.

Adding Transparency to an Image

Finally, before we wrap up this "Custom Art" section, we want to present a quick exercise in transparency. Many readers have asked us how to apply transparency to images to create "cut out" graphics on their Web pages, so we think you might appreciate this rundown. Although images are generally formatted in graphics programs, you can add transparency to a GIF in Office XP applications (including Word, FrontPage, Excel, and Microsoft PowerPoint), as well. Furthermore, numerous Clip Art images in Office XP are already formatted as transparent GIFs, so, in many cases, you can simply insert Clip Art onto your Web page that's already formatted as a transparent GIF (in Chapters 9 and 10, you'll hear more about Clip Art when we describe the ins and outs of creating Web pages in Word and FrontPage).

To apply transparency manually to a custom graphic in an Office program, you insert a picture and then assign transparency to the color of your choice. For this example, we apply transparency to an image in Word, but you can follow along using the same steps in Excel, FrontPage, or PowerPoint, if you prefer.

First, you need to obtain a GIF file that doesn't contain transparency. For this exercise, you can copy the newsguy picture from the *www.creationguide.com/newsguy* site or you can use your own image. To use the sample image:

1   Display *www.creationguide.com/newsguy*, right-click the GIF image with the orange background, and choose Copy.

2   Open a new document in Word, and click Paste on the Edit menu (or press Ctrl+V or right-click and choose Paste) to paste the image of the newsguy into your document. (If you're working with your own graphic, insert your graphic by displaying the Insert menu, choosing Picture, and then selecting From File.)

In the sample graphic, you're going to designate the orange color to be your transparent color.

3   If necessary, click the newsguy picture to display the Picture toolbar, and click the Set Transparent Color tool, as shown in Figure 3-21.

Figure 3-21   The Set Transparent Color tool enables you to designate a color as a transparent color.

4   In the picture, click the orange background.

The orange background color is set as the transparent color, and all portions of the image containing the color you clicked will appear transparent. To see the transparency in action, you can change the background color in your Word document.

Caution   If you click the background color of your image and it doesn't turn completely transparent, your background might consist of more than one color. For best results, you should use an image that has a solid, single-color background when you're creating a transparent GIF. In many cases, you can recolor a background as a solid flat color before you apply transparency—if you do this, ensure that the color you choose for your solid background color doesn't appear in the image; otherwise, you'll have transparent spots in your image.

---

5   To color the document's background, click Background on the Format
menu and then click a color square to apply a color background to
your Word document. Notice that when you add a color background to
your Word document, the color shows through the areas that were
orange in the newsguy image.

In this section, we've barely skimmed the surface of creating custom art, but
as you can see, custom art provides a lot of leeway for creativity. In addition to
using Word and Paint Shop Pro, you can use other Office programs and graphics
packages, as described in Chapter 5, as well as scan hand-drawn art pieces for
use in your Web pages. (We describe scanning in the next section.)

Photographs

You probably have at least one boxful of prime Web art resources lying around
your home—photographs. You can use new and old photographs to add art
to your Web pages. The trick is getting the hard-copy picture turned into information your computer can understand. To do that, you can use any of the following options:

- **Scanners**   Basically, a scanner takes a picture of your photograph
  and saves the picture information as a file on your computer. After you
  have a scanned picture, you can manipulate the file just as you manipulate other graphics files. You can use any flatbed scanner on the mar-
  ket to create Web graphics. You don't need to get a top-of-the-line
  machine, either. We use moderately priced scanners to scan most of
  our pictures. If you don't have a scanner and you aren't planning to
  purchase one, you can pay others to scan your pictures for you. For
  example, many copy centers also scan pictures for a small fee.

- **Film developers and online photo services**   The next time you
  drop off a roll of film for development, check out the services that the
  film developer offers. Many film developers can develop your film on
  CD, post your pictures to the Web, send your pictures through e-mail,
  create quality prints from digital pictures, and provide numerous other
  digitizing services. For a list of links to online photo services, visit
  www.creationguide.com/resources and click Online Photo Services.

- **Digital cameras**   A third option for obtaining photographic images is
  to use a digital camera. Digital cameras enable you to snap a photo
  and then instantly send the picture into your computer. If you're thinking about buying a digital camera, here are a few issues to consider:

- **Cost** Know your budget before you shop; most people don't need a top-of-the-line digital camera to get the job done. But, with that said, don't settle for "last year's" model just for the sake of saving a few bucks. Manufacturers are responding to the growing demand for digital cameras; thus, they're producing more cameras (which lowers per-unit cost) and improving the cameras' features. So buying a new camera at a camera shop can often result in a better value than buying an older model at a discount store.

- **Features** Digital camera features run the gamut, but if you're a beginner, make sure your camera has automatic and manual features. You'll probably want to use the automatic features at first to get the hang of digital photography. Then, after you're comfortable using your camera, you can start to experiment with the manual settings. Also, if you're buying the camera only for Web pictures, you can get away with a 1-megapixel (or lower) camera, but if you want to be able to use your pictures online and in print, consider getting at least a 1-megapixel (preferably at least a 2-megapixel or 3-megapixel, if you can swing it) camera. Higher megapixel cameras create better quality pictures and enable you to print quality pictures at sizes larger than the standard snapshot size.

Lingo   A *megapixel* refers to one million pixels, and it's a term used in reference to the resolution of graphics devices, such as scanners, digital cameras, and monitors.

Finally, remember that digital cameras are basically handheld computers. If you're going to be taking pictures under all sorts of circumstances and conditions, make sure you choose a camera that's built to withstand the torment. If you're planning for some truly extreme photography, consider checking out some of the "weatherproof" models.

- **File Format** Last but not least, a major point to consider when purchasing a camera is to determine how easy it's going to be for you to get the pictures out of the camera and into your computer. Will you need to use cables? Can you use infrared ports? Does the camera store the pictures on a CD? Make sure you know how the camera transfers pictures and that you're happy with the method before you buy.

Finally, as the last bit of advice in this chapter, regardless of how and where you obtain your Web page graphics, remember to optimize your images and save them as GIF and JPEG files. Make sure your images' file sizes are as small as possible without compromising quality. Furthermore, store your images in a central location on your hard disk, and don't forget to give every graphic a unique and meaningful name.

Key Points

- Online graphics are made up of pixels.

- Most browsers support GIF and JPEG images.

- GIF images are small, limited to a 256-color palette, and quick to download.

- GIFs can be interlaced, transparent, or animated.

- JPEG images can contain millions of colors and are frequently used to display photographs.

- By default, GIFs and JPEGs display line by line from the top down, but you can change the default by creating interlaced GIFs or progressive JPEGs.

- JPEG's compression scheme enables you to reduce the size of JPEG images, but the compression is "lossy," so compress with care (remember, the more you compress, the lower your picture quality).

- Size graphics in your graphics editing program to help make your Web page's graphics files as small as possible.

- Cropping images reduces file sizes.

- Consider using thumbnails to link to large online graphics.

- Graphic Web page elements include photographs, illustrations, buttons, logos, icons, bullets, horizontal rules, graphical text, and backgrounds.

- You can acquire Web graphics from clip art collections on CD-ROMs, online freeware, online art vendors, and graphic designers.

- You can create custom art by using various software programs as well as by scanning hand-drawn art.

- Photographs can be converted to image files by means of scanners, film developers, and digital cameras.

Chapter 4

Web Page and Web Site Design

You've read about Web text in Chapter 2, and you've looked over Web graphics in Chapter 3. Now you're ready for some *Web page* and *Web site* design theory. And that's what this chapter is all about—successfully blending Web text and graphics to create appealing and usable Web pages and sites. But before we dive into the mechanics of Web page and Web site design, we can't resist mentioning a couple planning issues. (Think of this section as preparation for Chapter 6, which discusses planning Web pages and sites in detail.)

Lingo   A *Web page* is a single page that displays in your browser; a *Web site* is a collection of related Web pages; and a *home page* is the main page (which usually serves as a table of contents or an introductory page) in a Web site.

Understandably, planning affects design in a couple major ways. Specifically, before you design for the Web, you should consider your audience and organize your *home page's* layout and Web site's structure (if you're planning to expand your solitary home page into a full-blown Web site).

Audience Reigns Supreme

Most likely, you're creating a Web page because you have knowledge to impart, a message to pass along, a service to provide, a group to keep organized, or entertainment to offer. But before you state your piece by creating a Web page or Web site, you should answer at least four audience-related questions:

- **What is the purpose of my page?**   Clearly define the goal of your Web page or Web site to yourself. For example, determine whether your site informs, entertains, serves as a Web portal (such as a search site or a directory of links), addresses a specific community (such as hobbyists, activists, employees, customers, and so on), presents an artistic expression, provides a personality profile (such as a personal page or resume), or fulfills another specific purpose. After you define the overall goal of your site, refine your site's topic. For example, let's say that you decide to create an informational site about pets. You chose an informational format—that's a start, but "pets" is a little broad. You could further refine your goal by deciding to provide information about caring for, say, pet lizards or, even more specifically, iguanas.

- **Who is my audience?**   Analyze who will be viewing your pages—corporate clients, cartoon-watching kids, local artists, armchair athletes, your extended family, and so forth. Be as specific as possible. Then think of a particular person—a real person—to represent a typical audience member that you can keep in mind while you design. For example, let's say you're creating a fan site for a basketball team. When you design this site, you should imagine the one friend, relative, neighbor, coworker, or acquaintance who proudly owns a full spectrum of team shirts, refuses ever to miss a game, and regularly yells at the TV set throughout the season. If you don't have one of those types around (you're definitely an anomaly!), you could focus on a well-known sports analyst (Jim Rome comes to mind), a sports-driven TV sitcom character, or even a character from a novel or movie as your ideal audience member. In other words, to create a dynamic well-focused site, you would design your site with a clear picture in mind of a particular sports fan—you wouldn't want to design your site with the vague notion that you're creating a Web site for anyone who has ever watched a basketball game. By the way, don't worry—you don't have to tell the person who's serving as your "ideal audience member" that you're using him or her as a design tool! Generally, designing for a real person is much more effective and enjoyable than designing for a generic audience profile.

- ■ **Who am I?**   Determine how you want to present yourself to your target audience. You should consciously choose how you want to communicate to your audience—casually, formally, professionally, comically, creatively, seriously, and so forth. Creating a perspective (or a persona) for yourself can keep you from straying toward inappropriate design decisions, such as including an adorable picture of your nephew at his first birthday party on your company earnings page.

- ■ **How will my audience view my page?**   Consider the technical capabilities of your audience. Basically, you need to think about how a typical person in your audience will be accessing your site. If your site is targeted to on-campus university faculty members, you probably won't have to worry about bandwidth because most universities have high-bandwidth networks. On the other hand, if you're designing pages for your friends who relocated all over the country (or the world) after graduation, you should create pages that will download reasonably quickly to accommodate dial-up modem connections.

Tip   Designing without an audience in mind leads to aimless design decisions. In contrast, pinpointing your audience provides recognizable boundaries and enables smart design choices.

As mentioned earlier, Chapter 6 covers Web site structure, planning, and audience analyses in greater depth, but your answers to the preceding questions should give you a feel for audience considerations. And as you'll soon see, knowing your audience comes into play when you make some of your design decisions. For example, we redesigned the New Frontiers for Learning in Retirement (NFLR) Web site to serve as a case study for this chapter. The site's main audience is the retirement community, who generally access the Internet at typical dial-up modem speeds (around 28.8Kbps per second to nearly 56Kbps per second) as opposed to high-speed cable modems, DSL (Digital Subscriber Lines), or *T1* lines. Therefore, when we redesigned the NFLR site, we kept the retirement community and their dial-up connections in mind.

Lingo   *T1* lines are high-speed communications lines that can provide Internet access at the rate of 1.544 megabits per second.

Storyboarding Your Web Site

After you identify your audience but before you start to create your Web pages, you should sketch your home page's layout as well as any relationships among ancillary pages—this visual representation is called a *storyboard*. You don't have to be an artist to create storyboards for your Web pages and Web sites. In fact, one of our favorite ways to sketch a site is on napkins at a nearby Italian restaurant. As with our preceding "consider your audience" chat, storyboarding Web pages and Web sites is also covered in more detail in Chapter 6. At this point, we simply mention sketching out your pages and site (if you're creating a site) as a design step. When you were thinking about text in Chapter 2, you might've come up with some site organization ideas based on your brainstorming results. Storyboarding simply entails roughly illustrating your organizational ideas by sketching the relationships among elements on each page as well as the relationships among your Web site's pages. At this point, you're focusing on the *structure* of your Web site, not the finer aspects of your content.

Figures 4-1 and 4-2 illustrate the concept of storyboarding. Figure 4-1 shows our sketch of the redesigned version of the New Frontiers for Learning in Retirement home page (NFLR2), and Figure 4-2 displays how we thought the NFLR site should be reorganized. Later in this chapter, you can see a couple of the storyboarded pages in the redesigned site take shape.

Now that you've at least briefly considered the concept of audience and page and site planning, let's move on to discuss how to best assimilate Web text and Web graphics into well-designed Web pages and Web sites. First we'll look at Web *page* design issues. Then later in this chapter, we'll address Web *site* design considerations.

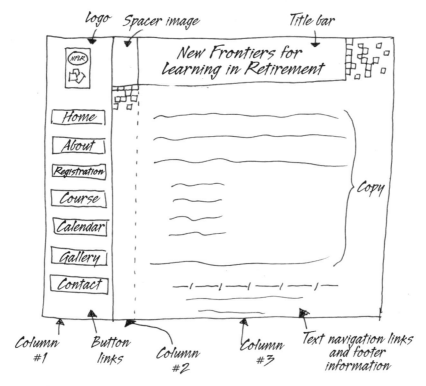

Figure 4-1 Our sketch of the redesigned NFLR home page shows the basic page structure used throughout the site.

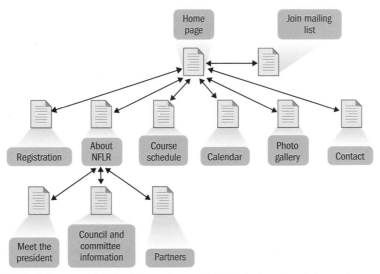

Figure 4-2 Our storyboard of the redesigned NFLR Web shows the site's overall structure and page relationships.

Web Page Design Rules That Won't Let You Down

Before you can create a Web site, you have to build a Web page—or maybe you're planning to build only a home page instead of a full-blown site. Either way, you can take advantage of some tried-and-true Web design tips. In this section, we address key Web page design issues and proven tactics. But we also have a small disclaimer because, first and foremost, designing Web pages and Web sites is a creative endeavor. We have no desire to take away a drop of your creativity—we'd much rather spark your imagination. Understand that the parameters we outline in this chapter (as well as throughout the book) are guidelines. We hope you'll experiment with your Web page designs in ways not mentioned in this text. We highly encourage you to do so. The information in this chapter will provide a strong foundation for you—a good base for custom designs. If you follow the advice in this book, you'll be able to create clean, attractive, and easy-to-navigate Web pages. Then you can take the fundamentals to new creative heights (and e-mail us when you do because we'd be happy to post a link to your Web page on *www.creationguide.com/readerpages.html*).

Tip   Keep in mind that most good page-design theories carry over into good site-design practices.

For discussion purposes, we've divided Web page design fundamentals into the following topics:

- Web page dimensions
- Page layout issues
- Color
- Navigation tools and hyperlinks
- Standard credibility components
- Text
- Graphics

Web Page Dimensions

Theoretically, Web pages are infinitely long and infinitely wide because they aren't bound by the size of cut paper. Of course, designing your page with measurements such as "infinity by infinity" in mind doesn't help you or your page's visitors. So let's look at a more reasonable way to select your Web page's boundaries. The best way to narrow down your page's parameters is to consider the browser window real estate on a lowest common denominator machine. In other words, you need to think about the amount of viewable content in the browser window of the user who has the most limited browser capabilities.

For Web page design purposes, the smallest monitor resolution out there displays 640 × 480 pixels at a time. Further, various browsers tend to show even less area than 640 × 480 pixels because of the browser's setup (including toolbars, scrollbars, status bars, Favorites or Bookmark windows, and so forth). For example, look at Figure 4-3. The two screens show Microsoft Internet Explorer on Microsoft Windows XP and Apple Macintosh OS X platforms along with the maximum available display area in the browsers' default setups. As you can see in the screens, Internet Explorer on Windows provides a display setting of 609 × 354, while Internet Explorer on OS X provides a display setting of 602 × 327. Further, users running Netscape Navigator obtain a maximum viewable area of 630 × 347 on a Windows-based system and 612 × 321 on a Macintosh.

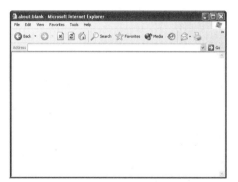 

Figure 4-3   The maximum viewable area in Internet Explorer on a Windows-based system using a display setting of 640 × 480 is 609 × 354. The maximum viewable area in Internet Explorer on a Macintosh system using a display setting of 640 × 480 is 602 × 327.

Therefore, by combining the smallest parameters of the available viewing areas in Internet Explorer and Netscape, you can see that approximately 600 × 320 (as you can see, we like to work with round numbers) is the smallest combined area when you take browser/system combinations into account—this is called the *safe area*. When you design your Web pages (particularly your home page), you should keep the safe area measurements in mind, and, as we describe next, make sure that your page's most important information appears within the safe area's boundaries.

With the mathematics of the safe area safely behind us, we now feel free to state that although you should design with the safe area in mind by placing your most important information in or as near the safe area as possible, most people view the Web on monitors set to the 800 × 600 screen resolution size. In fact, according to *www.statmarket.com* (February 17, 2001), a sample size of 50,465,595 Web sites revealed the following percentages (rounded to the nearest .5%) of people using the available screen resolution settings:

640 × 480: 7%
800 × 600: 53%
1024 × 768: 31%
1152 × 864: 2.5%
1280 × 1024: 2.5%
Other: 4%

Basically, the preceding numbers mean that you can focus your design on working best with the 800 × 600 screen resolution setting, although you should keep the other settings in mind (which means you should preview your pages in all settings to ensure no major problems exist).

But even after safe-area measurements and Web site statistics are taken into consideration, we have one last caveat for you regarding Web page dimensions—keep in mind that people don't always maximize their browser windows, especially if they're using large monitors. Thus, even when you're designing for 800 × 600, you won't be able to control exactly how people will size and view your pages. To counter the unpredictability of your page's presentation, we show you how to create *liquid pages* in the Part Two projects. Liquid pages automatically resize to a browser window as much as possible without losing the page's overall structure.

So given all the "unknowns" associated with Web page dimensions, you might be wondering if there's any hope for successfully designing a page that can be viewed by the masses. Of course there's hope; after all, you've surely seen a number of well-designed sites online. Basically, when it comes to Web page dimension considerations, your goal as a Web designer should be to ensure that your important information appears in the minimum safe area zone and you should consider creating liquid pages whenever possible. Using these two methods, you'll be able to present your information in the best possible light for most people on the Web.

Try This! If you have a fairly modern (Windows 98 or later) computer system, you can see the effects of viewing Web pages at various screen sizes. To do so, follow these steps:

1 Right-click a blank area on your desktop, and choose Properties.

2 In the Display Properties dialog box, click the Settings tab.

3 If you're using Windows 98, Windows Me, or Windows 2000, drag the slider control in the Screen Area section to change the screen setting to 640 × 480, click Apply, click OK (your screen might go black for a moment or two while it readjusts the screen area), click Yes, and then click OK.

If you're using Windows XP, the Settings tab in the Display Properties dialog box doesn't show a 640 × 480 screen resolution option by default. Therefore, to configure 640 × 480 on an XP machine, click the Advanced button on the Settings tab, click the Adapter tab, and click List All Modes. In the List All Modes dialog box, click a 640 by 480 setting, and click OK.

4 View *www.creationguide.com/nflr2* in your browser, and then minimize your browser window.

5 Repeat steps 1 through 3, changing the 640 × 480 setting to 1024 × 768 (if you're a Windows XP user, you won't have to visit the Adapter tab this time—you can simply drag the Screen Area slider control).

6 View *www.creationguide.com/nflr2* with the new settings, and then minimize your browser window.

7 Repeat steps 1 through 3 using the 800 × 600 setting (the most popular screen area setting), view *www.creationguide.com/nflr2*, and then close your browser window.

As you worked through the preceding process, the NFLR2 Web page's view should've gone through a metamorphosis similar to the changes shown in the accompanying figures.

640 × 480   800 × 600   1024 × 768

Tip   When you design Web pages, you should view your pages using various screen settings, color settings, and browsers to ensure that your page displays correctly for the majority of people. For instance, you should perform the steps in the Try This! exercise earlier in this chapter to view your Web pages at various sizes. Then, experiment with various sizes in other browsers and other color settings as well.

Page Layout Issues

Now that we've pinned down a target page size, let's look at page layouts. For the record, we'd like to state that just because the Web provides almost carte blanche publishing freedom, it doesn't mean that you can get away with simply uploading text and images willy-nilly—unless you don't care whether anyone visits your page long enough to read or even glimpse your content. A more successful approach—one that we highly recommend—involves following some basic rules for laying out pages.

The number-one layout rule is to apply basic template principles. A *template* (as you might know from hard-copy page design) is a grid that you can use as a guideline to lay out your page's elements. Although current limitations make it difficult for you to adhere to strict page layout rules and regulations for your Web pages as consistently as for printed text, numerous Web pages follow loosely defined templates to help contain the flow of information. For example, Figure 4-4 shows the very basic template we used to create the NFLR2 site. If you visit the NFLR2 site online (*www.creationguide.com/nflr2*) and click a few links, you'll see that every page adheres to the simple, straightforward template shown in Figure 4-4.

Using a template enables you to align elements and create consistent external and internal spacing between and around elements. When you devise templates, keep in mind that people generally scan Web pages from left to right and top to bottom; so design accordingly. Your primary design area is along the left side and top edge of the first screen that displays to users, which very nicely brings our discussion back to the "safe area" topic.

As we mentioned earlier, you can count on an area of 600 × 320 pixels as your safe area when your page loads into any browser, and a screen resolution of 800 × 600 as the most commonly viewed resolution (which has a cross-browser, cross-platform safe area of approximately 760 × 440). For the most part, users are willing to scroll down but not across. Therefore, when you create a Web page, stay within the width limitations as much as possible, but don't become overly concerned if your page flows below the safe area's height limitation.

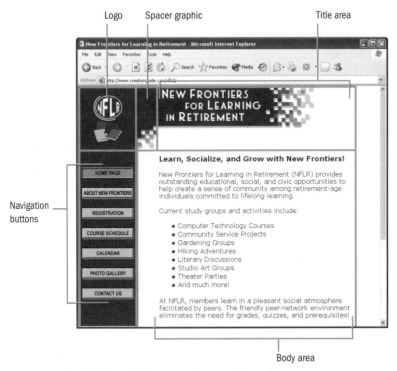

Figure 4-4 The NFLR2 site follows a simple geometric template.

Now, here's an even bigger tip: *The choicest spot of all within the safe area is the upper-left corner.*

Why? Because no matter how much a user resizes the browser window, the upper-left corner remains in view (or, in worst-case scenarios, it's the last area to go if window resizing gets completely out of hand). Therefore, the upper-left corner is prime property—the ideal place for you to insert your company's logo or other key information.

After the upper-left corner, the next-best area on your Web page is what journalists refer to as "above the fold." Newspapers carry the day's most notable news stories above where the paper folds, so that when the paper appears on newsstands passersby will see the top news stories and be tempted to purchase the paper. Obviously, users can't fold their monitors (not yet, at least), so your design "fold" is the bottom edge of the safe area's parameters. When you lay out your page's information, make sure that the most significant and eye-catching information appears on the opening view. Further, if your page scrolls below the fold, ensure that your design looks like it continues when viewers see the initial display. (Otherwise, users might not scroll at all.) You can indicate that a page continues by avoiding obvious page breaks (such as space between paragraphs) at the safe area's bottom limit.

Finally, you should include your site's main navigation links (such as a navigation bar, menu bar, or buttons) within the page's safe area—preferably along the left side or top edge. The NFLR2 site uses the very common left-edge navigation bar setup. The main navigational links on the MSN home page (*www.msn.com*) align across the top of the page. Secondary links align along the page's left edge.

In addition to using templates and designing within the safe area, you should incorporate fundamental Web page elements into your page, as shown in Figure 4-5. Most pages contain a title area, logo, navigation links, body, and footer text. You'll find numerous combinations and positioning of these elements, but the basic elements generally appear on most home pages in some manner.

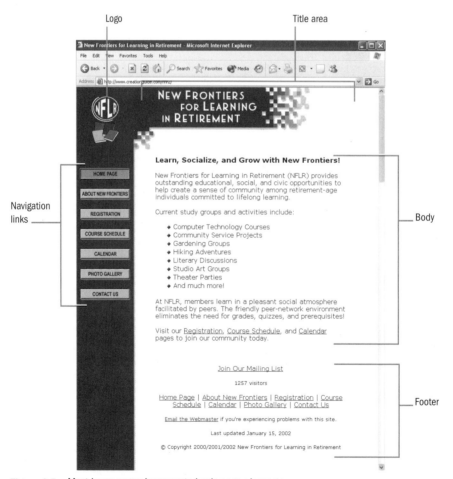

Figure 4-5   Most home pages incorporate basic page elements.

The remaining page layout considerations we want to impress on you encompass universal "good design" practices. Here are some common design principles that you should keep in mind and on-hand:

- **Blinking text and gratuitous animation**   Avoid blinking text and unnecessary animation; many people find these effects annoying and meaningless. On the other hand, many people appreciate a slick yet simple rollover effect for buttons.

- **Competition**   Search similar sites to see what's out there, and then make your site unique. By viewing similar or related sites, you can also get ideas of topics that need better coverage or that you've forgotten to address on your page.

- **Content**   Keep content fresh, simple, and smart. Further, aim to use at least 80 percent of your page to present your content (especially if you plan to use advertising on your page) and restrict navigation elements to 20 percent or less of your page area.

- **Cutting-edge technology**   Avoid using too many high-tech features or you'll lose the majority of your viewers. Most people don't want to download a plug-in (which is a small "helper" application that works with a browser to run a specific file type) just to view a Web page.

- **Download speed**   Ensure that your page downloads as quickly as possible; you have about 10 seconds before viewers itch to surf elsewhere.

- **Frames**   Use frames sparingly; they're tricky to implement properly and sometimes hard for users to navigate. Essentially, frames are used to divide a browser window so that users can view multiple pages at once, as we describe in Part Two in the Chapter 9 project.

- **Functional design**   Opt for function over form—every design element should also serve a purpose. If you're not sure whether a design element is functional, temporarily remove the element from the page and analyze the page without it. If your page works as well (or better) without it, the element is more ornamental than functional and should be dropped.

- **Important elements**   Size elements in proportion to their importance. Bigger means more important and draws attention quicker, whereas smaller equates to lesser importance.

- **Moderation**   Avoid using too much of any element or technique, including links, colors, scrolling, and so forth. Remember, too much emphasis results in no emphasis at all.

- **Sound files**   For the most part, don't automatically enable sound files. If you must include sound, provide an option to play an audio file. Most people don't like to listen to background sounds and many people keep their speakers turned down or off, which means that extraneous audio files only serve to slow download speeds considerably for no purpose. One way you can add sound if you're determined to do so is to add it in subtle ways, such as playing a short sound when viewers click a hyperlink (we show you how to do this in the Chapter 9 project).

- **The kitchen sink**   Don't get crazy and overload your home page (or any page, for that matter). If you have more than enough information for your home page, expand your page into a Web site by dividing information into logical chunks and placing each chunk on a separate subpage linked to your home page. Also, you don't have to use all your text and graphics just because you have the information on hand. Remember that Web pages are dynamic, which means you can selectively update and modify information on a regular basis, so opt to show pertinent information in a timely manner. For example, if you want to publicize the birth dates of your friends and family, consider showing just the current month's birthdays and updating the birthday listing monthly.

- **Visual appeal**   Verify that your page looks good in Internet Explorer and Netscape Navigator at various resolutions and color depths on Windows and Macintosh systems.

- **White space**   Create eye relief and visual space with strategically placed blank areas (white space), as described toward the end of the next section.

Color

After page dimensions and layout, you should consider your Web page's color scheme. A *color scheme* refers to your site's interface elements (not necessarily the colors used in images), such as title graphics, buttons, background, text, and so forth. Ideally, you should limit the number of colors used in your Web page's interface to three or four. The key is to use contrasting colors, especially if you're using a colored background. Also, keep your colors appropriate for your message. For example, if you're creating a Christmas edition of your site, use red and green (not pink and yellow), or use cool blues and purples if your site advertises a mountain ski resort. If you can't decide which colors will work best for you, you can always opt for black text on a white background—the standard black-on-white combination is pretty much bulletproof when it comes to read-ability and design sense.

In addition to using colors for your interface, you can use colors to call attention to certain content items on your page. For example, if you have a store site and you're running a special, you could highlight the information by placing a color background behind the text advertising your sale.

Overall, you should use your color scheme to create balance and unity throughout your site, but you should also use colors to draw attention to specific areas of the page, including links, titles, logos, key points, items of interest, and so forth.

Try This! To experiment with various background and text colors, visit a Web color selection page (see *www.creationguide.com/colortest*) or check out the Color Tools listed on this book's resources page (*www.creationguide.com/resources*).

Finally, when choosing a color scheme, remember to consult the Web-safe color palette we discuss in Chapter 3. Whenever possible, opt to use Web-safe colors to avoid unnecessary dithering. For example, the NFLR2 site's purple-blue background color uses the Web-safe color that's defined as having a red-green-blue (RGB) value of 51-51-102 and a hexadecimal value of #333366. (You can find the colors used on the NFLR2 page on the Web-safe color palette shown on *www.creationguide.com/colorchart*.)

Complementary to colors is *white space*, which we've already introduced a couple times in this book. As we mentioned, white space isn't necessarily white—white space is an area without content. The concept behind white space is to provide eye relief. You use white space to create visual space between and around images and body text. In essence, white space frames and draws atten-tion to your content.

Try This! To compare a site that uses Web-safe colors with one that doesn't, follow these steps:

1   Right-click a blank area on your desktop, select Properties, and then click the Settings tab in the Display Properties dialog box.

2   On the Settings tab, click the Colors drop-down arrow. (Note your current setting so that you can return to it in step 5.) If you're using Windows 98, Windows Me, or Windows 2000, select 256 Colors from the drop-down list, click Apply (your screen may go black for a moment), and then click OK.

   If you're using Windows XP (or Mac OSX), a 256 option isn't provided by default. You can view this example using the Medium (16 Bit) color setting on the Settings tab, or you can dredge up a 256 color setting. To access a 256 color setting in Windows XP, click the Advanced button, click the Adapter tab, click List All Modes, and select a monitor setting that uses 256 colors. Then, click OK, click Apply, click Yes, and click OK.

3   Open *www.creationguide.com/nflr1* in your browser. Notice the dithering that occurs on the Web page's background.

4   Now open *www.creationguide.com/nflr2* in your browser. As you can see, the page's colors appear clear and crisp, without dither, because the colors used to create the page are included in the Web-safe color palette.

5   Close your browser, right-click on your desktop, and return your color display to the original setting.

Navigation Tools and Hyperlinks

Navigation tools and hyperlinks include buttons, clickable logos, text links, and graphical links—basically, all the elements you provide on your Web pages that enable users to find additional information easily. Effective navigation elements tell users where they are, where they've been, and where they can go next. Therefore, all successful navigation tools and hyperlinks must use meaningful descriptors, whether the descriptors are graphical, textual, or both.

> **Tip**   As mentioned earlier in this chapter, remember to restrict your use of navigation elements so that they account for less than 20 percent of your Web page's area if possible. At times they might require more space, such as when you create a site or page that consists mostly of hyperlinks, or possibly you're creating a site with very little content and you want to visually balance the site.

To further clarify how to effectively use navigation tools, the following sections offer some rules of thumb for designing navigation elements.

Buttons

If you create a menu bar that uses buttons, keep the buttons consistent on the current page (same dimensions, color schemes, and so forth) and display the same group of buttons on every page. You can easily confuse viewers by offering different sets of buttons on various pages. To ensure consistency, we recommend using templates, as we emphasize throughout this book. Also, ensure that buttons are named so that they clearly indicate where viewers will go after they click a particular button. Finally, consider slightly modifying buttons to display the current page's button differently—such as slightly darker—so that viewers instantly know which button points to the current page.

Logos

If you include a logo on your Web pages, ensure that your logo is a high-quality GIF graphic that uses Web-safe colors. You want your logo to look great, regardless of a user's system capabilities. Ideally, you'll want to show your logo on your home page in the upper-left corner, a little larger than the logo's display on subsequent pages, and surrounded by a light padding of extra space to ensure that your logo stands out. Then on all ancillary pages, link a smaller version of your logo (also slightly padded by surrounding space) to your home page. That way, users can easily access your home page from anywhere within your site, while you reinforce your logo identity.

Logo Design   If you're designing a logo, keep in mind that logos are usually used in a variety of situations and sizes. One mistake that many people make when they create their first logo is that they create logos that are too complex. Complex logos become blurs and blobs when they're reduced to small sizes for business cards or other marketing materials. So keep it simple. Further, ensure that your logo appears sleek and legible in black and white as well as in color. You don't want to be disappointed when your logo, which looks so beautiful on your Web page, looks like an ink splotch when it appears in your newspaper advertisement. A great way to test your logo's durability is to re-size your graphic to an inch or two, print your logo, and then fax it to yourself. A good logo will be able to withstand this abuse and arrive intact after all's said and done.

Text Links

As mentioned in earlier chapters, you should always provide text links for all graphical links (including buttons, logos, and linked images). Doing so ensures that everyone—even those who opt to hide graphics in their browser window—can navigate within your site. Also, avoid embedding hyperlinks within paragraphs of text or linking viewers away from your page in midsentence.

Colorwise, if you don't use standard hyperlink colors (you can change link colors by using HTML code), ensure that you assign specific colors to nonvisited and visited hyperlinks and keep the colors consistent throughout your site. (Usually, sites use brighter colors for nonvisited links and darker colors for visited links—we talk more about formatting hyperlinks in Part Two.) Viewers frequently use visual cues to help them keep track of their online travels.

Paragraphwise, you should avoid embedding too many links within your body text. Embedding lots of links creates hard-to-read text, and simply begs readers to click a link and leave your site for good. Occasionally, you might want to include a link or two in a paragraph to provide relative information. If you feel inclined to embed a link, ensure that you provide enough information surrounding the link so that readers don't *have* to click the link for additional information unless they want to. Providing textual information around a link also serves as a safety net if the link dies an untimely death (due to server outages, standard archiving procedures, or simply because a site doesn't exist anymore). If readers have background information about a dead link and they desperately want to read the additional information, they might be able to successfully search for the information using a search engine.

Finally, on long pages, include a "Back to Top," "Top of Page," "Home," or another similar link at the base of the page (for instance, see *www.creationguide.com/resources*). And don't forget your bottom-of-the-page Webmaster e-mail link and copyright notice.

Try This!   To see links that take you to another part of the same page, visit *www.creationguide.com/ resources*. Each categorical group of links on the resources page is followed by a "top of page" link. Clicking a top of page link returns viewers to the list of resource categories displayed at the top of the page.

Graphical Links

On some sites, graphical elements, such as images, serve as hyperlinks. For example, a site might display thumbnails images (as explained in Chapter 3) that link to larger images. Or a site might use small icons or pictures that users can click to view additional information. If you use graphical links, ensure that users clearly understand that they can click the images for more information. Frequently, graphical links are accompanied by text links to make the association clear—we highly recommend this practice. For example, on retail sites, you might see a clickable picture of a coffee maker accompanied by hypertext (linked text) below the picture. In this setup, users can click either the linked image or the text to view detailed information about the coffee maker.

Tip   Above all else, avoid the cardinal Web page sin of providing dead links. To prevent this problem, check your links and run your site through an online validation service. A number of validation sites—including *validator.w3.org*, *http://validator.w3.org/checklink*, *www.htmlhelp.com/tools/ validator*, and *www.craigcecil.com/checkyoursite.htm*—will check your Web page's links and HTML code for free. Other fee-based validation services are also available online, such as *www.netmechanic.com*, among others.

Standard Credibility Components

Often when you view a Web page, you have no idea where the page's files are located, who created the page, or where the information you're reading came from. Anyone can post a Web site, and you shouldn't automatically believe everything you find on the Web—but you already know that! With that in mind, you should strive to make your Web pages as credible as possible. You can do that in a number of easy ways.

- **Attribution**   Give complete attribution, credits, bylines, and references for any quotes, graphics, or statistics you use on your Web page. Attribution gives credit where credit is due and strengthens your site's trustworthiness.

- **Contact information**   Make it easy for viewers to contact you and obtain more information through e-mail, mailing lists, telephone numbers, physical addresses, and so forth. One of the Web's biggest draws is its interactive appeal, so take advantage of this unique communication channel.

- **Copyright notice**   Include a copyright notice on your Web site to show that you care enough about your Web pages to take ownership of your site's content.

- **Dynamic content**   Keep your content up-to-date and modified regularly. If you show readers that you're serious about your page, they'll be more likely to take an interest in it.

- **Last updated**   Include text that shows when the page was last updated so that viewers know they're reading current information, and to reassure them that you haven't abandoned the page.

- **Personal information**   Provide information about yourself or a prominent person associated with the site (such as the club president); include your name (or the prominent person's name) and possibly a picture.

- ■ **Special interests**   State your point of view if your page presents commercial interests or advocacy issues.

- ■ **Spelling and grammar**   Check your spelling and grammar religiously. Not to sound preachy or melodramatic, but typos and grammatical errors are frequently construed as highly unprofessional, and they almost instantaneously jeopardize your credibility.

- ■ **Webmaster link**   Provide an e-mail link to the Webmaster in case viewers have problems or questions.

Text

In Chapter 2 we looked at how to write effective Web text, and in Chapter 3 we reviewed how to use text in graphical elements, such as title bars and buttons. In this section, we review effective ways to format nongraphical text.

As you know, text is used to present content and create hyperlinks. As a Web designer, you have the power to control your text's size, color, formatting, and style. A variety of thoughts are bandied about when it comes to text rules, but for your benefit, we've consolidated the basic premises that the majority of Web designers support, including preferences for font size, font style, and font formatting.

Font Size

Almost universally, Web designers recommend that you use the default font size for body text. This allows viewers to choose the font size through their browser's default settings. For special text, such as copyrights and other footer information, you can specify smaller font sizes to avoid disrupting your page's focus on the content. If you want to display larger text, such as headings, you should use the HTML default heading tags, as described in Part Two, instead of simply increasing the body text's font size.

Font Style

Even though thousands of font styles exist, all font styles can be categorized as either *serif* or *sans serif*. Serif fonts, such as Times, use "hooks," or short lines, on the ends of letters, whereas sans serif fonts, such as Arial, use plain-edged letters. On the whole, the Web design community voices a mixed response to the use of serif and sans serif fonts online. Personally, we generally prefer to use sans serif fonts rather than serif fonts when creating Web pages because we find sans serif fonts easier to read online as well as more visually appealing.

Tip   You should avoid displaying your text—both serif and sans serif—too small. A common (and slightly disturbing) trend seems to be emerging in which sites containing numerous links display the links in tiny font sizes. This setup can make the links illegible as well as hard to click for users whose browsers use a small default font size or who have smaller screen resolution settings. Clarity becomes even more of an issue when a serif font is used to display the tiny text and links.

In the past—when monitor resolutions left much to be desired (and were generally alien-glow green)—sans serif fonts were overwhelmingly recommended for on-screen text because serifs helped only to blur the text into further illegibility. Nowadays, monitors are much improved, so accounting for the blurriness factor doesn't hold much water (unless you opt to use very small text, which we don't recommend). But you're not off the hook—you still have font-related design decisions to address. For example, the NFLR2 site uses Verdana—an easy-to-read sans serif font—for the body text to present clear letters to accommodate viewers who might have vision problems.

If you've worked with print text, you might know that a common serif-related design technique is to use sans serif fonts for headings and serif fonts for body text. If you want to blend serif and sans serif text online to differentiate body text from headings, you can do so, but we recommend that you reverse the standard print practice. In other words, try using serif fonts for headings and sans serif fonts for text. Although you might feel odd at first when you reverse the age-old print standard, you'll most likely get over it quickly when you see that your online headings stand out nicely with serifs and your sans serif body text is easy-to-read.

Next, regardless of your serif preferences, you should stick with cross-platform fonts to ensure that users see your text similar to how you designed your page. Specifically, cross-platform fonts are common fonts that will display in most Macintosh and PC computers as well as display in Internet Explorer and Netscape browsers. Cross-platform fonts include the following:

Arial (or Helvetica)
Arial Black
Arial Narrow
Comic Sans
Courier New
Georgia
Impact
Times New Roman (or Times)
Trebuchet
Verdana
▶ 🏠 🚲 ♥ ⓘ ● ■ ? (Webdings)

Font Formatting

Last but not least among font design issues is formatting. Basically, not to sound dull or anything, but we advocate moderation (again!). For instance, when it comes to color text, avoid overusing it—use color (within your color scheme, of course) only to draw attention to items. Plus, think before using white text because users will need to do a little finagling before they will be able to print white text from your page. Instead of simply clicking the Print button, users will have to modify their browser settings to override the Web page's color scheme (if the browser supports that functionality) or they'll have to copy the text from your page into a text editing document (such as a Microsoft Word document), select the white text, recolor the text using a darker color, and then print the text from the text document.

Another formatting technique is to use italic and boldface. When it comes to italicizing and boldfacing, however, again limit your use. While monitors are improving all the time, italic type still tends to make online text harder to read, and liberal boldfacing weighs pages down, which drives readers away. Furthermore, overusing italic or boldface type waters down the emphasizing effect of the formatting technique. Now while we don't have much use for italics (other than titles of works, slang words, or annotations), we do believe boldfacing can come in handy on a fairly regular basis, as long as you use it with discretion. Ideally, when you use boldfacing on a Web page, the boldface type should make sense on its own. As discussed in Chapter 2, Web viewers scan pages before they read. A scanning eye will jump right to boldface type, so make sure your boldface type conveys a meaningful concept or idea and entices readers to stay a little longer.

If you really want to emphasize a point, consider offsetting or highlighting an example. Oftentimes, readers go straight for examples, Evel Knieveling right over your carefully devised and formatted chunks of body text. A good example can pique a reader's interest and possibly draw them into your main text.

Most important, do *not* underline nonlinked text. Users have become programmed to click underlined text—and there's no need to deprogram the masses starting with your site. Users can become highly annoyed if clicking underlined text doesn't take them somewhere, and nonlinked text that looks like a link ranks lower on the Web-page faux pas list than a dead link. So save everyone the hassle, and forget about underlining body text.

Finally, text alignment falls within the realm of font formatting. For the most part, use left-aligned text. For most people, left-aligned text is easy to read and readily adaptable to various browser window dimensions. Centered text is more difficult to read and creates jagged, unattractive visual lines all over your page's layout; so use centered text at your own risk or only in special circumstances (such as a poetry page, an introductory or "splash" page, or copyright text at the bottom of your page). Finally, right-aligned text, although occasionally successful as an avant-garde design technique, can get lost outside the safe area or turn readers off if they find jagged left-edges too distracting. Therefore, consider using left-aligned text on most of your Web pages, and use white space to add shape to your text on the page.

Graphics

In Chapter 3, we took an in-depth look at Web graphics. As far as graphics and Web page design go, you should adhere to the following four practices in addition to the techniques discussed in Chapter 3:

- Avoid large graphics that seem to take days to download on a 28.8-Kbps modem.

- Steer clear of meaningless graphics. If a user has to wait to see a graphic, make sure that the graphic contributes to the user's experience.

- Ensure every graphical link has a text link equivalent.

- Include an ALT tag for every graphic. (*ALT* stands for *alternative*, as in text that serves as an alternative for a graphic.) An ALT label provides the pop-up text when you move your mouse over a graphic (as shown in Figure 4-6) as well as displays in graphical placeholder areas when graphics are turned off (as shown in Figure 4-7). These days, ALT tags also provide text for page reader utilities, which read content to computer users who are visually impaired (for more information about using a page reader or "narrator" utility in Windows XP, see the Try This! exercise later in this chapter).

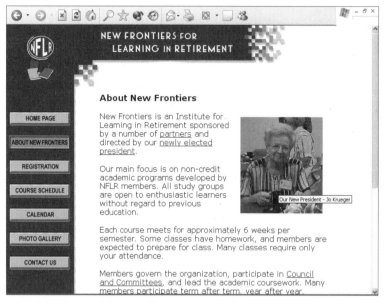

Figure 4-6   An ALT label can display image information in a pop-up window.

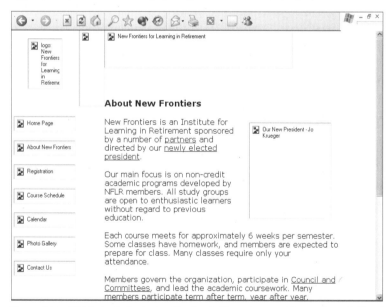

Figure 4-7   ALT labels display in graphic placeholders when graphics are turned off and provide text for narrator utilities.

Try This! ALT tags can provide an accessibility feature for vision impaired Web surfers. When you use ALT tags, a narrator utility can read the ALT tags' contents. If you're using Windows XP, you can easily hear this feature in action. To do so, ensure that your speakers are on and then follow these steps:

1　In your browser, display *www.creationguide.com/nflr2/about.html* to serve as a sample page.

2　On the Start menu, choose Programs, choose Accessories, choose Accessibility, and then click Narrator.

3　In the dialog box that describes the Narrators' function, click OK. The Narrator dialog box opens and the Narrator feature is active.

4　Click the About New Frontiers Web page to make the browser window active.

5　After the narrator reads the Web page title, point to various elements on the page (such as buttons, the picture, and hyperlinks) to hear the narrator read the tool tip text (note that "tool tip" text is the ALT text on a Web page).

6　Click Exit in the Narrator window to turn off the feature, and click Yes.

Web Site Design Rules to Live By

Now that you've been inundated with good-Web-*page*-design techniques, let's take a quick look at good-Web-*site*-design techniques. Fortunately, good Web site design mostly involves applying good-Web-page-design techniques across the board. Therefore, make sure that you use the following two Web site design theorems in conjunction with the numerous Web page design techniques presented earlier in this chapter.

As far as Web site design goes, our goal is to have you leave this section with two main Web site design concepts painlessly emblazoned in your mind—consistency and structure.

Consistency

Web site consistency means that when viewers move from page to page throughout your site, they can visually see and intuitively grasp that they remain within your site. Viewers should recognize instantly when they've surfed to a page that's not yours. To create consistency, you use common design elements throughout your Web site, such as similar title bars, a consistent navigation bar, a universal color scheme, standard graphical text styles, consistent body text fonts, and so forth. Most important, users should be able to find your pages' navigation tools and logo in approximately the same area on every page in your site.

> **Tip**   Remember, you can use templates and style sheets to help achieve consistency throughout your Web site.

As you can see, if you create a solid home page, achieving site consistency is a snap; you've already taken care of all the "hard" work, such as devising color schemes, creating navigation bars, customizing title bars, and so forth. Ancillary pages simply need to mold the elements to their needs and use a complementary template. One of the benefits of using a consistent template and standard components on every page in your Web site is that it enables you to cover your "backdoor." Frankly, you never know when a reader will enter your site through a backdoor page (or subpage). Some people will inevitably find your site through search engines or links on other Web pages, and the search results and referring links won't always take readers to your Web site's home page. When you include basic components on your pages, people can quickly understand your Web site's structure and purpose as well as easily access ancillary pages in your site.

> **Lingo**   A *site map* is a Web page that shows all the links in a site in hierarchical structure, enabling users to gain an overview of the Web site as well as access to every link in the site. To see a site map in action, visit *www.creationguide.com/sitemap.html*.

Structure

Similar to consistency is a site's structure. And one of the most important points about site structure is to have one! In other words, you should outline your site's structure up front (as described earlier in the chapter when we discussed storyboards) and stick to your building plans so users won't get lost and turned around within your site. When creating structure, keep the following points in mind:

- Create a clean, logical structure. Aim to keep your site three clicks (or three levels) deep or less. (For example, see the storyboard shown in Figure 4-2.)

  > **Tip**   A highly effective way to keep users informed of their location within your site's structure is to display title bars on each page that depict the page's content and to slightly modify navigation bar buttons to indicate the current page. Figure 4-9 in the next section shows examples of modified buttons and page titles.

- Ensure that your navigation links clearly outline your site's hierarchy. On larger sites, consider including a *site map*. Frequently, we click site map links whenever we visit a new site to quickly see what's offered. We're usually pleasantly surprised at the number of treasures (cool links) we find on site maps that are otherwise hard to find on main Web pages.

■ Use page titles on every page. Further, make the home page's title text larger and ancillary page's titles slightly smaller to visually indicate the page's place in the hierarchy.

Case Study Practice

To wrap up this chapter, we present the original and redesigned versions of the New Frontiers for Learning in Retirement home pages and About New Frontiers Web pages. (You can see online versions of the sites at *www.creationguide.com/nflr1* and *www.creationguide.com/nflr2*.) Figure 4-8 shows the original NFLR pages, and Figure 4-9 shows the redesigned pages. Compare the four pages, and identify the Web page and Web site design issues and modifications that we've addressed in this chapter.

Figure 4-8 The original New Frontiers Home and About New Frontiers pages break many of the standard design rules outlined in this chapter.

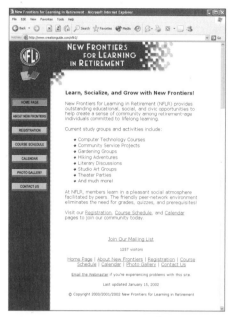

Figure 4-9   The redesigned New Frontiers Home page incorporates a number of good design techniques. The redesigned About New Frontiers Web page takes advantage of tried-and-true subpage design rules.

Key Points

▨   Remember that the audience reigns supreme—always design with a specific audience member in mind.

▨   Storyboard your home page and Web site's page relationships—think *structure*, not content details.

▨   Keep the lowest common denominator computer screens in mind, but feel comfortable using liquid pages and designing for an audience using 800 × 600 screens.

▨   Use templates and grids to guide your layout.

▨   Reserve your Web page's upper-left corner for your most important information.

▨   Display main concepts "above the fold."

▨   Include navigation links within the safe area.

▨   Incorporate a title area, logo, navigation links, body text, and footer text into each Web page.

▨   Use moderation in almost all areas of design—too much of any one element can kill a page.

- Implement a color scheme, preferably limited to three or four colors.

- Employ white space to create eye relief and draw attention to main elements on your page.

- Keep your navigation tools easily accessible, clearly defined, and consistent throughout your site.

- Link your logo to your home page throughout your site.

- Build credibility by providing contact information and clear channels of communication and by supplying attribution, credits, and references.

- Use the default font size for body text, and stick with cross-platform fonts whenever possible.

- Never underline nonlinked text.

- Include ALT tags with every graphic.

- Create consistency throughout your site by repeating your color scheme, title text, navigation tools, and other page layout elements on every page of your site.

- Ensure that users can easily identify a clear and logical structure for your site.

Chapter 5

Stockpiling the Goods

When you create Web pages, you need to have at least a couple (probably more) Web page creation tools on hand. Mind you, we're not talking about hardware—we're sure you've realized the importance of having a computer as well as possibly having access to a scanner, printer, and camera (digital or standard). In this chapter, our focus falls on the array of software that you can use to create, edit, and manipulate Web pages. As we show you in Part Two, you can create, edit, and publish Web pages by using a number of software applications and tools, and we find that we frequently mix and match our weapons of choice. Likewise, knowing your choices will help you create a working environment that best suits your needs and personal style.

To get started, let's look at two of the most basic "tools" you'll need during your Web creation endeavors—an Internet connection and server space.

Internet Connectivity and Server Space

No matter how astounding your Web page, it will live in virtual anonymity if you can't connect to the Internet and transfer the page's files to a server. (Recall from Chapter 1 that a *server* is a powerful computer that is connected to the Internet's backbone data lines, stores Web page files, and responds to users' requests to view the stored Web pages.) You must be connected to the Internet or have access to an Internet connection before you can achieve an online presence.

Granted, you can *create* most Web pages without an Internet connection, but you'll be dead in the water when it comes time to publish your pages online.

Tip If you use your computer to surf the Web, rest assured—you have an Internet connection. Using a standard dial-up Internet connection, you can copy Web page files from your computer onto a server that's connected to the Internet.

In addition to the basic prerequisite of Internet connectivity, you might need to purchase some space on a server for your Web files. We say *might* because in a lot of cases server space is freely given away or provided in addition to other paid services. For example, your Internet service provider (ISP) might give you 30 MB (give or take 20 MB) of free server space in addition to your Internet connection. The notion of *free server space* catches many people by surprise—but it's out there, and it's a thriving online practice. Not surprisingly, though, you'll find benefits in purchasing server space as well as using free space.

Free Space Online

It's true. You can create and display a Web site at this very moment for free, as in $0. All you need to spend is a little time and creative effort (and we make your task even easier by showing you how to create and display a free MSN Group Web site in Chapter 7). You don't need any additional software or fee-based Internet accounts—nothing but your text and a few pictures, if you want to include them. Of course, you face a couple of minor limitations when you take this approach (such as a long Web address and possibly limited page-layout options), but depending on your ultimate goal, the limitations might not affect you all that much. So consider yourself informed—free Web space is readily available. As we mentioned, we've run into more than a few people who were sincerely amazed to discover this fact.

The number-one way to become the proud owner of a free Web page is to turn to an *online group or community*. One of the benefits of joining an online group or community (other than the "free" factor) is that most online groups and communities enable you to create Web pages by providing templates or wizards that you can use.

Lingo An *online group or community* is a virtual area on the Web where people with similar interests gather and share information.

Among the many free online groups and communities, three popular ones come quickly to mind (which are also listed on *www.creationguide.com/resources*):

■ MSN Web Groups (*http://groups.msn.com*)

■ Lycos Tripod (*http://www.tripod.lycos.com*)

■ Yahoo! GeoCities (*http://geocities.yahoo.com*)

The biggest drawbacks of online groups and communities are that your Web address is usually fairly long, you generally have a limited amount of server space, your choices of page layouts are usually somewhat limited or controlled, you might have to tolerate pop-up advertisements each time you visit your page, and, if you don't want to use a group's or community's templates, customizing your page can sometimes be tricky.

Note Most companies who sponsor online groups and communities make their money through advertising and selling upgrades and add-on features and services.

Similar to online groups and communities, another free way to get on the Web is to create site-specific pages. During your surfing, you might find that some Web sites offer free Web space to registered members. For example, you can create an About Me page on eBay (an online auction site located at *www.ebay.com*) if you're a registered site participant. The purpose of eBay's About Me pages is to introduce eBay users to other people who visit eBay.

Yet another type of "free" online Web space—which technically isn't free— is Web space that you get from your ISP. Because you most likely cut a check to your ISP on a regular basis (or at least record an automatic payment), we can't exactly label ISP server space as free; it's more like prepaid, available space. When you signed up with your current ISP (assuming you have one), they probably informed you in an excited voice or a sentence ending in an exclamation point that you get "*X* megabytes of free server space!" At the time, you probably didn't know what that meant, so you might have just thought "Oh, that's nice" and moved on to the next detail. Now that you're thinking about creating a Web page, you should revisit the "free server space" component of your ISP agreement. Most likely, you'll find that you have anywhere from 10 MB to 50 MB of server space at your disposal.

Try This! To find free Web space, type *free Web space* in any search engine—you'll be rewarded with a slew of sites offering to host your page. Or check out the 100 Best Free Web Services Web site at *www.100best-free-web-space.com*. This site provides reviews and site rankings, which makes it a great resource for locating and reviewing free Web hosting services.

The upside of ISP server space is that you're already paying for it, so you might as well use it. The downside is that you'll probably have to live with a cumbersome Web address, similar to online group and community Web addresses. For example, a couple of our ISPs (we have several) grant "free" server space, but the Web addresses' formats are *www.domain.com/~username/filename.html* and *members.domain.net/username/filename.html*. For most people, the preceding naming formats are a little long and not easy to remember. Another advantage of ISP server space over online groups and communities is that you generally have greater freedom regarding how you create and display your pages (which could be a disadvantage if you prefer to work with the precon-figured templates that seem to be standard fare on many online community sites).

All in all, the main point about free online sites is that Web space is instantly available to you. And as long as you don't mind a longish home page Web address, some design limitations, and possibly pop-up advertisements, then free space is a great way to initiate yourself to the Web.

Purchasing Server Space

In contrast to using free Web space, you can shell out a few clams for a Web page that uses the Web address of your choice as long as someone hasn't beaten you to the name. When you take this route, you have the following two main consider-ations: choosing and registering a Web address name (such as *creationguide.com*), and signing up with a provider that will host (or store) your Web pages (unless you're going to run your own server—but that topic is best saved for more advanced books). Let's look at how to register a Web address and obtain a host-ing service.

Registering a Web Address

Before we go any further, let's nail down some simple vocabulary. Namely, instead of *Web address*, we really should say *domain name*. Loosely speaking (very loosely), a domain name is a Web address. As you may or may not know, all Web addresses are actually groups of numbers (called *Internet Protocol*, or IP, numbers) that serve as Internet addresses. Being a human, you probably also know that, for most people, remembering a meaningful name is much easier than remembering a series of numbers divided by dots. Therefore, the *Domain Name System* (DNS) came into existence. Fundamentally, DNS simply assigns textual names (such as *creationguide.com*) to numbered Internet addresses (such as 207.155.248.5). Thus, to appear as if you know what you're doing, you should use the term *domain name* in place of *Web address*.

When you're ready to obtain your own domain name, you can pick a domain name (such as *creationguide.com*—although we can tell you right now that the name is already taken), see whether it's available, and, if it is, register the domain name as your very own for a nominal annual fee. By nominal, we mean somewhere around the price of a good meal or slightly more per year.

Choosing and registering a Web domain name is straightforward after you access a legitimate registration site. Fortunately, InterNIC (which is under the umbrella of the U.S. Department of Commerce) hosts a Web page that lists all the acceptable domain name registration Web sites. Many hosting sites also offer name registration services (as we discuss in the next section). To see the official list of domain name registrars, visit *www.internic.net/alpha.html.*

While visiting the InterNIC site, check a few registration sites to review their pricing schedules and policies (or visit *www.creationguide.com/resources*, and we'll link you to a couple of our favorite hosting services). When you've found a site you like, you can generally type your proposed domain name in a text box. Then, the site will inform you whether the name is available. If it is, you work out a payment arrangement (usually by credit card) and the site registers your domain with InterNIC. Your next step is to find an ISP that will host your domain name and Web pages.

Finding Space for Your Domain

If you don't run your own server—and most people don't—your next step is to find an ISP or hosting service that's willing to provide a home for your domain name, that is, if you didn't complete this step during your domain registration process (as described in the preceding section). You can find numerous hosting services online—type *Web hosting* in any search engine and you can have a field day researching various Web hosting providers. Or better yet, visit *http://hostindex.com*, a comprehensive site devoted to providing information about numerous aspects of hosting services, including a monthly list of the top 25 hosts. Finally, as mentioned a moment ago, you can visit *www.creationguide.com/resources* for links to hosting services and domain name registrars. Regardless of how you conduct your research into finding server space, remember to check a few key facts, including fees, network configuration, Microsoft FrontPage Server Extensions (if you're using FrontPage features, as discussed in Chapter 10), and reliability. On average, basic Web hosting services charge a nominal monthly fee along with a one-time setup fee (see each hosting service's Web site for specific prices). Unless the rates seem outrageous, don't let the fees rule your decision. Before signing on with a Web hosting service, find out how the host handles the following features:

- **Bandwidth**   Most hosting companies are connected to the Internet by T1 and T3 lines; anything less and you might as well choose another company. Basically, a T1 line can carry up to 1.5 megabits of data per second, and a T3 line can carry 45 megabits per second. Thus, a T3 connection provides much more bandwidth and speed. In addition to Internet connections, you should check to see how many clients are hosted on each machine. If a hosting service overloads its machines, performance will be slow despite high-speed connection lines.

- **Space**   When you sign up for Web hosting services, ISPs and hosting companies assign you a certain amount of server space (just as your computer has a certain amount of disk space that you can use to store files). Most ISPs and hosting services offer more space on their servers than you'll need (at least initially). However, you should get at least 10 MB of server space. Most hosts provide at least 25 MB.

- **Support**   Technical support is an important element when you're choosing a Web hosting company—if you run into problems, you'll want to be able to turn to someone who can help. The most basic support consideration you should look for is the number of hours per day the technical support staff is available. Many sites offer 24×7 support, so look for round-the-clock support when you're weeding out potential companies. Round-the-clock support is important because you'll most likely be updating your pages during off hours, so off hours are the times you'll probably need support the most. Also see whether the site publishes its support response rate. Finally, check to see whether you can readily identify the avenues of support the company offers, including phone numbers (look for 1-800 numbers), fax numbers, e-mail addresses, online informational reports and FAQs, and a snail mail address.

- **Extras**   You might want to check to see what "extras" each company offers to entice customers. For example, most hosting services provide e-mail accounts you can use with your domain name (such as mm@creationguide.com or jc@creationguide.com). You can generally set up anywhere from 5 to 20 e-mail accounts with a single Web hosting agreement. Other features you might check out include the cost of adding space to your site, in case your site grows larger than your originally allotted space; the cost of upping your traffic quota, in case more people visit your site than you anticipated; whether FrontPage Server Extensions (if you're using FrontPage) and streaming media are supported; and available add-on services, such as adding chat groups and site search features.

Now that you've considered your domain name, hosting services, and basic Web space options, we're ready to move closer to home and talk about desktop applications. In the next section, we take a look at software applications you can use on your system to create, edit, and publish Web pages and Web page elements.

Web Page Creation Tools

In this section, we outline the types of tools you might need to create Web pages, name a few applications we find helpful, and point you down the path of finding other utilities that best suit your needs. As you might imagine, because of the Web's booming popularity, lots of software vendors have busied themselves by creating Web page creation programs. In this chapter we introduce many tools (but nowhere near all the available utilities), and in Part Two we show you how to use some of them to create complete Web sites. Ultimately, though, we leave you with the responsibility of choosing the software packages that feel most comfortable for you.

To simplify our approach in this chapter, we've divided basic Web page development tools into the following three main categories:

- Text editors and HTML editors
- Graphics applications
- FTP (File Transfer Protocol) utilities

Text Editors and HTML Editors

Overwhelmingly, when you create Web pages, you'll be spending the greatest amount of time interacting with a text editor or an HTML editor. You use editors to create HTML files that contain display instructions for Web browsers and provide content for your Web pages. When you use an editor, you have the option of working with basic editors, in which you enter HTML code manually, or using more advanced WYSIWYG (what you see is what you get—pronounced *wizzy-wig*) editors, which create HTML code for you while you type text, insert images, and drag elements around in a Web page layout view. Finally, and not surprisingly, some applications keep a foot in both camps by qualifying as an upscale basic editor but not quite an advanced WYSIWYG editing application—we take a quick look at all three types of editors in the next few pages.

Tip You can download many of the applications (or demos of the applications) mentioned in this chapter from shareware sites such as *www.tucows.com*, *www.shareware.com*, or *www.download.com*. *Shareware* can be best summed up as "try before you buy." When you download a shareware program, you try it out for a while for free. If you like it, you send the developer the requested fee. Too bad all merchandising isn't so user friendly!

Basic Text and HTML Editors

When you use a basic text editor, you type in all the HTML commands and your Web page's text into a blank document. The most basic of the basic text editors is the Notepad application that comes with the Microsoft Windows operating system. Figure 5-1 shows Notepad containing some HTML text.

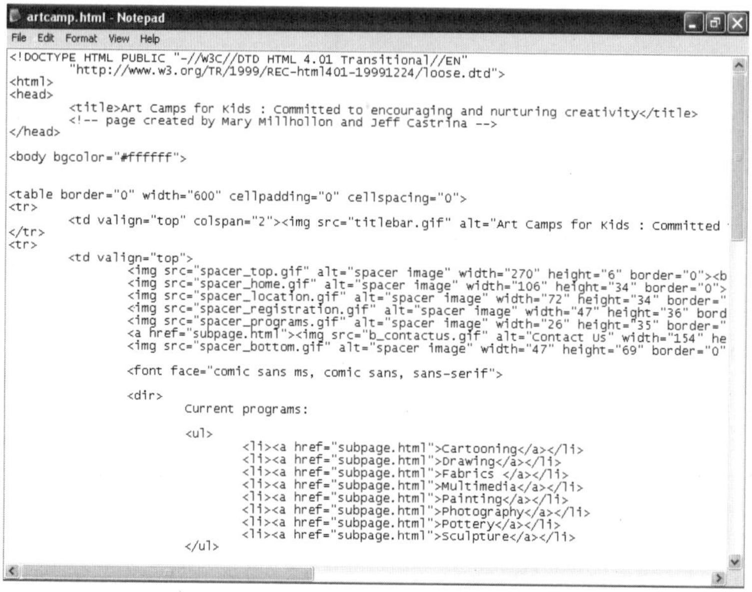

```
artcamp.html - Notepad
File Edit Format View Help
<!DOCTYPE HTML PUBLIC "-//W3C//DTD HTML 4.01 Transitional//EN"
        "http://www.w3.org/TR/1999/REC-html401-19991224/loose.dtd">
<html>
<head>
        <title>Art Camps for Kids : Committed to encouraging and nurturing creativity</title>
        <!-- page created by Mary Millhollon and Jeff Castrina -->
</head>

<body bgcolor="#ffffff">


<table border="0" width="600" cellpadding="0" cellspacing="0">
<tr>
        <td valign="top" colspan="2"><img src="titlebar.gif" alt="Art Camps for Kids : Committed
</tr>
<tr>
        <td valign="top">
                <img src="spacer_top.gif" alt="spacer image" width="270" height="6" border="0"><b
                <img src="spacer_home.gif" alt="spacer image" width="106" height="34" border="0">
                <img src="spacer_location.gif" alt="spacer image" width="72" height="34" border="
                <img src="spacer_registration.gif" alt="spacer image" width="47" height="36" bord
                <img src="spacer_programs.gif" alt="spacer image" width="26" height="35" border="
                <a href="subpage.html"><img src="b_contactus.gif" alt="Contact Us" width="154" he
                <img src="spacer_bottom.gif" alt="spacer image" width="47" height="69" border="0"

                <font face="comic sans ms, comic sans, sans-serif">

                <dir>
                        Current programs:

                        <ul>
                                <li><a href="subpage.html">Cartooning</a></li>
                                <li><a href="subpage.html">Drawing</a></li>
                                <li><a href="subpage.html">Fabrics </a></li>
                                <li><a href="subpage.html">Multimedia</a></li>
                                <li><a href="subpage.html">Painting</a></li>
                                <li><a href="subpage.html">Photography</a></li>
                                <li><a href="subpage.html">Pottery</a></li>
                                <li><a href="subpage.html">Sculpture</a></li>
                        </ul>
```

Figure 5-1 Many Web designers turn to Notepad when hand-coding HTML documents.

You might wonder why Web designers would opt to manually code their Web pages. The answer varies, but, for the most part, Web designers hand-code their Web pages for some of the following reasons:

- **Control** Hand-coding enables you to use the codes you want instead of the codes a WYSIWYG editor inserts. For example, you might want to use two blank line breaks, but a WYSIWYG editor might insert a paragraph marker. Furthermore, some WYSIWIG editors create "messy" code; hand-coding can keep code orderly and easy-to-read, with code alignment set to the designer's preferences.

■ **Quick fixes**   Knowing how to manually create and modify HTML code enables Web designers to make quick changes to a Web page, regardless of how the Web page was initially created. For instance, if you want to update your site's copyright date, you can update and save the change in a text editor in less time than it would take to simply open the page in a WYSIWYG editor.

■ **Code cleanup**   Many advanced HTML editors (as discussed later in this chapter) add extra code to documents. If you know how to create and edit standard HTML code, you can clean out extra code and reduce the size of your HTML files. And remember—on the Web, size matters, and the smaller the better. Furthermore, because HTML editors are only designed by humans, at times HTML editors might miscode your page. In those instances, you can save yourself lots of time and aggravation by changing the HTML directly instead of hunting down the proper dialog box setting in the HTML editor.

■ **Fine-tuning**   Another habit of advanced HTML editors is that they sometimes use HTML tags that not all browsers support. You can use text editors to modify HTML code so that it conforms to the capabilities of most browsers.

Of course, learning HTML is a prerequisite to creating your pages in a text editor. In Chapter 8, we walk you through the process of using HTML to create a Web page to give you an idea of HTML's form. (Don't worry—you can do it.) That chapter is just an introduction, however. You'll need to access additional resources if you really want to get serious about HTML. If you're interested in learning HTML or having an HTML reference nearby, you'll find that a generous collection of HTML books line the shelves at your local bookstore. You can also find pages and pages of helpful information online. (We've also listed some HTML references at the end of Chapter 8.)

Text editors can range from barely offering you a hand to coming fully equipped with customized HTML-specific features. To help illustrate the range, we've provided short descriptions of some of the most popular text editors in use today:

- **BBEdit**   (*www.barebones.com/products/bbedit.html*) This HTML editor from Bare Bones Software is popular among Macintosh Web developers. BBEdit enables you to edit, search, transform, and manipulate text. Like the other HTML editors, BBEdit provides an array of general-purpose features as well as many features specifically developed to meet the needs of HTML authors.

- **HomeSite**   (*www.macromedia.com/software/homesite*) Macromedia HomeSite is a popular code-only HTML design tool used by many professional Web developers. This text editor includes HTML-specific features to help you create effective, clean HTML pages. For example, it includes an HTML Tag Inspector, split-window editing, an image map utility, and more. You can download a 30-day trial version to test the product.

- **Notepad**   Notepad comes with the Microsoft Windows operating system and is about as bare bones as it comes when talking about text editors. Beware, though: if you're working on a very long document, you won't be able to use Notepad. For longer documents, you'll have to use WordPad (described later in this list) instead.

- **NoteTab**   (*www.notetab.com*) The NoteTab text editor, by Fookes Software, is Notepad on steroids. This program includes a number of features that can simplify your job of hand-coding Web pages. For instance, you can display HTML utilities along the left side of the window pane in the Clip Bar. Then, you can insert HTML code by double-clicking menu items, including clicking the New Web Page menu item to insert the basic code structure for an entire HTML document. One drawback, which is typical of many text editors, is that the free trial program only supports one level of Undo; if you want to undo a number of actions, you'll have restore the information manually.

- **TextPad**   (*www.textpad.com*) TextPad, created by Helios Software Solutions, serves as yet another beefed up version of Notepad. In TextPad, you can view an HTML tag menu while you work as well as keep tabs on the documents you're currently working on. TextPad supports multiple Undo actions, which can come in handy when you're playing with HTML.

■ **UltraEdit** (*www.ultraedit.com*) IDM Computer Solutions provides UltraEdit to serve as a text-editing package that you can use on a trial basis for 45 days. After you download and install the application, click About UltraEdit on the Help menu and then close the Help window to activate the program. Although this application is designed for some-what advanced users (such as programmers), it includes features that you might find handy. For instance, you can easily preview your pages in your browser and use the accompanying dictionary to spell check your documents.

■ **WordPad** WordPad is a step up from Notepad. If you're running Windows, you can open WordPad by clicking Start, pointing to Programs and then Accessories, and then clicking WordPad. WordPad offers more word-processing features than Notepad, and it supports longer documents. Figure 5-2 shows an HTML document in WordPad.

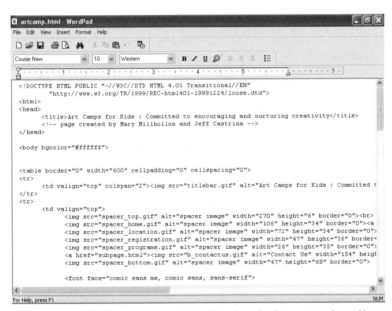

Figure 5-2 WordPad serves as a good text editor when the document you're working on is too long for Notepad to handle.

Try This! Display *www.creationguide.com/artcamp* (or any other Web page of your choice) in your browser, and then click Source (or View Source) on your browser's View menu. A Notepad document opens that displays a text version of the Web page's HTML code.

Midrange Text and HTML Editors

The next level of HTML editors starts to enter the realm of WYSIWYG. We could call midrange text editors WYSIWYG-lite applications because the applications offer text editor features along with a limited amount of advanced HTML editor capabilities. Because most applications are either text editors or full-fledged HTML editors, we recommend just one main application in this category—Microsoft Word version 2002.

Note   Similar to Word version 2002, other Office XP (version 2002) programs—such as Microsoft Excel and Microsoft PowerPoint—also let you save your documents as Web pages.

Word 2002 enables you to use a familiar word processing interface to create HTML documents through the Save As command. When you save a Word document as a Web page, Word automatically creates the HTML source code for the document. Chapter 9 shows you how to use Word to create a Web site. Figure 5-3 shows an HTML document in Page Layout view as well as in the HTML Source view. You can obtain Word 2002 by purchasing (or upgrading to) the Microsoft Office 2002 suite.

Figure 5-3   Word 2002 offers a Web Layout View as well as the HTML Source View.

Advanced HTML Editors

The third group of HTML editors includes the advanced applications that enable you to create and edit Web pages by using graphical interfaces. In most advanced editors, you can view and edit the HTML source code directly as well as work in the WYSIWYG interface. Furthermore, most advanced editors provide a preview feature, which enables you to view how a Web page will display online before you view the page in your browser. Web-specific features are frequently incorporated into advanced HTML editors as well. (We know that last bit sounds a little vague, but when we create a Web page in FrontPage in Chapter 10, we introduce you to a few high-end Web-specific tools so you'll know what we mean.) Popular advanced HTML editors are well documented online, so instead of wasting page space here summarizing online statistics, we've provided pertinent URLs for the Web sites that offer the applications appearing in our short list. Although other editors are readily available, these six are some of the most popular programs. (Check each product's Web site address to assist you in comparing features and prices.)

- Adobe GoLive (*www.adobe.com/products/golive/main.html*)
- CoffeeCup HTML Editor (*coffeecup.com/editor*)
- HotDog Professional (*www.sausage.com/professional/overview.html*)
- HoTMetaL Pro (*www.hotmetalpro.com*)
- Macromedia Dreamweaver (*www.macromedia.com/software/dreamweaver*)
- Microsoft FrontPage 2002 (*www.microsoft.com/frontpage*); also comes with the Microsoft Office 2000 XP Developer suite
- NetObjects Fusion MX (*www.netobjects.com/products/html/nfmx.html*)

Note In addition to HotDog Professional, Sausage Software offers a WYSIWYG HTML editor for beginners, called HotDog PageWiz, and an HTML editor for kids ages six and up, called HotDog Junior. Surf around the Sausage Software home page to find other useful Web page creation utilities. After all, if you ask us, any company named *Sausage Software* that offers HTML editors named *HotDog* deserves a little extra attention.

Among the preceding applications, Dreamweaver is probably the most popular (yet most challenging to learn) Web editor among design professionals for a number of reasons, including the fact that it maintains hand-written code, enables users to preview pages in various browsers, and automatically checks for browser conflicts. On the other hand, FrontPage (shown in Figure 5-4) is the easiest advanced HTML editor for beginners to learn and provides nice clean HTML code. Furthermore, FrontPage is popular with the business community. As we mentioned, you'll get a feel for creating Web pages in FrontPage in Chapter 10.

Note Keep in mind that your Web page creation environment doesn't have to be an either/or kind of setup. At times, we find it's quicker to use an advanced WYSIWYG application (especially when resizing tables), but at other times a quick edit in Notepad serves us best.

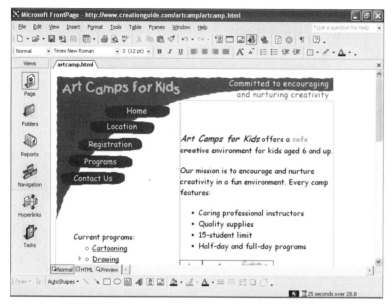

Figure 5-4   Microsoft FrontPage is a popular high-end Web development program that's fairly easy to learn.

Graphics Applications

When it comes to Web page development, graphics applications come in a strong second behind the all-important text or HTML editor. After all, most pages use graphics, and you'll want to either create or tweak the graphics you use on your Web pages. Therefore, you'll need to have a graphics package installed on your system. Our personal favorites (or at least the programs we seem to use most frequently) are Jasc Paint Shop Pro and Adobe Photoshop—both appear in the graphics application list that you're about to run into after the next paragraph.

Regardless of your graphics package, the five main skills you'll need to acquire when using a graphics program are cropping, cutting, resizing, recoloring, and saving as a different file format. So check your application's help files to brush up on your technique. Now, here are five popular graphics programs along with their Web addresses (we recommend that you visit the listed Web sites for product details and pricing):

■   **Fireworks**   (*www.macromedia.com/software/fireworks*) This application is easy to use and especially convenient when you need to create buttons and other basic Web site graphics. Macromedia developed Fireworks specifically for creating Web graphics.

■   **LView Pro**   (*www.lview.com/index1024.htm*) LView Pro is a popular shareware graphics program. It includes typical graphic features as well as Web page utilities, such as a tool to create online photo gallery pages.

- **Paint**   Microsoft Paint is a graphics program that comes with Windows. Paint is a scaled-down graphics package compared to other graphics programs, but it serves as a handy graphics tool when you're in a pinch or want to quickly make minor adjustments.

- **Paint Shop Pro**   (*www.jasc.com/products/psp*) Paint Shop Pro is an affordable, all-purpose graphics program used by many designers. Visit the Jasc Web site to download a free trial demo.

- **Photoshop**   (*www.adobe.com/products/photoshop*) Photoshop is probably the leading image-editing program. It can be a little tricky to use when you're first learning it, but once you get the commands mastered, you'll be highly satisfied with the application's flexibility. We frequently mock up sites using Photoshop before we create actual Web pages in an HTML editor. The overriding drawback of Photoshop is that it's fairly pricey for casual designers.

In addition to the preceding graphics applications, you can also use illustration programs to create *vector-based graphics*. In a vector-based graphic, you can move, resize, and otherwise manipulate an image's elements (such as moving an entire shape around within an image). Vector-based illustration programs that frequently come in handy when creating Web pages include Adobe Illustrator (*www.adobe.com/products/illustrator*), Macromedia Freehand (*www.macromedia.com/software/freehand*), and CorelDraw (*www.corel.com*).

Lingo   *Vector-based graphics* are images made with lines and shapes instead of shaded computer pixels.

Try This!   If you want to include an animated GIF on your Web page but you aren't itching to build one from scratch, you'll be glad to hear that the Office XP media CD-ROM contains a number of small animations you can use on Web pages. To insert an animated GIF:

1   Open Word (or other Office application), display the Insert menu, choose Picture, and click Clip Art.

2   In the Insert Clip Art pane, search for a clip art item, and double-click an item that displays with a gold star.

3   To see the animation in action, open the File menu and click Web Page Preview.

As we've suggested before, insert animated components in moderation. Animation can quickly become overly distracting, which will detract from your page rather than add to its appeal.

**GIF Animators, Image Map Applications, Banner Programs, and
More**   Web pages incorporate all kinds of specialty knickknacks—including elements created with "mod" sounding technologies such as Active Server Pages, Java, Flash, and so forth. In addition, you can create audio and video files for use on the Web. Although we're just as fascinated with these topics as with basic Web page design techniques, creating those elements is beyond the scope of this book. Our goal is to get you up and running on the Web. Therefore, we'll save the "fancy" stuff for another book. If you're itching to acquire some extra-credit Web page creation skills, we suggest you start by creating animated GIFs, image maps, and banners. Following are some sites you might find useful:

- **Animated GIFs**   (*www.mindworkshop.com/alchemy/gifcon.html*) The GIF Construction Set Professional uses wizards to walk you through the entire process of creating an animated GIF and consistently earns top ratings from reviewers.

- **Banners**   (*www.animation.com*) The Animation.com site enables you to instantly create advertising banners.

- **Image maps**   (*www.globalscape.com/products/cutemap*) GlobalSCAPE CuteMAP is a shareware application that simplifies creating image maps. You can download a free trial version.

Keep in mind that you can find quite a few animated GIF builders, banner creation utilities, and image map creators online. Furthermore, some of the graphics programs we mentioned earlier in this chapter (such as Fireworks and Paint Shop Pro) have built-in animated GIF and image map features. The preceding three applications are mentioned merely as samples to help get your search rolling.

FTP Utilities

Last but not least, you might need one of those mysterious FTP utilities. Actually, FTP utilities aren't at all mysterious, but whenever we mention "FTP" to people who've never heard of it before, the color seems to drain from their faces. Basically, FTP utilities are programs that allow you to copy entire files from your computer to another computer across the Internet. For example, whenever we complete a chapter, we FTP the chapter's graphics to Microsoft Press in Redmond, Washington, even though we're in (overly) sunny Arizona and (overly) rainy Oregon.

Tip   You might not need to use an FTP program if you're creating an online group or community Web page. Furthermore, if you're using Microsoft's Web Publishing Wizard, Network Places, or an advanced HTML editor's publishing utility to upload pages, you won't need to use an FTP program up front. Eventually, though, you might want to use an FTP utility to delete, copy, and otherwise manage online files. In Chapter 11 and Chapter 12, we fill you in on the details of online file management, where being comfortable with an FTP application can come in handy.

You can find numerous FTP programs online, many of which are shareware programs. Popular FTP programs include the following:

■ **BulletProof FTP**   (*www.bpftp.com*) BulletProof provides an intuitive drag-and-drop interface, similar to other top FTP programs.

■ **CoffeeCup Direct FTP**   (*www.coffeecup.com/software*) This program serves as an FTP application that also lets you edit HTML pages online. On the site's Download page, you'll find that CoffeeCup Software also provides image map, button creation, and animated GIF applications, among other products.

■ **CuteFTP**   (*www.globalscape.com/products/cuteftp*) This easy-to-use and popular FTP application has been around for a while, and it's our personal favorite for the PC. Using CuteFTP, you can drag-and-drop files to transfer files from your machine to a remote machine and vice versa. Among other applications, GlobalSCAPE also offers an HTML editor (CuteHTML) and an image map application (CuteMAP).

■ **Fetch**   (*www.fetchsoftworks.com*) Recently, Fetch was updated to version 4.0.2 (before that, it hadn't been updated since 1997!). Fetch is designed to make accessing FTP sites as simple as possible. It's available free of charge to educational institutions and nonprofit organizations; others should pay the shareware fee.

Now that you know vaguely what FTP programs do and that you can download them from the Web, don't worry too much about them. At this point, knowing that they exist is enough—if you're really gung ho, you can download an FTP application so that you're ready to upload pages after you create them, but you don't need to do that now. We'll help you out with FTP programs and file management later in the book, in Part Three. But before we do that, we want to tackle the fun stuff in Part Two—creating your Web pages.

A Bit about Browsers

We'd be completely remiss if we wrapped up this chapter without addressing the most obvious software application tool of them all—a browser. You need to have a browser (or a few browsers) installed on your computer so that you can preview your pages before you publish them online. Remember that browsers are applications that interpret HTML pages. Unfortunately, not all browsers interpret HTML in exactly the same way. Therefore, a page you design and then view in Microsoft Internet Explorer could very easily display as a shocking mess in another browser. Even well-designed pages appear slightly differently in various browsers. To see an illustration of this phenomenon, view the various screen shots in Figure 5-5.

Tip   No two browsers (or browser versions) process HTML code in exactly the same way; therefore, when you design Web pages, view your pages in as many browsers as possible before publishing your site.

In Figure 5-5, you can see the following anomalies:

■   The default bullets in Netscape Navigator are bigger on both PC-based and Macintosh machines than those in Internet Explorer.

■   The margin spacing (or *offset*) around page perimeters varies by browser. Notice that the Internet Explorer browser windows leave more margin space around the top-left graphic than do the Navigator browser windows.

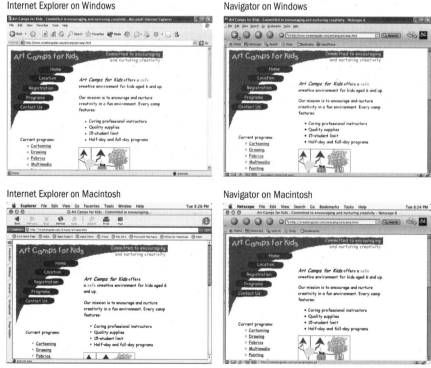

Figure 5-5   Viewing the same Web page in various browsers demonstrates the small anomalies that crop up in your pages when they're viewed online (to see a larger view of these screens, visit *www.creationguide.com/differences*).

■ The default font size is smaller on PCs than on the Macintosh in both Internet Explorer and Navigator, which can affect how text displays and wraps.

■ Due to font and spacing size differences, varying amounts of information appear above the Web page's "fold."

■ Browser window widths vary. Notice how the title bar graphic spans the entire window in a couple instances and it appears with extra white space in the other instances.

We designed the Arts Camps for Kids page to work cleanly in both Internet Explorer and Navigator, but you can see that slight differences remain that are beyond a designer's control.

A number of browsers exist on the Web. You may or may not want to verify that your pages display appropriately in all browsers out there. For most designers, ensuring that pages display properly in the biggies—Internet Explorer and Navigator—is plenty; combined, these two browsers account for over 90 percent of all browsers accessing the Internet. Of course, you must always consider your audience. If you *know* your viewers will be using Opera browsers, you'd better ensure that your page looks good in Opera. For edification purposes, here's a short list of additional browsers you can find lurking on the Web:

■ America Online uses an adapted version of Internet Explorer (*webmaster.info.aol.com*).

■ Lynx is an all-text browser (*lynx.isc.org/current*).

■ Mozilla is a Web browser designed for people who want to create Mozilla-based products and packages (much of the Netscape Communicator browser is based on Mozilla code), but the general public can use the browser for free as well (*www.mozilla.org*).

■ Opera is a small application with extremely quick download times (*www.opera.com/download*).

You might want to download additional browsers to see how your pages display in alternate browsers. Previewing your Web pages simply entails displaying your HTML files in a browser window locally—so the process is quick and simple. Most important, though, you should ensure that you have access to at least one version (PC or Macintosh) of Internet Explorer and Navigator for testing and previewing purposes. Don't worry—we'll remind you a few more times in Part Two about the importance of previewing your Web pages in more than one browser as well as in more than one version of each browser, if possible.

Key Points

- You need Internet connectivity and server space to display a Web page online.

- You'll find that free Web space is readily available online, particularly in online groups and communities.

- You can purchase a domain name and buy server space to have full control over your Web site and Web address.

- You can use text editors to create Web pages.

- HTML editors range from all-text programs to advanced WYSIWYG interfaces.

- Graphics applications enable you to create Web graphics, edit pictures, and create mock-ups of future Web pages.

- You can find GIF animators, banner creation sites, and image map utilities online (in addition to lots of other freeware and shareware programs).

- FTP programs enable you to copy files from your computer onto a remote computer.

- Not all browsers are created equal—different browsers display the same Web page in various ways.

- You should always view your Web pages in Internet Explorer and Navigator (at least) before publishing your Web pages online.

Chapter 6

Planning Your Attack

Now that you're overflowing with Web-centric knowledge from Chapters 1 through 5, we're going to walk you through a Web site planning process. You're aware of all the elements you need to consider; now it's just a matter of consolidating the information into some concrete review questions and checklists. As you've probably heard throughout your life, a little planning up front can save more than a few headaches down the road. Not surprisingly, this philosophy holds true with Web development as well—a little preparation and forethought go a long way toward smoothly achieving success on the Web.

You might've noticed that this is the final chapter in Part One. We hope that you'll see this chapter as a bridge between Web theory and practice. In Part One, we've covered a lot of Web design basics; in Part Two, you'll have a chance to apply what you've learned to the hands-on exercises and projects in which you'll be creating the overall structure of four Web sites (one per chapter).

In Part Two, you can either re-create the Web pages exactly as we describe or use the sample Web pages as templates for custom pages. For each Web site we present in Part Two, we summarize the planning process we completed before we created the actual page. Every chapter in Part Two also includes a short planning section, so you'll know how each page evolved during the site's planning phase and where the project is taking you regarding your hands-on page-development actions. If you're going to customize any of the Web sites we've included as samples, you'll need to do some custom planning as well.

Eventually, after you've graduated beyond this book (and we have every confidence you will), you'll need to conduct your own planning sessions. Therefore, we designed this chapter to clearly outline each planning stage succinctly and in an easy-to-reference format. In the future, if you're ever stumped about setting goals for your Web site, defining your audience, designing your framework, or building your Web pages, grab this book off your shelf and turn to this chapter to help jump-start your thought processes.

To help illustrate the planning process, let's look at the evolution of the Curiosity Shoppe Web site. Figure 6-1 shows the final version of the shop's home page (*www.creationguide.com/cshoppe*). In the upcoming sections, we address some of the issues we considered when planning the Curiosity Shoppe Web site and explain what impact our decisions about those issues had on the final design.

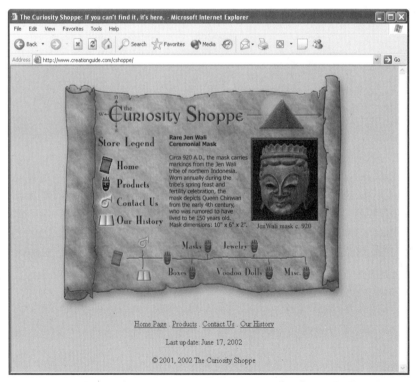

Figure 6-1   The Curiosity Shoppe home page presents a store front for a collectibles shop's Web site.

Defining Your Goals

Before you create a Web page or Web site, you must first address the project from a wide-angle perspective. You need to clearly consider your site's purpose and your goals for your site. Namely, you need to answer the following questions:

- Why do I want a Web page or Web site?
- What are my immediate goals for my Web site?
- What are my long-term goals for my site?
- What is my timeline?

For the Curiosity Shoppe site, the answers to the preceding questions were fairly straightforward. First, the Curiosity Shoppe owners wanted to make their shop easily accessible to more customers through an online presence. The owners' immediate goals were to inform people about the store, provide a means of contact, and advertise their products and store location. Their long-term plans are to offer their entire line of products for sale online and update the home page daily with a featured item. Finally, the owners' timeline can be summarized like this: static site online (*live*) within 2 months of the home page's inception; sales feature fully functional within 6 months after the home page has gone live; and a full line of online products available within 12 months from the date the initial home page went live.

Most likely, your goals and timeline will be less complex than those of the Curiosity Shoppe. For example, your goals might simply be to create an online résumé and have the résumé go live by next month, with updates occasionally added as necessary.

Getting to Know Your Audience

After you've outlined your goals for your site, you need to consider who's going to be visiting your Web pages. In other words, you need to think about your audience. You must have at least some perception of the people you want to visit your Web space. You need to address this planning step early in the process because (as mentioned in Chapter 4) many design and content decisions are based on your audience.

The best way to get to know your audience is to talk to them, if possible. Consider interviewing or surveying the people who will view your pages. For example, if you're making a family site, call your family members and find out what they'd like to see on the site. In addition, consider how users will be connecting to your page. Are they typical Web surfers with dial-up connections? If so, keep your page sizes small and your layouts fairly simple. Are you designing a site for online gamers? Then take advantage of high-speed connections and cutting-edge technologies. Designing for kids? Bright colors work well. You get the idea. To help analyze your audience, answer the following questions:

- **Who makes up the core of my target audience?**   Your answer might include such categories as customers, students, employers, family members, kindred spirits, club members, and so on.

- **What does my audience want to find out from my site?**   This question is different from asking yourself what you want to tell your audience—here's where you should really listen to prospective site users so you can design accordingly.

- **How experienced with the Web are the members of my audience?**   You'll need to figure out whether the bulk of your users will be novices, casual Web surfers, or cyberspace champions. Knowing users' level of expertise is key, because, although experienced users can frequently figure out "what's going on" in complex or uniquely designed sites, beginning users generally require a little more guidance. For example, if you're catering to beginning surfers, you should make it a point to clearly and consistently identify the site's structure through simple navigation elements; save avant-garde designs and navigation schemes for more advanced audiences.

- **What types of Internet connections and bandwidth capabilities will my users have?**   Knowing whether your audience is connected through a simple modem, an internal corporate network (called an intranet), or a high-speed connection such as a Digital Subscriber Line (DSL) will make a difference in how you design your Web site, including the types of elements you'll incorporate. For example, if you're certain that your viewers will be accessing your Web site on high-speed connections, you'll be freer to include video clips and numerous graphics with a minimal risk of losing viewers. If you include video and numerous graphics on a Web site accessed by users with dial-up connections, however, you'll risk losing those viewers before your site displays because they'll understandably get tired of waiting for the large elements to download.

- **Where is my core audience located?**   You'll need to determine whether people will visit your site while at work, on campus, in home offices, in living rooms, at cyber cafés, in your neighborhood, and so forth. This specification relates closely to the preceding question—if you know where your core audience is located, you'll most likely get a good feel for the types of connections they'll be using to access your site. Furthermore, location can come into play if you're designing a regional site versus a national site. For example, a David Bowie site might have an international audience, whereas your Block Watch site would probably cater mostly to your neighborhood. This differentiation is similar to the variations of information found in a newspaper's front-page section (which would correspond to a nationally or internationally focused Web site) compared to the local section (which would correspond to a locally oriented Web site).

■ **What's the typical age group among my audience members?**
You want to be sure that your site appeals to the age group you're targeting. This question is rooted in common sense—whether you like it or not, you can make some minor sweeping (albeit conservative) assumptions based on your audience's age, and these assumptions can help you throughout the Web page creation process. Knowing your audience's typical age ("typical" being the key word) helps you to make appropriate design decisions. For example, preteen Barbie-pink backgrounds don't work well on sports sites that target 18–40-year-old males. Furthermore, age parameters help you to choose words (particularly slang and colloquialisms) wisely, such as whether to "dude" or not to "dude." In addition, age information enables you to create meaningful metaphors—for example, will retirees really know (or care) what it feels like to get kicked in the head in a mosh pit? Finally, age specifics can help you determine the types of information you'll include on your Web pages. For example, if you're creating a kid's site, you wouldn't feature AARP information, but you might seriously consider including a Harry Potter trivia feature.

■ **How will users find out about my site?**   You'll want to know whether people will hear about your site by word of mouth, from online directories, from hard-copy Web directories or phone books, through links from a "parent" page, as a result of search engines, through paid commercial advertisements on TV or radio, and so on, so that you'll know best how to advertise and publicize your site.

Tip   After you've interviewed, surveyed, and talked to people; listened to feedback; and summarized your data, remember to specifically visualize a real live person instead of a generic profile while you create your Web site and design your Web pages.

Drawing the Blueprints for Your Site

After setting your goals and defining your audience, you're ready to design your Web site's framework. If possible, your first step should always be to collect your content before you design. As we assert in Chapter 2, organizing your content—or at least its main concepts—can help you organize your overall site in a logical manner.

After you gather the main types of information you want to include on your site (don't worry—your text and graphics don't have to be polished at this point), you need to figure out how best to present your information. For example, you can organize your site in any number of ways, including the following:

- Alphabetically
- Chronologically
- Graphically
- Hierarchically
- Numerically
- Randomly (not recommended—but it's out there)
- Topically

By far, most sites are organized hierarchically. A hierarchical site presents a home page that contains catchy introductory text and links to the site's main pages. This setup is widely used by designers and greatly appreciated by users (who mostly just want to use Web pages—not figure out how they're organized).

Another critical (though certainly less exciting) aspect of organizing your site involves naming your files. After all, when you boil it all down, your site is entirely made up of files—so organizing your site must include systemizing your files. Before we get to the Site Planning Checklist, let's take a look at some file-naming practices that you can mull over now and implement later.

Keeping Your Files in Line

As you now know, Web pages usually consist of a few files working together to create the appearance of a single page. Furthermore, a Web site consists of multiple Web pages (which in turn consist of multiple files). Because of this multifile nature of Web pages and Web sites, you're going to have to come up with a plan for naming and organizing your Web site's files. (In each chapter in Part Two, we explain how we've organized each site's files, so you'll have lots of chances to get the hang of naming and organizing files before the end of this book.) For the most part, a standard Web site can consist of the following simple structure, which is shown in Figure 6-2:

- **Main directory**   Contains HTML files and an images directory. You can provide any name for this directory when designing your pages on your local machine. When you upload your pages to a hosting service, you'll probably place the main directory folder's contents into an online folder named "Web" and copy the entire images folder (folder and all) into the Web folder.

- **Images directory**   Contains GIF and JPEG (or JPG) image files used on your Web pages. This directory is usually stored within the main directory.

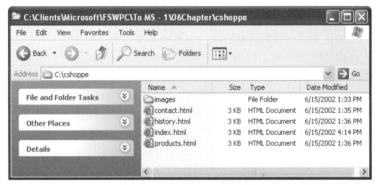

Figure 6-2   You store directories and files for your Web site locally before you copy them to a server linked to the Internet.

Notice in Figure 6-2 that the main directory currently holds four HTML files—contact.html, history.html, index.html, and products.html—one file for each of the Web site's main pages. Keep in mind that an HTML file's name is the name that appears in the Web page's URL address. For example, to visit the Curiosity Shoppe's Products page, you would enter *www.creationguide.com/ cshoppe/products.html*. As you can see, the preceding URL consists of the domain name (*www.creationguide.com*), the directory or folder name (*cshoppe*), and a filename (*products.html*).

For most home pages and many subpages, you might've noticed that you don't have to enter a filename. For example, when you visit Microsoft's home page, you simply type Microsoft's domain name, *www.microsoft.com*, or, if you visit the Creation Guide Resources page, you type *www.creationguide.com/ resources*. If no HTML filename is indicated after a domain name or directory (folder) name, most servers will display a particularly named file by default—most likely index.html, although some servers also cater to index.htm, default.htm, or default.html. Ask your hosting service which name you should use for your home page (or test each filename online to see which one works by default); 9 times out of 10 (and probably more frequently than that) index.html is the way to go when naming your home page, and it's your safest bet when you're unsure.

Because your HTML filenames will appear within your Web page's URL, you should follow a few simple rules to keep life simple for you and your users:

- **Keep filenames short, simple, and meaningful**   Users might want to access a subpage directly, so make the URL easy for them to type and remember. For example, use a file named "products.html" instead of "p1-2002m.html."

- **Avoid symbols and punctuation**   Most people find typing symbols and adding punctuation slows their typing speeds considerably and dramatically decreases their typing accuracy. Furthermore, symbols and punctuation can create new avenues for confusion. For example, if your page is named *www.creation-guide.com*, users could easily forget the hyphen and type *www.creationguide.com* (thereby missing your page altogether and visiting ours by mistake!).

- **Use an underscore (_) to indicate a space**   Some older servers don't recognize spaces, so use underscores instead to indicate blank spaces. Furthermore, you run into the same problem with spaces as you do with symbols and punctuation—spaces are easily forgotten and leave room for errors (lots of them).

- **Use all lowercase letters**   Once again, think "ease of use" for your Web site visitors. Filenames in URLs are case-sensitive, and a randomly uppercased letter can lose more than a few visitors. All lowercase filenames are easy to type and easy to remember.

Tip   Make sure that every HTML filename has an .htm or .html extension and that every image filename has a .gif, .jpeg, or .jpg extension.

Naming Images In addition to naming your HTML files, you'll need to name your image files. Generally, users don't access image files directly; instead, HTML pages reference image files whenever they need to be displayed. Therefore, you have more leeway when it comes to labeling your images. One handy image-naming trick that we use is to identify an image's purpose with a simple prefix incorporated into the file's name, which helps us to quickly identify and find files when we need them. Specifically, we precede image names with *p_*, *b_*, or *t_*. A p_ image is a picture. For example, p_mask indicates that the image is a picture of a mask. A b_ image is a button. For example, b_products indicates that the image is the navigation bar's Products button. And a t_ image refers to a title bar. For example, t_contacts specifies that the image is the title bar graphic used on the Contacts page.

By now, you should be realizing that organization plays an important part in Web site planning. You need to streamline your thoughts as well as start to consider how you'll systemize your files (which, again, are basically your Web site's Web pages and graphics). You can streamline the site-organization phase by performing the tasks and addressing the issues presented in the upcoming Site Planning Checklist.

After (or while) you address the items on the Site Planning Checklist, you should storyboard your site's structure as described in Chapter 4, in the "Storyboarding Your Web Site" section. In other words, you should illustrate the relationships among your site's pages and information to ensure that you've created a clear site layout that includes all your information in an easily accessible format. Figure 6-3 shows one of the Curiosity Shoppe's initial storyboards. You can make storyboards even more detailed than the one shown in Figure 6-3 by including short descriptions of what's going to appear on each page. For example, in the storyboard shown in Figure 6-3, you could add notes such as, "The contact.html page contains an e-mail link and a map showing the shop's location."

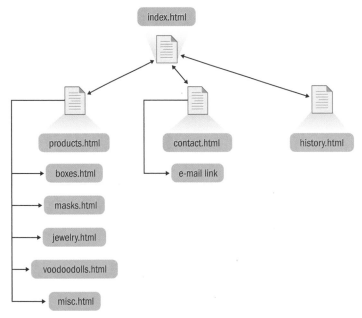

Figure 6-3   The Curiosity Shoppe storyboard shows the filenames used within the initial site.

Site Planning Checklist

The items on this checklist outline the basic tasks you should perform while planning your Web site. Address each listed task and issue, and sketch your site's informational relationships as you plan:

❑   Visit similar sites to see what you like and don't like, and figure out how you can make your site unique.

❑   Be sure that your site specifies who you are and (if appropriate) your enterprise's identity.

❑   Pick colors that evoke an appropriate emotion for your site. Ensure that your color scheme presents a clear contrast for easy reading, analyze whether the colors work to further your site's goals, and try to use colors from the 216-color Web-safe palette. For a quick refresher on Web-safe colors, see Chapter 3 and our online color chart at *www.creationguide.com/colorchart*.

❑   Verify that the main point of your site is clearly identified up front, not buried a page or two deep into your site or missing, and that each page clearly identifies its purpose. You don't want readers to visit your home page or find your site through a backdoor and then wonder what they're supposed to do now that they've found your Web site.

- ❏ Classify your site to yourself so that you don't lose your focus. For design purposes, label your site as commercial, informational, educational, entertainment, navigation, community, artistic, or personal, or as some other type of site.

- ❏ Design the site to reflect how users will most likely navigate through your pages. You can get an idea of what users want during your audience-analysis stage. Make sure that you include umbrella topics (main topics—not outdoor gear topics) on your home page, and then provide more specific links on each subpage. For example, provide a Contacts link on the home page and provide departmental links on the Contacts page.

- ❏ Ensure that your site offers viewers a few ways to contact you—physical address, e-mail address, phone number, carrier pigeon, and so forth.

- ❏ Name your files appropriately (as discussed earlier in this chapter).

- ❏ Create easy-to-understand button names that clearly reflect your site's structure. Cryptic buttons might look awesome, but they tend to confuse readers (especially when no explanatory text accompanies your esoteric creation).

- ❏ Divide your content into logical units. Don't divide one page into two just because it seems like the page is getting too long. On the other hand, if you see a logical break in a long page, by all means, divide the page (but make sure you don't lose the newly created page by burying its link deep within your site).

- ❏ Analyze your information, and make your most important information the most prominent and accessible.

- ❏ Determine ways in which you can create a unifying look or theme throughout your site. Don't forget to include a logo and use consistent navigation links on every page. Keep in mind that the nitty-gritty design aspects of your site's look and theme are addressed more thoroughly in the next planning stage, when you design your home page and subpages.

- ❏ Include at least one element that will encourage users to return, such as a daily or weekly updated element or a chat room.

Try This! Quick—think of three sites you've visited recently. Now analyze why and how those three sites made an impression on you. Are there any elements you can adopt and modify for your site? Were those sites easy to navigate? Does an element that you didn't like stand out in your mind? Use your personal experience to your benefit. After all, you know what you like when you're surfing the Web.

Laying Your Home Page's Foundation

After the site-planning dust settles, you can clean off your slate and start to design your home page (and subpages). By now, you should have a very strong idea of what your home page should include—logo, title bar, links to your site's main pages, and so forth. For the most part, you should have taken care of the practical side of page design, such as determining a file-naming structure, analyzing your audience, determining hardware limitations, and so forth. At this point, your creative juices get to take over while your organizational synapses rest and rejuvenate. In this design phase, focus your attention on how you can creatively present all the necessary home page components in a way that reflects your site's goals, optimizes your site's theme, and elicits the proper "emotional" response from users. For example, the Curiosity Shoppe wanted to convey the feeling that the store sells treasures that have been discovered throughout the world. Therefore, we came up with the treasure map theme and the N-S-E-W "C" logo for the Curiosity Shoppe's owners.

After you start to think of creative ways to present your ideas, start to sketch various layouts and ideas. You'll begin to see what works best, and ideas will breed off one another until you come up with a page design that does the trick. Figure 6-4 shows a sketch of the Curiosity Shoppe's home page. Because we designed the home page to make a unique impression, its design is notably different from the layout of the site's subpages. Therefore, we also sketched the Products page to illustrate how title bars and navigation links would display on subpages, as shown in Figure 6-5. While you're sketching your home page, refer to the Home Page Planning Checklist that starts on page 132 to ensure that you've covered all your bases.

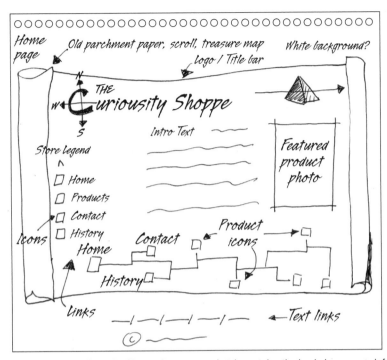

Figure 6-4   The Curiosity Shoppe home page sketch contains the basic home page information.

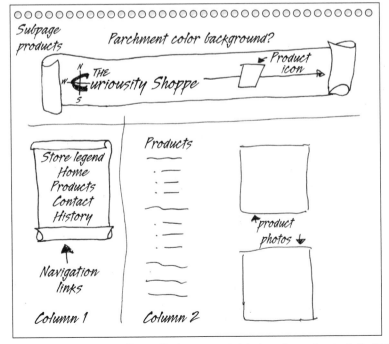

Figure 6-5   The Curiosity Shoppe Products page sketch shows how subpages in the Web site differ significantly from the home page.

Home Page Planning Checklist

You need to verify that your home page includes the elements listed in the following Home Page Planning Checklist. If you purposely omit certain elements, be sure you understand why. Keep in mind that the list doesn't weight the importance of elements by order—in fact, the list is alphabetized specifically to avoid promoting any elements over others. (We're tricky like that.) Make sure that one way or another you address *all* the following elements in relation to your home page's design:

❑   Creation or revision date

❑   Easily identified and consistently displayed navigation links or buttons

❑   Home page icon or logo that can be used throughout the site

❑   Important information displayed above the fold

❑   Informative title

❑   Intentional emotional effect or theme created by means of words, colors, layout, font, and so forth

❑   Logo or other identifying graphic, such as a family crest or departmental code

❑   Opening page "hook" to catch viewer's interest (Home pages generally vary at least slightly from subpages.)

❑   Quick loading approach (It's true—gigantic images make extremely poor backgrounds, and you really don't need to show 90 pictures on your home page.)

❑   Site's purpose is clear and viewers know what steps they can take next (beyond clicking the Back button)

❑   Subheads break up long text (if necessary)

❑   Text links display along the bottom of the page

❑   Upper-left corner is put to good use, preferably with your logo

❑   Your identity or your organization's identity

Tip   Even though the Home Page Planning Checklist looks lengthy, your home page shouldn't. At all costs, avoid overloading your home page. You're better off adding a couple links to your navigation menu instead of cramming information into every corner (and beyond) of your users' screens.

Gathering Supplies and Preparing to Build

As you might remember from Chapter 5, after you've specified your goals, met your audience, organized your site, and designed your home page's layout, one final planning component remains—rounding up your tools and supplies. This stage includes ensuring that you have well-written and edited text, appropriately sized graphics (which you might have to tweak a little when the actual page design process begins), scanned or otherwise digitized pictures, and the tools to arrange all the items on your Web pages. As you can see, the tasks in this stage are concrete and straightforward, but completing them generally takes a significant amount of time—so plan accordingly. Luckily, although this stage usually takes the longest, we can describe the process fairly succinctly. Basically, before you create your Web page, you need to gather the supplies listed in the following Supplies Checklist.

Note   We're not trying to discourage you by stating that the supplies stage of the Web game can be time-consuming. It's just that gathering, creating, and modifying text and graphics almost always seems to take slightly longer than planned (at least that's been our experience—and not just because we inherently tend to enjoy creating, modifying, and playing with graphics and text!). Fortunately, you don't need to worry about "gathering supplies" types of delays at this point. Remember, our goal in this book is *faster smarter* Web page creation. To that end, in each chapter in Part Two, we've listed the supplies necessary to create the chapter's Web pages. Then you can download the images and copy the text you'll need from the Creation Guide Web site. So never fear: the hunting and gathering stages detailed in Part Two are brief and painless.

Supplies Checklist

Before you start to create your Web pages, you should have the following elements on hand and easily accessible—or at least in the process of being finalized:

- ❑ Text—edited, spell checked, and proofread
- ❑ Photographs, graphics, and illustrations (including buttons, title bars, and a high-quality logo)
- ❑ Page sketches and templates
- ❑ HTML editor, text editor, or Web page creation tool (such as an online community wizard)
- ❑ Graphics program
- ❑ Domain name (either purchased or assigned)
- ❑ Server space

Tip   Remember, if you decide to purchase a domain name, the name should be short, simple, and influenced by your Web site's purpose.

Now that the theory and planning phases are fully covered, you're ready to get your hands dirty and tackle Part Two of this book. So roll up your sleeves—it's time to create!

Key Points

- Define your Web site's goals.

- Know your audience.

- Outline your Web site's hierarchy, organizational flow, and overall feel.

- Sketch your home page and subpages.

- Gather your supplies and tools.

- Get ready to create Web pages and go live!

Part II

The Walk: Creating Web Pages

When you learned to drive a car, you probably spent some time listening to an instructor, watching defensive-driving movies, memorizing street signs, and studying driving-related facts in the Department of Motor Vehicles handbook. Sure, those learning exercises were helpful, but most likely, the art of driving truly sank in only after you got behind the wheel as a student driver and took a few spins around town with your driving instructor. Experience counts quite a bit in the real world. This sentiment isn't exactly new—Einstein summed it up pretty well when he said, "One cannot learn anything so well as by experiencing it oneself." In Part Two we're going to put you in the driver's seat and let you put the theories you learned in Part One into practice.

In this part you'll find four project chapters designed to help you acquire some well-rounded, hands-on experience as you test drive the Web site creation process. Throughout these chapters, we've tried to make the learning process as enjoyable, straightforward, and intuitive as possible. To that end, we've arranged the chapters progressively, from simplest to most complex, so that you can ease your way into more advanced Web page creation tasks. In addition, each Web site is created using a different tool that is either already on your computer or is easy to obtain.

Chapter 7

Posting a Web Page Within an Hour (or So)

Let's say you decide that you're more than ready for a relaxing beach house vacation. Most likely, your first thoughts turn to money—so you set a budget and figure out how much cash you'll need to save or whether your vacation money stash can cover your expenses. Next, you choose a destination and reserve a beach house. Then you purchase plane tickets, line up a rental car, and promise yourself that you'll exercise more regularly. Finally, weeks or months later, you pack your bags, including at least one new bathing suit; take care of last-minute minutiae so your pets and plants won't waste away; and, as a result of your careful planning and preparation, take off to enjoy a most-deserved oceanside escape. Planning a Web site follows the same pattern (without the added workouts, of course)—you start with the "big picture" goal and work down to the details.

To create the Web site described in this chapter, you'll need the following "supplies":

- An Internet connection
- A browser (ideally Microsoft Internet Explorer version 6 or later)
- Access to *www.creationguide.com/msn* and *http://groups.msn.com*

Introducing Online Groups and Communities

Here's some good news—by reading this chapter and following along with the online project's steps (located at *www.creationguide.com/msn*), you'll have a live Web site in no time. Furthermore, you won't need to partake in any deep-breathing exercises, calisthenics, or caffeine-laden drinking binges to get your Web site up and running. In other words, this is going to be fast and easy! So let's get going.

For this project's purposes, let's imagine that your goal is to have some information online today. Let's also say that you'd prefer not to spend any money at this point for an online presence. Amazingly enough, this goal is realistic and easily achieved. (As we mention in Chapter 5, you'd be surprised at the number of people we meet who have no idea that free space is readily available online.) You can quickly create a free Web site by taking advantage of the simplest and least expensive Web publishing approach around—*online groups and communities*.

Lingo   *Online groups and communities* are areas on the Web designed to enable people to create Web pages at no charge and then share them with others who have similar interests.

As we explain in Chapter 5, online groups and communities are areas on the Web where you can post Web pages for free—all you need to invest are some graphics (if desired), text, and a little time. Our tool of choice for this chapter's project is the MSN Groups site, which is located at *http://groups.msn.com*. But first, let's take a quick look at online groups and communities in general.

The goal of many online groups and communities is to enable people to share common interests with others online. As a group or community participant, you can create, visit, and join groups and communities free of charge. The key to participating in groups and communities is to join the online service. Joining an online group or community generally entails filling out a form and gaining a username and password. For example, before you can create an MSN Groups Web site, you must have a .NET Passport, as described later in this chapter.

In addition to requiring membership, online groups and communities usually outline parameters you need to stay within. Common parameters address issues such as:

- Length of nicknames and personal descriptions
- Maximum number of Web pages in your site
- Maximum number of people allowed in your group or community
- Membership (usually, you must complete a membership form)

■ Minimum system requirements

■ Size and number of documents stored on the Web site

■ Size and number of messages in your message board

■ Size and number of pictures and images

■ Total available storage space (which dictates how large and complex your site can become)

As you can see in the preceding list, many online group and community limitations make sense. By freely providing resources in a reasonable way, online services can provide the maximum service to the greatest number of people. But, as someone who's about to create an online Web presence, you should know the ins and outs of the service that will be supporting your site. Therefore, before you choose to create Web pages using an online group or community, be sure that you check out the site's offerings as well as the limitations. As mentioned, for this project we show you how to create a Web site on the MSN Groups Web site. To view the limitations of MSN Groups, follow these steps:

1   Visit the *http://groups.msn.com* Web site and click Help.

2   In the Help window, search for Help topics using the term *restrictions*.

3   In your search results, click the Limits And Restrictions topic heading or another similar heading.

MSN lists the parameters each MSN Groups site must abide by. You should keep the parameters in mind when you plan and create your Groups Web site.

Getting Acquainted with MSN Groups

Now that we've looked at online services' limitations, let's look at some of the benefits offered by MSN Groups. You can glean quite a bit of information about MSN Groups from the MSN Groups home page. As you can discover online, with MSN Groups, you can visit and join existing groups that interest you, store documents online, and create custom groups. When you create a custom group, you become the manager of the group, which enables you to determine how the Web site looks, what features and information it contains, and who can visit your site and join your group.

Generally, MSN Groups sites consist of various combinations of the following features, including (but not limited to):

- **Calendar** A page that looks like a calendar and helps members keep track of dates and events.

- **Chat room** A private space on the site where members can exchange messages in real time. In other words, members can hold online conversations as if they're on the phone, except that they type their messages instead of speak them.

- **Community settings** A Web page that depicts the Web site's community settings, including the site's description, access and membership policies, e-mail distribution list policy, rating, and directory listing. Members can view the community settings, but only site managers can alter the settings.

- **Custom lists** Lists that members can customize for any purpose.

- **File cabinet** An area that members can use to store, exchange, and access files.

- **Home page** The first page that visitors see when they visit your site.

- **Invite someone or recommend to a friend** A tool that enables members to introduce other viewers to the sites they like and have joined.

- **Member list** An up-to-date list of the site's members, including each member's nickname, role, and join date.

- **Member profile** An area where a member can alter profile settings, including changing a nickname, revising a self-description, specifying an e-mail address, and canceling membership.

- **Message board** An area where site members can read and reply to messages and share files.

- **Photo album** A page where members can display photos accompanied by short descriptions for other members to view.

- **Recommendations** An area where members can rant or rave about books, music, movies, and Web sites.

- **Site e-mail** A utility that enables site managers and members to easily send messages to all members on the site's e-mail distribution list.

■ **Site manager**   The person who has the greatest control over a site and who is responsible for overseeing the site. Generally, the site manager is the person who created the site or someone the site's creator has assigned to the manager role. By default, you'll be the site manager of the site you create in this project.

After you create an MSN Groups Web site, you (as the site manager) can add and remove elements to customize your site. Additionally, after other users sign up with your group and become members, they can participate in your site's activities by leaving messages on the message board, participating in chats, posting pictures in the picture albums, and so forth.

Now that you have an idea of where we're headed, let's get started with your first Web site creation project. As with all Web pages, this project starts with a planning phase. In this project we show you how to create an MSN Groups Web site for a 6th-grade class, but you can use the instructions for this project as guidelines to create any site that best suits your needs. Our goal in this project is to get you off on the right foot—where you wander from here is up to you.

> **Note**   You can re-create Ms. Kathy's 6th Grade site using the text and graphics we provide online (see *www.creationguide.com/msn*), or you can use your own content. We think a Groups Web site for a class is a good practice site to build because it uses many of the features that can also serve as a basis for family, sports team, project team, workgroup, and friend sites. Feel free to follow this project's instructions verbatim or to replace sample text and graphics with your own. Although creating the class site should be fun and informative, you might be more satisfied with your customized results. (Nothing against Ms. Kathy, of course!)

Planning an MSN Groups Site

Planning your site is your first task in any Web publishing endeavor—even when you're using an online group or community site, such as MSN. Generally, online communities—MSN Groups included—simplify the planning process by providing wizards, templates, clip art, and other Web page creation resources and utilities. MSN Groups offers a number of helpful tools, most notably Web page templates. A *template* is a preformatted Web page layout that you use to plug in custom information, similar to Microsoft Word templates that you use to build formatted documents, letters, Web pages, and so forth. In contrast, a custom home page offers you a blank Web page, which you need to fill on your own.

> **See Also**   *In Chapter 9, we show you how to create a Web site using the Web Page wizard and Microsoft Word templates.*

On the MSN Groups site, you can create Web pages by using templates and creating custom pages. At this point in the book, taking advantage of MSN's easy-to-use page creation tools and templates is the way to go. Then we'll show you how to add some custom touches. Furthermore, after you acquire more advanced Web page creation skills by working through later chapters in this book, you can return to your MSN Groups site to customize and liven up your existing Web pages even more. By using an online service's page creation tools and templates, you can get online quickly and easily—plus this approach gives you a taste of how satisfying and entertaining it is to see and share your pages online.

Because we opted to take the template route for this project, our planning process for this project's Web site didn't require any Web site storyboards or home page sketches. Instead, our planning process involved checking out a few of the MSN Groups classifications, viewing existing pages, and determining which resources offer the most useful set of possible MSN features to the majority of users. Also, during our planning stages we received an inside scoop that Ms. Kathy was anxious to have a Web site for her 6th-grade class. Ms. Kathy's 6th graders have frequent access to the computer lab so that they can participate in interactive studies. Therefore, we opted to create a class MSN Groups site for Ms. Kathy to help her organize her class's activities and to help provide a means to reinforce computer skills with her students. You're free to use Ms. Kathy's pictures, which are available from *www.creationguide.com/projects/chapter7/ images*, when you practice creating your own MSN Groups site.

After selecting MSN features and a topic, our planning process entailed obtaining a few key pictures from Ms. Kathy and talking to her about her goals for the site.

As you can see, the planning stage was fairly brief. Furthermore, because MSN Groups sites are easily customizable, we knew that we had the benefit of being able to add and subtract features at will after the initial Web site was up and running. To summarize our MSN Groups Web site planning process, we completed the following simple steps:

- Chose an online service (MSN Groups)
- Specified a site topic and target audience (Ms. Kathy's 6th-grade class)
- Determined basic content
- Obtained a few graphics

Now that a general plan for the online Groups Web site is taking shape, our next step is to join the community.

> **Note**   You don't necessarily need to gather graphics to get started with an MSN Groups Web page. Using MSN Groups, you can easily add and delete graphics after you've created your Web site. Remember, you can use Ms. Kathy's pictures or MSN clip art for now, and then you can delete the temporary pictures and insert your own images whenever you have digitized pictures ready for online viewing.

Becoming an MSN Member with a .NET Passport

Universally, free online communities require you to join their sites. Luckily, joining usually only involves completing an online form. Being a member of an online community serves a number of purposes, including providing membership security and enabling custom settings. Having a member profile allows you to customize the Web sites you build and provides information to others whenever you become a member of another Web site within the group or community. As you'll see in a moment, obtaining MSN membership doesn't require you to divulge any retirement savings account numbers, credit card PIN passwords, or other sensitive information, so the process is hardly a scary prospect.

To join MSN Groups, you first need to obtain a Microsoft .NET Passport. If you are the proud owner of a free Hotmail e-mail account (available at *www.hotmail.com*) or an MSN e-mail account, you can use your information as your passport. If you don't have a Hotmail or MSN account, you'll need to acquire a .NET Passport. Obtaining a passport entails (you guessed it) filling out an online form. To go about getting your .NET Passport, visit *www.passport.com* (shown in Figure 7-1) and click the Sign Up For Your Free Passport Today button. Clicking the sign-up button displays the sign-up form. Simply work through the form to acquire a .NET Passport.

> **Note**   You can also access a passport registration page by clicking the Passport link on the MSN Groups home page. But because Web pages change frequently, we thought it was better to go straight to the source by pointing you to the .NET Passport home page.

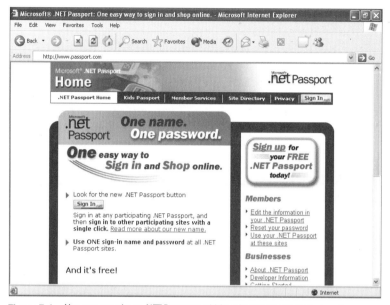

Figure 7-1   You can acquire a .NET Passport within minutes by signing up online.

Note that one of the requirements of signing up for the .NET Passport is to supply your e-mail address. If you don't have an e-mail address or if you prefer not to use your existing e-mail address, you can click the Hotmail link to sign up for a free e-mail account (or visit *www.hotmail.com*). Whichever route you take, you must enter a legitimate e-mail address before Microsoft will grant you .NET Passport privileges.

> **Tip**   During the .NET Passport registration process, you're asked if you want to share your e-mail address with other Web sites that use the .NET Passport technology. To view a list of sites and businesses that use the .NET Passport technology, click the Use Your .NET Passport At These Sites link on the Microsoft .NET Passport home page, as shown in Figure 7-1. If you're unsure about sharing your information, pass on this option for now—you can always change your preferences later.

After you complete the .NET Passport registration process, you'll soon receive two e-mail notices in your e-mail application's Inbox—a welcome message and a "verify your e-mail address" message. As you'll see, the "verify your e-mail address" message contains a ridiculously long Web address that you must visit to validate your e-mail address. If the address is highlighted in your e-mail application, simply click it; if the address isn't highlighted, copy the entire address (from *https* all the way to the end of the long string of letters and digits) and paste it into your browser's address box. Either way, your browser will quickly display a page that states *Your E-mail Address Has Been Verified*.

If you see the e-mail verification page—Congratulations! You're officially registered as a .NET Passport holder, and you're ready to create an MSN Groups Web site.

Creating an MSN Groups Web Site

After you obtain your .NET Passport, you're ready to complete this chapter's companion project. We provide the instructions for the Chapter 7 project online to compensate for the fact that online groups and communities frequently change. We didn't want to print today's online steps in this chapter only to have the steps change a couple months after the book went to press. Therefore, in an effort to make this information as helpful as possible for you, we've posted the project's steps online at *www.creationguide.com/msn*. That way, if the MSN Groups site changes, we can update the steps accordingly.

As you can see on the Creation Guide Web site, you can view the project's steps online, or you can click the Print Version link to open the project as a Word document. If you open the Word document version of the project, you can print the document, which might make following along a little easier. That way, you won't have to switch back and forth between the Creation Guide Web site and the MSN Groups Web site while you work. Instead, you can lay the printout of the steps on your desk while you build your MSN Groups Web site.

Regardless of how you proceed, Chapter 7's project steps describe how to complete the following tasks:

- Set up an MSN Groups Web site
- Invite others to join your group
- Customize your Web site
- Edit your site's text and content
- View the HTML behind your page
- Modify your Web site's features
- Delete your Web site

> **Note**   Keep in mind that because you're creating the Web site, you'll be its site manager by default. Furthermore, you must be signed into the MSN Groups Web site using your .NET Passport before you can make any changes to your site.

If you have any questions throughout the Web site creation process, feel free to contact us through the Feedback page (*www.creationguide.com/ feedback.html*) or by sending an e-mail to us at mm@creationguide.com or jc@creationguide.com. And by all means, after you've created your masterpiece, feel free to share it with us. We'd enjoy seeing your site!

Additional Resources

As with all Web creation projects, you'll find that you can benefit from accessing design and troubleshooting resources. For MSN Groups sites, your best trouble-shooting resources can be found on the MSN Groups Help pages. To access the Help pages, click Help in the MSN Groups menu bar. If you're interested in HTML resources, refer to the section "Additional Resources" near the end of Chapter 8.

Key Points

■ Online groups and communities enable you to create Web sites quickly and easily.

■ Generally, you must join an online community before you can create a Web site. To join the MSN Groups site, you must have a .NET Passport.

■ Planning an online group or community site often entails logging into the Web site, using a template or wizard to build your site, gathering pictures, and thinking about the site's content.

■ By default, you're the site manager of the sites you create.

■ As a site manager, you control your Web site's content and activity.

■ As the manager of an MSN Groups site, you can add images and e-mail addresses, edit text, change background colors, manage site proper-ties, and delete your sites.

■ Help is never far away on the MSN Groups site. Whenever you're feel-ing a little lost, simply click MSN's Help link.

Chapter 8

Demystifying Basic HTML

Can you remember the intense and conscious effort it took to learn the sounds and shapes of the alphabet way back when? Eventually, after lots of practice, you got it. After you learned about letters, you slowly began to understand how to combine the letters into words, words into sentences, sentences into paragraphs, and so on. At this point, reading probably seems natural to you. Most likely, you read the newspaper and surf the Web without thinking much about individual letter sounds and shapes. That's because over the years, you've developed your foundation in letters and words into a seemingly innate ability to read. Learning how to create HTML documents from scratch—by using tags and understanding how HTML works—is a lot like learning to read. The process might take some patience and lots of practice at the beginning, but if you take the time to learn about HTML now, you'll eventually be able to use HTML to create Web pages almost as naturally as you read.

Gathering Project "Supplies"

To create the Web pages described in this chapter, you'll need the following "supplies":

■ A basic text editor, such as Microsoft Notepad or WordPad (applications that are included with Microsoft Windows) or TextEdit (which comes with Macintosh OS X)

■   A browser and an Internet connection (An Internet connection is necessary only to download the sample project's graphics from this book's companion Web site.)

Tip   If you're Zip savvy, you can download just the zip_images8.zip file and extract the images locally.

■   The following figures downloaded from *www.creationguide.com/ projects/chapter8/images*:

b_background.gif	b_lessons2.gif	picture.gif
b_background2.gif	b_performances.gif	sendnote.gif
b_competitions.gif	b_performances2.gif	t_background.gif
b_competitions2.gif	b_recitals.gif	t_competitions.gif
b_contact.gif	b_recitals2.gif	t_contact.gif
b_contact2.gif	bg.gif	t_home.gif
b_home.gif	footer.gif	t_lessons.gif
b_home2.gif	logo.gif	t_performances.gif
b_lessons.gif	p_chris.jpg	t_recitals.gif

To obtain the figures to use with this chapter's project, display *www.creationguide.com/projects/chapter8/images*, as shown in Figure 8-1, right-click an image's filename, and select Save Target As to save a copy of the file to a folder named C:\music\images on your computer. For detailed downloading steps, see the section "Getting Your Folders and Graphics in Place" later in this chapter.

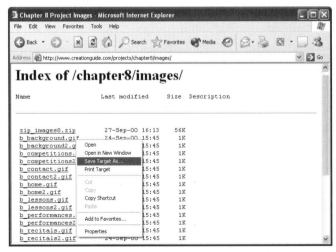

Figure 8-1   Before you can complete this project, you need to download the project files from the Internet.

Why HTML?

In the Part One chapters we briefly introduce you to HTML. Basically, we explain that you construct Web page documents by including HTML commands (also called HTML tags) within the body of a basic text document. Although other technologies (such as XML and CSS, also known as Extensible Markup Language and Cascading Style Sheets) are beginning to have a significant impact on Web page development, HTML is the foundation of most Web pages today—and if you're going to create Web pages, you need to know about HTML.

Now we understand that you might not feel ready to create a Web page from scratch using only a blank document and a vaguely familiar-sounding technology named HTML. But believe it or not, you're ready—so for now, just go for it. We're having you use HTML in the first major Web page project in this book because you'll find that understanding HTML's basics will come in extremely handy whenever you create Web pages in the future—no matter how you create those pages. Therefore, we're taking a baptism-by-fire approach in this chapter, which means that you'll be writing your own HTML documents before long.

In some ways, you might find that the project in this chapter is the most important project in all of Part Two. If you're going to create Web pages, you'll be well ahead of the game if you master some basic HTML commands and concepts. Someday, when you're much more comfortable with Web page creation, knowing at least some HTML will enable you to modify and tweak pages to suit your preferences, even if the pages you're modifying have been generated by an HTML editor. Furthermore, knowing HTML means that you'll be able to remove unnecessary (and sometimes proprietary) HTML commands that many HTML editors tend to add to Web page documents. Removing unnecessary codes can make your HTML documents smaller, which in turn means that your pages will load faster. Finally, as you become more proficient using HTML commands, you might find that you can make changes more quickly and precisely by adding, deleting, or modifying HTML code instead of modifying a Web page in an HTML editor.

We're now ready to get started. The first order of business, before we commence creating a Web site, is to briefly (very briefly) go over some basic HTML theory. By the way, when we say theory, we're talking clear, helpful information—not complex rhetoric. Think of the upcoming theory discussion as spreading a blanket before picnicking—you might as well get somewhat comfortable and discourage at least a few of the pests up front.

So You've Heard about Cascading Style Sheets Cascading style sheets (or CSS) is a technology that enables you to define a Web site's page formatting in a single place—either in a separate document or in a special area within each Web page document. In many Web designers' and developers' eyes, everyone should be using CSS as soon as possible. But the reality of the situation is that the Web is a ways off from being fully CSS-compliant, and many many Web sites don't incorporate style sheets. Fortunately, the Web continues to support older formatting techniques along with the newer CSS commands.

In relation to you, the goal of this chapter is to teach you HTML; therefore, we decided to omit teaching you how to use style sheets in this chapter. After you learn HTML, you'll be able to move on and learn CSS at your leisure (who knows—maybe we'll write a book about CSS to help you along!). To help whet your CSS appetite, we show you how to modify the autogenerated style sheets in the projects in Chapter 9 and Chapter 10.

In relation to CSS, you might hear that some of the HTML tags and attributes we show you in this chapter are *deprecated*, such as the ⟨FONT⟩ tag. A deprecated element can be (and is) used on the Web; it is simply earmarked for eventual elimination. You can see a list of HTML tags along with notations regarding which are classified as deprecated at *www.w3.org/TR/1999/REC-html401-19991224/index/elements.html*.

Finally, due to the various levels of CSS and HTML compliance on the Web these days, you can help browsers interpret your Web pages by specifying whether your page is strictly compliant with the latest standards, transitional (includes deprecated HTML elements), or framed (includes deprecated HTML elements and frames within the Web site). To do this, you insert a particular version of the ⟨!DOCTYPE...⟩ HTML tag in your Web pages, as described here as well as in this chapter's project steps:

■ If your Web page adheres to CSS and HTML 4.01 standards, insert:

```
<!DOCTYPE HTML PUBLIC "-//W3C//DTD HTML 4.01//EN"
"http://www.w3.org/TR/html4/strict.dtd">
```

■ If your Web page adheres to HTML 4.01 standards and includes deprecated HTML elements and attributes (most of which concern visual presentation), insert:

```
<!DOCTYPE HTML PUBLIC "-//W3C//DTD HTML 4.01 Transitional//EN"
"http://www.w3.org/TR/html4/loose.dtd">
```

■ If your Web page adheres to HTML 4.01, includes deprecated HTML elements and attributes, plus uses frames, insert:

```
<!DOCTYPE HTML PUBLIC "-//W3C//DTD HTML 4.01 Frameset//EN"
"http://www.w3.org/TR/html4/frameset.dtd">
```

Because the project in this chapter includes deprecated HTML elements but not frames, your documents will use the second statement—the transitional statement—in the preceding list. We'll show you how to add this statement to your HTML document in the project steps later in this chapter.

HTML Basics

Fundamentally, HTML commands serve as instructions that tell a browser how to display a Web page's content. In other words, HTML commands provide format information that controls the display of your Web page's text and graphics. Keep the purpose of HTML commands in mind. You'll see later how HTML commands weave their way in and around your Web page's content in an HTML document, but, basically, an HTML document contains two types of information:

- Content information, including text and pointers to graphics
- HTML commands, which are used to manipulate how content displays

In this chapter, we show you how to enter HTML commands and page contents into a plain-text document to create Web pages. Furthermore, you'll link the pages you create so that they can work together to create a Web site. To accomplish this feat, you'll need to use a text editor, such as those mentioned in Chapter 5, including Notepad or WordPad (if you're running Windows) or Text Edit (if you're using a Mac OS X, or SimpleText if you're using Mac 9x or earlier operating systems). Figure 8-2 shows how fully coded HTML documents appear in TextEdit, WordPad, and Notepad, respectively. When you start this chapter's project, you'll start with a blank page. To open Notepad, click Start, point to Programs, point to Accessories, and then click Notepad. To open WordPad, click Start, point to Programs, point to Accessories, and then click WordPad. To open TextEdit, double-click the TextEdit icon on your hard disk.

Note Don't be alarmed at the seemingly incomprehensible conglomeration of HTML commands shown in Figure 8-2. HTML can look complex, but it really consists only of combinations of letters, numbers, and symbols with a little organization thrown in. You're obviously familiar with letters, numbers, and symbols, so rest assured that learning to use HTML commands is well within your skill set.

As we mentioned, HTML tags take care of formatting your page. In contrast, your content is the information that displays on your page (text, graphics, headings, and so forth). In other words, HTML takes care of how information displays (bold, italic, left-aligned, and so on), and content specifies what is displayed. Knowing how to incorporate the proper HTML tags throughout a Web page's content is the key to making a Web page in a text editor. So let's look at how to use HTML tags.

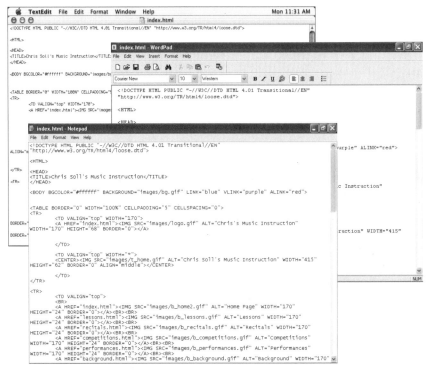

Figure 8-2   Viewing an HTML document in TextEdit, WordPad, and Notepad.

Using HTML Tags

In this section, we introduce the basic rules of HTML along with a few common tags. Keep in mind that this section does not define every HTML tag out there; quite a few HTML tags exist, and plenty of books devoted to HTML provide comprehensive command lists. (If you want to find out more about HTML than what we cover here, check out any of our favorite HTML references, which are listed in the section "Additional Resources" near the end of this chapter.) Our philosophy is that if you learn the basic rules of using HTML tags, you'll be able to use any of the tags you discover online or in HTML books.

Let's start our discussion of HTML tags with a simple rule: *HTML tags consist of commands that appear within angle brackets (<>).*

For example, one of the first tags in a Web page's source code is typically <HTML>. This tag tells a browser right off the bat that the text document is an HTML document. The browser knows that any text within angle brackets (<>) is an HTML command that needs processing and that all text outside angle brackets (<>) is content that needs to be displayed.

Lingo *Source code* refers to the contents of the HTML document that creates a Web page. Most browsers enable you to view a Web page's source code. For example, to display a Web page's source code in Microsoft Internet Explorer, display a Web page, click the View menu, and click Source.

Here's the second rule you need to remember: *HTML tags are not case-sensitive.*

This rule isn't earth shattering, but it's convenient to know. It means that browsers don't care whether the text between the angle brackets is capitalized or lowercased. Therefore, <B> and <b> are essentially the same tag (which, incidentally, is a tag that instructs the browser to display the text following the tag in boldface). Similarly, <HTML>, <html>, <HtMl>, and any other combination of capital and lowercase letters represents the same tag.

Here's rule number three: *HTML tags almost always come in pairs.*

Because most HTML tags are used primarily for formatting purposes, HTML tags often come in twos: a starting tag and an ending tag (also referred to as an *opening tag* and a *closing tag*). This pairing enables you to tell browsers where a particular formatting attribute (such as boldfacing) should start and where it should end. Think about when you go to the movies with a few friends and two friends go in to save seats while the rest of the group goes to the concessions counter. The two people saving the seats sit separately at each end of the saved seats to mark a span of seats that will contain the friends. If the seat-savers were HTML tags, they'd tell the browser that all the seats between them should be formatted as their friends' seats.

Starting tags and ending tags have very specific purposes—namely, a starting tag indicates when an action should start, and an ending tag indicates when an action should stop. (See, we're not talking rocket science here!) While starting and ending tags appear very similar they have a minor, albeit critical, difference. Ending tags are differentiated from starting tags by the inclusion of a forward slash (/) just after the left bracket, like this: </HTML>. The last element in HTML documents is usually the </HTML> command, which indicates the end of the Web page's display. Going back to the movie theater example, let's say that one seat-saver is sitting in an aisle seat and the other seat-saver is sitting in the middle of the row. The seat-saver sitting in the middle of the row is wearing a red shirt. Suddenly, a new arrival asks the seat-saver sitting in the aisle seat whether the seats are taken. The aisle-side seat-saver would say something like, "Yes—all the seats down to the person in the red shirt are taken." That's the role of a starting tag. The red-shirted seat-saver serves as an ending tag. For example, a <B> tag tells a browser, "Please boldface all the text between me and that </B> tag over there."

For further illustration, let's look at an example of text that uses HTML tag pairs. The following sentence includes HTML starting and ending tags that format the sentence as a paragraph (<P></P>), display the phrase *butter flavoring* in italic (<I></I>), and format the word *popcorn* in boldface (<B></B>), as shown in Figure 8-3:

```
<P>Do you want <I>butter flavoring</I> on your <B>popcorn</B>
or do you like it plain?</P>
```

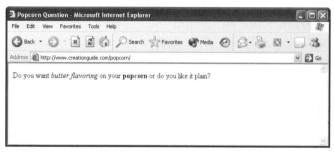

Figure 8-3   If the popcorn question is included in an HTML document, you could view the formatted question in a browser, as shown here and on *www.creationguide.com/popcorn*.

The popcorn sentence also illustrates an interesting concept called *nesting*. In HTML documents, nesting has nothing to do with twigs and feathers and everything to do with the order in which HTML tags appear. In the popcorn sentence, the italic tag set (<I></I>) and the boldface tag set (<B></B>) are nested within the paragraph tag set (<P></P>). Here's a key rule you should follow when you're nesting HTML tags: *Nested HTML tags should close in the reverse order in which they open.*

That rule might seem a little confusing, so let's look at an example. Basically, opening and closing HTML tags shouldn't get their lines crossed. Here's a correct pattern:

```
<HTML>  <P>  <B>  </B>  </P>  </HTML>
```

In this example, the <B> (boldface) tags are nested within the <P> (paragraph) tags, which are nested within the <HTML> (document identifier) tags. This setup would result in bold text within a paragraph within an HTML document. The following setup would also work:

```
<HTML>  <P>  <I>  </I>  <B>  </B>  </P>  </HTML>
```

Notice that this nesting example uses the same pattern as the popcorn sentence. In this example, the italic tag set and the boldface tag set aren't nested inside each other, but both tag sets are nested within the paragraph tag set.

Now let's lighten up the discussion a bit and look at a more clear-cut rule: *By default, HTML documents display a single space between text elements.*

This rule might seem odd to mention, but spacing issues are a great concern on the Web for a number of reasons (mostly because designers have to deal with content that resizes and reflows—issues that are nonexistent in printed documents). In an HTML document, adding any number of spaces within your code by using the spacebar, Tab key, or Enter key results in a single space. Therefore, you could embed the following four code snippets in an HTML document:

```
<I>Music Instruction</I>
<I>Music                          Instruction</I>
<I>            Music Instruction            </I>
<I>
Music Instruction
</I>
```

and the text will appear as shown in Figure 8-4. (You can view the Web page and source code online by visiting *www.creationguide.com/spacing*.)

Figure 8-4   Text displays with a single space between words, even when extra space is added between words in the HTML document.

Now you're ready for the next rule, which adds some spice to HTML tags: *Some opening HTML tags can contain properties (also called attributes), which further refine an HTML tag's instructions.*

In other words, you can frequently customize the instructions related to an HTML formatting command. For example, you can add a COLOR attribute to the <FONT> command to change the display color of text, like this:

```
They say the <FONT COLOR="green">grass</FONT> is greener.
```

If you inserted the preceding sentence into an HTML document, the text would display the word *grass* in green, as you can see online at *www.creationguide.com/greengrass*.

Finally, here's the last rule in this section: *Numerous variations exist when it comes to the HTML nesting theme, properties, and use of tag sets.*

As with all rules, you'll find that although most of HTML is predictable, the technology is as consistent as spelling rules, which means that you'll frequently find exceptions to the rules. For example, if you want to add a line break in

HTML, you enter <BR>. There's no closing tag for a line break—you either have a line break or you don't. Similarly, you insert a horizontal rule with the <HR> tag; again, no closing tag required.

Don't worry if you're feeling slightly confused. You'll start to get a feel for HTML as you work on the Web site project in this chapter. There's nothing like hands-on experience to gain knowledge. We'll introduce you to additional HTML tags and concepts in the project as we go. For added assistance, you might want to keep Table 8-1 handy while you work.

Table 8-1   HTML Tags Used in the HTML Project

Tags	Function
`<A HREF="xxx.xxx"></A>`	Marks the *anchor*, or clickable, portion of a hyperlink. The HREF attribute points to the information that should be displayed after the anchor's content is clicked. Anchor content is specified between the anchor tags (`<A></A>`) and can include text and images.
`<B></B>`	Indicates to display text between the `<B>` and `</B>` tags in boldface.
`<BLOCKQUOTE> </BLOCKQUOTE>`	Offsets a paragraph from the regular body text, usually by indenting the paragraph's left and right margins.
`<BODY></BODY>`	Marks the start and end of the Web page's displayable content.
` `	Inserts a line break. The ` ` tag doesn't have a closing tag, and this tag is frequently used consecutively to create white space on a Web page.
`<CENTER></CENTER>`	Centers the enclosed information on the page or within a table cell.
`<!DOCTYPE...>`	Specifies the Web page's document type definition (DTD), such as whether the page uses strict HTML and CSS coding, transitional HTML coding (including deprecated HTML tags), or frames.
`<FONT></FONT>`	Enables you to specify the enclosed text's font color, face, and size.
`<H1></H1>`	Specifies heading text. Heading sizes range from H1 through H6, with H1 being the largest heading size.
`<HEAD></HEAD>`	Provides an area in which you can display your Web page's title, include search engine information, add advanced formatting information, embed CSS coding or link to a style sheet, and write scripts. Other than the text within the embedded `<TITLE></TITLE>` tags, most head information doesn't display directly to viewers.
`<HTML></HTML>`	Delineates the start and end of an HTML document.
`<I></I>`	Indicates to italicize the text appearing between the `<I>` and `</I>` tags.
`<IMG SRC="xxx.xxx">`	Displays an image on a Web page. The SRC attribute points to the particular image that should be displayed.
`<LI></LI>`	Identifies a list item within an unnumbered (bulleted) list `<UL>` or an ordered (numbered) list `<OL>`.
`<OL></OL>`	Specifies an ordered (numbered) list.

Table 8-1 HTML Tags Used in the HTML Project   *(continued)*

Tags	Function
`<P></P>`	Indicates the start and end of a paragraph. By default, paragraphs display left-aligned. The closing `</P>` tag is optional. (In other words, you can simply insert the `<P>` tag at the start of each new paragraph to format your HTML contents without typing `</P>` at the end of each paragraph.) We've included the closing `</P>` tag throughout this chapter for added clarity. Browsers typically insert a blank line (plus a little extra space) before starting a paragraph.
`<TABLE></TABLE>`	Delineates the start and end of a table.
`<TD></TD>`	Defines the start and end of a cell within a table. `<TD>` tags are nested within `<TR>` tag sets.
`<TITLE></TITLE>`	Enables you to insert the Web page's title text that should display in the browser's title bar.
`<TR></TR>`	Indicates a table row. `<TR>` tags are nested within a `<TABLE>` tag set.
`<UL></UL>`	Specifies an unnumbered (bulleted) list.

Just as a last note in this section, we want to make a minor disclaimer. Although we're confident that you can create an HTML document from scratch, please keep in mind that this chapter serves only as an introduction to creating Web pages in HTML. Unfortunately, covering all the available HTML commands in a single chapter is unrealistic, but this chapter is packed with helpful coding tips and you'll find some leads on good HTML references in the "Additional Resources" section near the end of the chapter. If you create the Web site described in this chapter's project, you'll gain a strong foundation in HTML coding as well as have a template that you can customize to create unique Web pages. (We even tell you how to use the site as a template later in this chapter.)

Handling HTML Documents and Web Graphics

When you create Web pages, you usually work with multiple files. You'll have your home page HTML file (generally named index.html or index.htm), a graphics file for each graphical element on your page, and additional HTML files for linked pages. Therefore, before you start creating, you have to think of an organizational scheme so that you don't drive yourself crazy later. We highly recommend that you create a folder to contain all the HTML files used in your Web site, and, within the main folder, create a subfolder named images. Then you can store all your HTML documents in the main folder and place your graphics in the images folder. To illustrate, see Figure 8-5, which shows the HTML documents and images necessary to create this chapter's project site.

Keeping your files organized is imperative when you're adding graphics and creating hyperlinks because you must include instructions in your HTML document regarding where the browser should look for a particular graphic or linked page. Furthermore, being organized can greatly simplify the file upload-ing process when you're ready to go "live" by transferring your local files to a Web server. Your best bet is to create a folder that you can use consistently throughout the Web page and Web site creation process.

Along with being organized, you should religiously save and preview your Web pages throughout the development process.

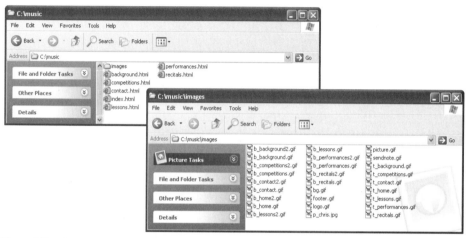

Figure 8-5   You should keep your Web site's files and folders organized in a simple yet logical manner.

Saving and Previewing HTML Documents

When you create Web pages—especially when you're hand-coding HTML—you should save and preview with abandon. Speaking from firsthand "We can't believe we just lost all that data" experiences, we can recommend without res-ervation saving your work frequently—that pretty much goes without saying whenever you're working on any file on any computer. (If monitors grew grass, our mice would wear out well-worn diagonal paths to the Save button—not to mention that we both knowingly contribute to the slow erosion of our *Ctrl* and *S* keys by pressing Ctrl+S every so often.)

Tip   "Save, save, save!" should be one of your mantras when you're working with computers.

In addition to frequently saving your files, you should preview the Web pages you build numerous times throughout the creation process. Previewing an HTML page simply means looking at your HTML document in a browser (or a couple browsers) as opposed to staring at the text and HTML code version of the document in a text editor. Performing this exercise, you can see how the HTML is formatting your content and you can troubleshoot display problems early. We'll often alter a site's layout simply because what looks good on paper doesn't transpose well to an online page.

To preview a Web page in your browser, use any of the following procedures after you've created an HTML file:

- Display the contents of the folder containing the HTML document, and double-click the HTML document's icon.
- Open your browser application (such as Internet Explorer), and type in the HTML file's location.
- Open your browser application, open the folder containing the HTML document, and drag the HTML file's icon from its folder into the browser window or the browser's Address bar.

Note We suggest specific points at which you should save and preview the project Web site in the next section. Feel free to save and preview your files more frequently than we suggest, however, especially if you take a break while creating.

We've covered a good bit of theory; now it's the witching hour. If you've read the previous few pages, you're ready to tackle the HTML Web page creation project. You should have a workable knowledge of basic HTML tags, realize that you should save your HTML documents and images in designated folders, and recognize the importance of frequently saving and previewing your Web pages throughout the creation process. We're satisfied that you're ready, so let's get the project rolling.

Planning the HTML Site

For the HTML project, we decided to create a Web page for Chris Soll, a professional musician and music instructor. Our first planning step involved meeting with Chris and finding out what types of information she wanted to include on her Web site. In our initial consultation, we found that she had a number of student-specific as well as professional-specific topics she wanted to incorporate into her site. Based on this information, we initially attempted to design a two-tier navigation bar, but the design started to look too cluttered. We determined that we could make a cleaner site by using specifically named buttons and providing a quick Site Overview section on the home page. The final design resulted in a clean, flexible layout.

After you create Chris Soll's Web site—which we quickly began to refer to as "the music site" during our consultation, based on the overwhelming presence of her baby grand piano, flute collection, and stacks of sheet music and music books in her studio—you can use your HTML document as a template to create similar Web sites that have a completely different look and feel. (Don't worry—we describe how to use the music site's code as a template later in this chapter.) Figure 8-6 shows the storyboard we came up with to illustrate the pages we wanted to include in the music site. Figure 8-7 shows a finalized sketch of the music site's home page.

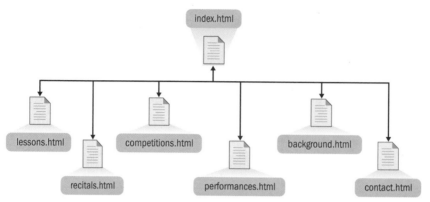

Figure 8-6   The music site's structure enables people to access any page in the site from every location.

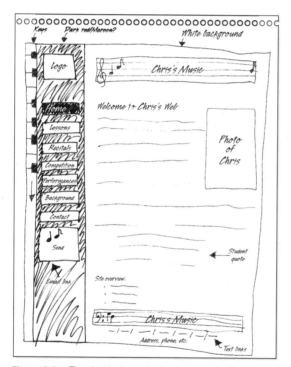

Figure 8-7   The sketch shows the basic layout for the music site's home page design.

Note   Notice in Figure 8-7 that we initially planned to insert the address information below the site's text links along the bottom of the page. Later, during the design process, we realized that placing the address above the links made better design sense. The links were already listed in the navigation bar on the left, so we wanted to present the "new" and more important address information before repeating the text link information.

Getting Your Folders and Graphics in Place

As we mention earlier in this chapter, your first task is to create a folder for your Web files and organize your graphics. Here's the process we suggest you follow (though feel free to change the folder location and name to suit your preferences):

1   Create a folder on your C:\ drive and name the folder *music.*

2   Open the music folder, and create a subfolder named *images.*

3   Open your browser, and display *www.creationguide.com/projects/ chapter8/images.*

4   Right-click the b_backgound.gif image (or right-click the Zip file, if you're familiar with Zip files and your system can extract them), and select Save Target As (if you're using Internet Explorer).

5   In the Save As dialog box, browse to the C:\music\images folder, and then click Save.

6   Right-click the next graphic and save the file to the images folder.

7   Repeat step 6 until you've saved all the graphics files to your computer.

Tip   After you finish this chapter and are done experimenting with the music Web site, you can delete the C:\music folder if you like.

As you download the graphics for the music site, notice the naming scheme we've used to label images:

- **b_*xxx***   Specifies that the image is a button. A *b_* graphic appended with the number *2* (for example, *b_background2.gif*) indicates a second version of the button that displays whenever the associated page is displayed. (You'll see what we mean later.)

  Therefore, b_background.gif is the Background button, and b_background2.gif is the "current page" version of the Background button, as shown in Figure 8-8.

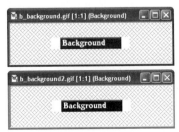

Figure 8-8   Each button in the music site consists of a regular button and a current page version of the button.

- **bg.gif**   Specifies the background graphic. The music site uses the same background graphic throughout the site, so only one bg.gif file is required.

- **footer.gif**   Identifies the graphic as a running footer graphic used at the bottom of the site's pages.

- **logo.gif**   Identifies the logo graphic. The music site uses the same logo graphic throughout the site, but it's possible that you'd have a few versions of a logo graphic (especially if you're using a smaller or modified version of the logo on subpages).

- **p_xxx**   Specifies that the graphic is a picture. The music site has only one photograph, and it's on the home page.

Note   The picture.gif file is a placeholder graphic used on the template discussed later in the chapter. You won't use the picture.gif file in the music site.

- **sendnote.gif**   Identifies the graphic as the "send mail" icon. Later, you'll link this icon on the music site so that users can click the sendnote.gif graphic to open a preaddressed e-mail message when they want to send a message to Chris Soll.

- **t_xxx**   Specifies that the image is a title bar banner graphic. For example, t_background.gif is the Background page's title bar banner graphic (which displays the word Background and is placed at the top of the page that presents background information about Chris Soll), as shown in Figure 8-9.

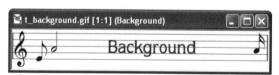

Figure 8-9   A graphic file is used to create a title bar banner on each page in the music site.

When you create your own Web pages and Web graphics, you'll probably devise your own naming scheme. We've shown you the method we used to name our graphics to give you an idea of how helpful having a naming system can be. You'll see the benefit of a well-planned graphics-naming scheme as you start to insert HTML code in a few moments.

Preparing Your Home Page File

After you have your folders and graphic files in place, you're ready to begin creating your site's home page. To begin the creation process, you need to create an HTML document that contains the standard tags that appear in all HTML documents. The standard tags are (see Table 8-1 presented earlier in this chapter):

- `<!DOCTYPE...>`
- `<HTML></HTML>`
- `<HEAD></HEAD>`
- `<TITLE></TITLE>`
- `<BODY></BODY>`

Notice that, with the exception of the `<!DOCTYPE...>` tag, the standard tags all come in sets. Figure 8-10 shows the proper way to nest the standard HTML tag sets in an HTML document and shows how to insert title text. After you type the standard HTML tags in a text document, you need to save the text document as an HTML document, as described in the upcoming procedure.

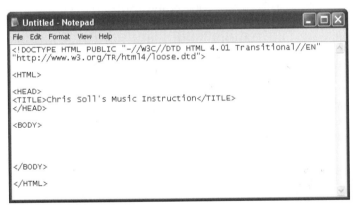

Figure 8-10 This document contains the standard HTML tags with title text inserted between the `<TITLE>` tags.

> **Note** Remember that HTML isn't case-sensitive, so you can type `<HTML>`, `<html>`, `<HtMl>`, or any other combination of capital and lowercase letters and your tag will be fine. In this chapter, we used uppercase letters for HTML tags throughout to make spotting them easy.

To begin creating the music site's home page and save it as an HTML file, follow these steps:

1 Open Notepad, WordPad, or TextEdit. We use Notepad throughout this project.

2 Click in a new blank document and type the following document type definition (which indicates that the document contains deprecated tags):

```
<!DOCTYPE HTML PUBLIC "-//W3C//DTD HTML 4.01 Transitional//EN"
"http://www.w3.org/TR/html4/loose.dtd">
```

> **Note** If you don't want to type the !DOCTYPE information shown in step 2, you can copy the information from the *www.creationguide.com/music* Web page's source code (display the Web page in your browser, view the source code, and copy the entire <!DOCTYPE...> tag.

3 Press Enter twice.

4 Type <HTML>, and then press Enter twice.

5 Type <HEAD> and press Enter.

6 Type <TITLE>Chris Soll's Music Instruction</TITLE>, and then press Enter.

7 Type </HEAD> and press Enter twice.

8 Type <BODY>, press Enter a few times (to give you some breathing room when you enter your Web page's content information), type </BODY>, and press Enter twice.

> **Note** Content text—text that displays between and outside HTML tags—displays in the same case as it is entered in the text document. Thus, if you type *chris soll's* instead of *Chris Soll's* in step 4, Chris's name will appear in all lowercase letters on your Web page. Also, remember that you don't have to worry about putting too many spaces (including blank lines) between content text and HTML tags. When a browser displays the document, it ignores the extra spaces.

9 Type </HTML> to complete the standard HTML tag setup.

You're now ready to name and save the file to your C:\music folder.

10 On the File menu, click Save.

11 In the Save As dialog box, type **index.html** in the File Name box and ensure that Text Documents is selected in the Save As Type drop-down list. (If necessary, click the arrow to select the Text Documents option.)

12 Use the Save In drop-down list and navigate to the C:\music folder on your computer.

13 Click Save and close Notepad.

The file should now display as index.html in your C:\music folder, and the icon should indicate that the file is an HTML document. At this point, you can already view your file in your browser. To view your newly created HTML file, double-click index.html. The file should open in your Web browser. Notice that the only content is the Web page's title text, which displays in your browser's title bar.

Now that the Web page's title and standard HTML tags are in place, let's add the page's background image and default link colors.

Specifying the Background and Link Colors

You can include attributes in the <BODY> tag to add background colors, background images, default text link colors, and so forth, as described in the following steps:

1 Open Notepad, WordPad, or TextEdit, and then open the C:\music\index.html file from within the text editor. If you don't see the file index.html listed in the Open dialog box, ensure that the Files Of Type list box displays All Files (*.*). If you're using Mac OS X, TextEdit automatically displays an HTML document as a Web page by default. To open and display the HTML code instead of the Web page, select the Ignore Rich Text Commands check box in the Open File dialog box (note that you can select this option in the program's Preferences dialog box as well, if you don't want to select the check box on a case-by-case basis).

> **Tip** You must open your HTML file by using the text editor's Open command, by dragging the document's icon into the text editor's window, or by right-clicking the HTML file and choosing Notepad on the Open With menu. If you double-click an HTML file in folder view, you'll display the HTML document in your Web browser.

2 In the <BODY> tag, click after the Y and before the >, press the spacebar, and then enter the following attributes and values, including the quotation marks:

```
BGCOLOR="#ffffff" BACKGROUND="images/bg.gif"
LINK="blue" VLINK="purple" ALINK="red"
```

The <BODY> attributes you just added are defined as follows:

● BGCOLOR defines a background color. Although the music site uses an image for the background, we defined a white background for folks who view the site with images turned off. In the color chart on *www.creationguide.com/colorchart*, you can see that #ffffff is a hexadecimal number that equates to white.

● BACKGROUND enables you to specify a graphics file to use as a background image. Remember that browsers automatically tile background images to fill the browser window. The music page uses the bg.gif file, which is stored in the images subfolder of the music folder, as a background image. Because both the index.html document and the images folder reside in the music folder, you don't have to indicate the image's complete address. If your image was saved elsewhere (that is, not within a subfolder of the folder that contains the index.html document), you'd have to enter the entire address that points to the image.

Lingo   *Tiling* refers to repeating an image across a window's area and down until the entire window is filled with the repeating image.

● LINK enables you to specify the color in which unvisited text hyperlinks display.

● VLINK enables you to specify the color in which visited hyperlinks display. In other words, after a user visits a site's Contacts page, any text links pointing to the Contacts page will display in the visited link color (purple, in this case).

● ALINK enables you to specify the color in which links display while users click the links. Showing a different color while the users click links clearly indicates to users that they are activating a hyperlink.

Your HTML code should now display as shown in Figure 8-11.

Figure 8-11   Some page formatting attributes can be added within the <BODY> tag. (The newly added code is highlighted in orange.)

Tip   Whenever you enter HTML code, always verify that you've included all angle brackets (<>) and quotation marks ("") in your HTML code as well as spelled the HTML commands properly. Missing small elements or misspelling commands can cause your Web page to display incorrectly or not at all. We've included screen shots of the code you're creating throughout this chapter so that you can easily check your work.

---

3 Save your HTML document, open your browser, and view index.html in your browser window. (You don't have to close your text document, but you do have to ensure that you've saved your most recent changes.) The index.html file should now display the background image in your browser window.

Tip If the changes you make in your HTML document don't show up on the preview page in your browser, click the Refresh button to update your view.

Now that the standard HTML tags, default background image, and link colors are in place, the next step is to begin to format your Web page's <BODY> area.

Creating a Table

In this section, we show you how to create a table that will contain all the elements of your Web page. Controlling elements on a Web page is a little tricky because of the variable nature of browsers and browser windows, so many sites are designed using tables with hidden borders to help lay out Web pages. Eventually, style sheets will take over the job of formatting and aligning Web pages, but for now thousands and thousands of Web pages rely on tables to control the display of Web page elements. Of course, not every Web page uses a table, but you'll find tables to be an extremely useful tool.

Basically, tables use three tags:

- <TABLE></TABLE> delineates the start and end of a table.

- <TR></TR> indicates a table row. <TR> tags are nested within a <TABLE> tag set.

- <TD></TD> defines the start and end of a cell within a table. <TD> tags are nested within a <TR> tag set.

In the music site, you'll create a two-column, three-row table:

1 If necessary, open Notepad, WordPad, or TextEdit, and then open C:\music\index.html from within the text editor. If you don't see the index.html file, remember to ensure that the Files Of Type list box displays All Files (*.*).

2   In the index.html file, click below the opening <BODY> tag (the <BODY> tag
should now contain the attributes you added in the previous section), type
<TABLE BORDER="1" WIDTH="100%" CELLPADDING="5" CELLSPACING="0">
and press Enter. Notice the quotation marks around the attribute's values.
Make sure you include beginning and ending quotation marks throughout.
Here's the purpose of each of the attributes included in the opening
<TABLE> tag:

- BORDER defines the width of the table's outline in pixels. For now,
  we're showing a 1-pixel border to aid in seeing the table while you
  design. After the page design is complete, you'll change BORDER="1" to
  BORDER="0" to hide the table borders on your Web page.

- WIDTH defines the table's exact pixel width or specifies the percentage of the browser's window that the table should fill. We're
  using a table to format the entire page, so the table is sized to fill
  100 percent of the browser's window space.

- CELLPADDING creates a space (measured in pixels) between the cell
  contents and the table border. After sampling a few spacing parameters, we found that adding a CELLPADDING value of "5" did the trick.
  This type of setting exemplifies the value of testing settings, saving,
  and previewing your HTML page during the creation process.

- CELLSPACING specifies the amount of space (in pixels) between
  cells. In the music site, we didn't need to specify any spacing
  between cells, so we set the attribute to "0".

Tip   For added assistance, you can refer to Figure 8-12 while you work through the
table creation process.

---

3   Type <TR> to start the first table row.

4   Press Enter, press Tab to make reading your code easier, and type <TD
VALIGN="top"> to begin the first cell in the first row. The VALIGN="top"
attribute indicates that you want to align the cell contents to the top of
the cell (by default, cell contents align to the middle). You can align
cell contents using the values top, middle, bottom, or baseline. Also,
by default, cell contents align at the left. (Later we show you how to
change the default alignment by centering contents within a cell.)

5   Press Enter twice, press Tab, and type </TD> to mark the end of the
first cell in the first row.

6 Press Enter twice, press Tab, and type `<TD VALIGN="top">` to create the second cell in the first row.

7 Press Enter twice, press Tab, and type `</TD>` to mark the end of the second cell in the first row.

8 Press Enter and type `</TR>` to complete the first row of your table.

9 Press Enter and repeat steps 3 through 8 to create the second table row (or copy and paste all the code starting with `<TR>` and ending with `</TR>` to create a second table row, as described in the tip).

10 Press Enter after creating the second table row, and then create a third row by retyping the commands in steps 3 through 8 or by copying and pasting the table row code.

11 After entering the third table row, press Enter and type `</TABLE>` to complete the table tags.

Tip   If you prefer not to retype the table row commands when creating the second and third table rows, click before the first row's `<TR>` command and drag to select all the text up to and including the `</TR>` closing command. Then press Ctrl+C to copy the selected code. Click after the `</TR>` command, press Enter, and press Ctrl+V to paste the copied HTML code into your text document. Press Ctrl+V again to create the third table row.

Finally, you'll add a `WIDTH` attribute to the two cell tags (`<TD>`) in the first row of the table. You can assign column width by percentage (for example, the left column could be assigned to take up 50 percent of the browser window), or you can insert an exact pixel measurement. By default, if you don't include the `WIDTH` attribute in table cells, the table sizes the columns based on the size of the cell content and the size of the browser window. You need to add the `WIDTH` attribute to only one cell in a column (and if you have conflicting measurements in cells in the same column, the browser will use the largest setting by default). To keep our setup orderly, we'll add the `WIDTH` attribute to the cells in the first row:

Note   If you don't define column widths in tables by adding the `WIDTH` attribute to `<TD>` tags, browsers automatically size the columns based on each column's widest item and the browser's window size.

---

12 In the first cell in the first row, click after "top", press the spacebar, and type `WIDTH="170"` to set the first column to 170 pixels wide.

13 In the second cell in the first row, click after "top", press the spacebar, and type WIDTH="*". The asterisk in place of a pixel number indicates that the browser should allow the second column to be as wide as necessary to fill the remaining table width. Because this table is formatted as 100 percent of the browser window, the asterisk instructs browsers to expand the second column to fill the remainder of the browser window area.

14 Save your HTML document. Your HTML code should look like the code shown in Figure 8-12.

Now that your table is in place, you're ready to enter content into the table. The first order of business is to insert the logo into the top-left corner.

Figure 8-12 The table code creates the structure for your Web page's contents. (The added table code is shown in orange.)

Inserting and Linking the Logo

We're creating a standard page design, so we opted to insert the logo in the top-left (prime real estate) corner. We plan to use the home page as a template for all subpages, so we're going to link the logo to the home page. That way, when you use the home page as a template, all subpages will automatically include a logo that links to the site's index.html home page.

When you insert a logo, you're basically inserting an image. To insert an image in an HTML document, you use the `<IMG>` tag with the `SRC` attribute, which points to a particular graphic. For example, to specify the music site's logo, you'd type `<IMG SRC="images/logo.gif">`. Similarly, when you insert your logo and format it as a hyperlink, you use the same HTML codes that you use to link any graphic. So pay attention to the following steps—you'll find yourself using these commands quite a bit. First, let's insert the logo graphic (we take care of linking the graphic in just a bit):

1 If necessary, open your text editor and open index.html.

2 In the first cell in the first row, click after the `<TD VALIGN="top" WIDTH="170">` tag, press Enter, press Tab, and type the following HTML tag, which points to the logo image:

```
<IMG SRC="images/logo.gif" ALT="Chris's Music Instruction"
WIDTH="170" HEIGHT="68" BORDER="0">
```

Tip Adding spaces and returns in your HTML code won't affect your Web page's appearance, so you don't need to add returns in your HTML document to match the examples in the text. Our text examples had to be shortened to fit properly within the book's page design. Your code can be entered as shown in the project's HTML reference figures included throughout this chapter.

With the exception of the `SRC` attribute, the `<IMG>` tag's attributes used in the music site are optional (but very useful) and are defined as follows:

- `SRC` specifies the filename of the image (the source of the image) to be displayed.

- `ALT` enables you to provide descriptive text that displays when the cursor is placed over the image area.

- `WIDTH` and `HEIGHT` specify the image's width and height. You should specify the sizes of your images because doing so helps browsers display your Web page's layout faster. Keep in mind that any actual image resizing (as in making an image larger or smaller) should be done in your image editing program and not by using `WIDTH` and `HEIGHT` attributes in your HTML document—ideally, you want your images to be sized as closely as possible to the size you'll display the images on your Web pages.

■   BORDER specifies the thickness of the border around the image. By
      default, a 1-pixel border appears around graphics that are formatted as
      hyperlinks. Generally, designers change the default by setting the
      BORDER attribute to `"0"`.

Lingo   An *anchor* is either the clickable text or graphic component of a hyperlink or a specified
target area within a document. Most notably, anchor text is surrounded by the `<A></A>` tag set
in HTML documents.

Next you'll format the logo.gif image to serve as a hyperlink to the home page.
Basically, creating a hyperlink entails marking some text or a graphic as an *anchor*
by using the `<A></A>` tag set around the text or image you want to serve as a hyperlink, and then specifying to the browser what should be displayed after the anchor
element is clicked. To make the logo a hyperlink, follow these steps:

1   Click before the `<IMG...>` tag and type `<A HREF="index.html">` to
      specify that when users click the logo, they will be taken to the home
      page. (As mentioned earlier, this linking information will come in
      handy when you copy the home page to create subpages.)

2   Click after the closing `>` of the `<IMG...>` tag and type `</A>` to specify
      the end of the anchor's contents.

Tip   If you're using Notepad and your code goes beyond the edge of the window,
open the Format menu and choose Word Wrap. When Word Wrap is activated, Notepad automatically wraps your text and displays all your text in the current window.

---

3   Save index.html. Your HTML code should look similar to the code
      shown in Figure 8-13.

Figure 8-13   The newly added code inserts a logo and links the logo image to the home page.

Inserting the Home Page Banner Graphic

After inserting the logo, inserting the home page's banner graphic will be a piece of cake. This step entails inserting an image in the second cell of the first table row. You won't have to link this graphic, so the procedure is fairly straightforward. The only twist to inserting the banner graphic is that you'll want to center the graphic within the table cell by nesting the `<IMG>` tag within the `<CENTER></CENTER>` tag set. To insert a banner graphic on the home page, perform the following steps:

1. If necessary, open your text editor and open index.html.
2. In the second cell of the first row, click after the `<TD VALIGN="top" WIDTH="*">` tag, press Enter, press Tab, and then type the following:

```
<CENTER><IMG SRC="images/t_home.gif" ALT="Chris Soll's Music
Instruction" WIDTH="415" HEIGHT="62" BORDER="0" ALIGN="middle">
</CENTER>
```

3. Save index.html. Your HTML code should display as shown in Figure 8-14.

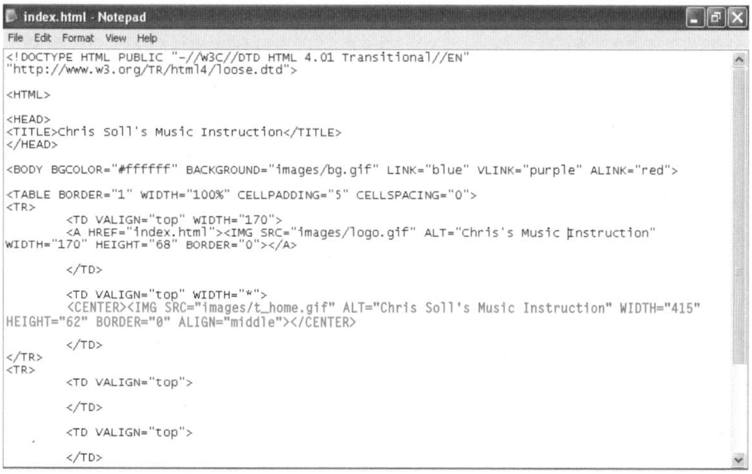

```
<!DOCTYPE HTML PUBLIC "-//W3C//DTD HTML 4.01 Transitional//EN"
"http://www.w3.org/TR/html4/loose.dtd">

<HTML>

<HEAD>
<TITLE>Chris Soll's Music Instruction</TITLE>
</HEAD>

<BODY BGCOLOR="#ffffff" BACKGROUND="images/bg.gif" LINK="blue" VLINK="purple" ALINK="red">

<TABLE BORDER="1" WIDTH="100%" CELLPADDING="5" CELLSPACING="0">
<TR>
	<TD VALIGN="top" WIDTH="170">
	<A HREF="index.html"><IMG SRC="images/logo.gif" ALT="Chris's Music Instruction"
WIDTH="170" HEIGHT="68" BORDER="0"></A>

	</TD>

	<TD VALIGN="top" WIDTH="*">
	<CENTER><IMG SRC="images/t_home.gif" ALT="Chris Soll's Music Instruction" WIDTH="415"
HEIGHT="62" BORDER="0" ALIGN="middle"></CENTER>

	</TD>
</TR>
<TR>
	<TD VALIGN="top">

	</TD>

	<TD VALIGN="top">

	</TD>
```

Figure 8-14 The banner image code specifies to browsers which image should display as the banner on the index.html Web page.

4. Open index.html in your browser. (If index.html is already open in your browser, click the Refresh button to update your view.) The browser should display your version of index.html as shown in Figure 8-15. In the figure, notice that the table borders for the first row display around the inserted graphics. Hold your cursor over the logo or banner graphic to display the image's ALT text.

Tip You must save your HTML document before you can view the document's
changes in a browser window. If your most recent changes aren't displaying in your
browser, ensure that you've saved your HTML document. If you still aren't seeing the
changes, click the Refresh button in your browser to ensure that you're viewing the
most up-to-date version of your page.

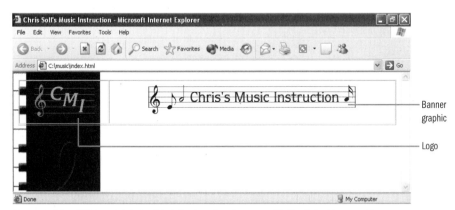

Figure 8-15 At this point, index.html displays in a browser with the linked logo and home page
banner graphic, which were positioned using a table.

In the next section, you'll see how to create a navigation bar that you can
use throughout the music site.

Adding Navigation Links

Creating a navigation bar for the music site entails inserting button graphics and
linking each graphic to a Web page. You've already inserted the logo and banner graphics, so you know how to use the <IMG> tag. Furthermore, you've linked
the logo, so you're also familiar with the <A></A> anchor tags. The only slightly
tricky part about using navigation buttons in the music site is that each page
shows a custom button for the current page. For example, whenever a user visits
the home page, the black version of the Home button displays, and whenever a
user visits another page in the site, the standard maroon Home button displays.
This setup will become clearer as you progress through this section. To create a
navigation bar on the home page, follow these steps:

1   If necessary, open your text editor and open index.html. You'll place
the navigation bar in the first column of the table's second row, which
will cause it to display on the left side of the page.

2 After the second <TR> tag, click after the first <TD VALIGN="top"> tag, press Enter, press Tab, and type <BR> to insert a blank line between the logo graphic and the upcoming navigation bar.

In the next few steps, you'll embed each button's image tag within an anchor tag that links the button to an appropriately named Web page. You haven't created the subpages yet, so take note of the filenames provided in the anchor tags. The subpage's filenames will have to match the filenames in the anchor references. In all, you need to add seven buttons. You'll start by adding the current-page version of the Home button. (Recall that you downloaded two versions of each button—the current-page version of each button has a "2" at the end of the button's filename.)

3 Press Enter, press Tab, and type the following:

```
<A HREF="index.html"><IMG SRC="images/b_home2.gif" ALT="Home Page"
WIDTH="170" HEIGHT="24" BORDER="0"></A>
```

4 Type

 to add two line spaces, press Enter, and press Tab.
You're now set up to enter the next button link and graphic.

Tip You can repeatedly type the HTML code with varied HREF file references, SRC file-names, and ALT information, or you can copy the code you type in steps 3 and 4 and paste the copied code into the table cell six times. Then, replace the HREF file references, SRC filenames, and ALT text definitions in each entry, as shown in Figure 8-16.

---

5 Type the following:

```
<A HREF="lessons.html"><IMG SRC="images/b_lessons.gif" ALT="Lessons"
WIDTH="170" HEIGHT="24" BORDER="0"></A><BR><BR>
```

6 Press Enter, press Tab, and type:

```
<A HREF="recitals.html"><IMG SRC="images/b_recitals.gif"
ALT="Recitals" WIDTH="170" HEIGHT="24" BORDER="0"></A><BR><BR>
```

7 Press Enter, press Tab, and type:

```
<A HREF="competitions.html"><IMG SRC="images/b_competitions.gif"
ALT="Competitions" WIDTH="170" HEIGHT="24" BORDER="0"></A><BR><BR>
```

8 Press Enter, press Tab, and type:

```
<A HREF="performances.html"><IMG SRC="images/b_performances.gif"
ALT="Performances" WIDTH="170" HEIGHT="24" BORDER="0"></A><BR><BR>
```

9 Press Enter, press Tab, and type:

```
<A HREF="background.html"><IMG SRC="images/b_background.gif"
ALT="Background" WIDTH="170" HEIGHT="24" BORDER="0"></A><BR><BR>
```

10 Press Enter, press Tab, and type:

```
<A HREF="contact.html"><IMG SRC="images/b_contact.gif" ALT="Contact"
WIDTH="170" HEIGHT="24" BORDER="0"></A><BR><BR><BR><BR>
```

Notice that there are four <BR> tags at the end of step 10. The extra line spaces are included because we also want to insert the Send Us A Note icon to give users an easy way to send e-mail messages to Chris. When you create an e-mail link, you use a special HREF format in the anchor tag, as follows.

11 Press Enter a couple times to separate the Send Us A Note HTML code from the main navigation bar HTML code, press Tab, and then type

```
<A HREF="mailto:mm@creationguide.com">
```

except replace mm@creationguide.com with your own e-mail address so that users will open a blank e-mail message addressed to you when they click the Send Us A Note icon.

12 Insert the Send Us A Note icon and close the anchor reference by typing:

```
<IMG SRC="images/sendnote.gif" ALT="E-mail Chris" WIDTH="170"
HEIGHT="77" BORDER="0"></A>
```

13 Save index.html. Your HTML code should look similar to the code shown in Figure 8-16.

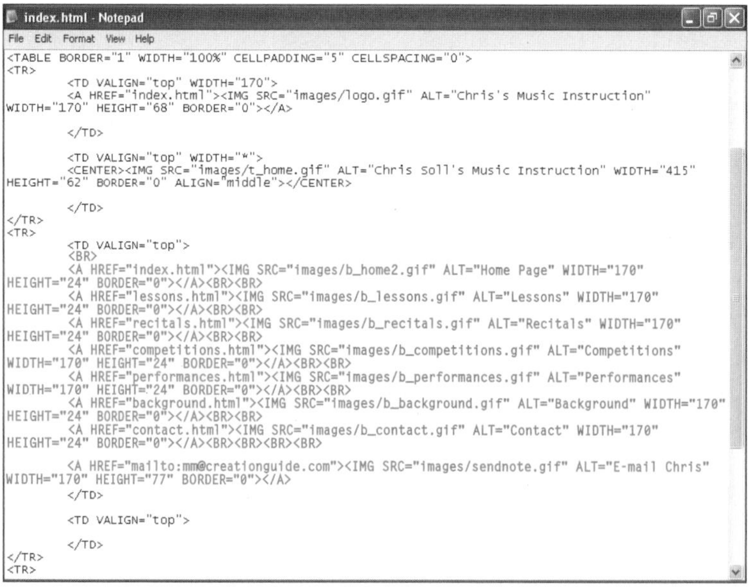

Figure 8-16   The navigation bar HTML code is inserted into a single table cell.

14 Open index.html in your browser. Your home page should now include a navigation bar on the left, as shown in Figure 8-17. Notice that the Home button displays differently than the other buttons to show that users are currently viewing the home page. Click the logo and Home button to make sure that the home page redisplays. (Clicking any other button in the navigation bar will display an error because you haven't created those pages yet.) Hover your cursor over each button to ensure that the ALT text is correct throughout. Click the Send Us A Note icon to ensure that a blank e-mail message opens and is addressed to you.

Figure 8-17 You can test some of your HTML coding by clicking the Home button and the Send Us A Note image in the navigation bar.

Inserting Footer Information

You next need to add the footer information. The music site's footer includes a footer graphic, the address and phone number information, text links that correspond to the navigation bar links, and some copyright text.

The process of inserting a footer graphic is similar to the process of inserting the header graphic described earlier in this chapter. The main difference in the footer area is that you're going to place the footer graphic in the second cell in the third row and you're going to insert some additional information in the cell along with the graphic (as described in the next section). Because you're going to include other information below the footer graphic, you'll nest the footer graphic within paragraph tags (<P></P>) to ensure that space will be included above the graphic. Let's start to create the footer element by inserting the footer graphic:

1   If necessary, open your text editor and open index.html.

2   In the third row of the table, click after the second <TD VALIGN="top"> tag, press Enter, press Tab, and then type <P ALIGN="CENTER"> to indicate the start of a paragraph and to specify to center align the paragraph's contents. (By default, paragraphs are left-aligned.)

Tip   For added assistance, refer to Figure 8-18 as you insert the Web site's footer information.

---

3   Specify the footer image's information by inserting the image tag with the following attributes:

```
<IMG SRC="images/footer.gif" ALT="Chris Soll's Music Instruction"
WIDTH="415" HEIGHT="62" BORDER="0" ALIGN="middle">
```

4   Type </P> to indicate the end of the paragraph section. The closing </P> is optional, but adding it makes the code clearer.

Next you'll insert a second paragraph that centers the address and phone number information.

5   Press Enter twice, press Tab, and type:

```
<P ALIGN="CENTER">1234 Songbird Alley, Mesa, AZ 85201<BR>
555 555-5555</P>
```

Notice the <BR> tag in the preceding HTML code between the address text and the phone number. Adding the <BR> tag inserts a line break and displays the phone number below the address on the next line.

Now you'll add some text links in the footer area that correspond to the navigation bar's buttons—that way, if any users have graphics turned off, they can still navigate around your site. To add text links, you follow a procedure similar to creating graphic links. The difference between the two tasks is that you enclose text between anchor links instead of enclosing an IMG tag, as shown in the following steps. First, you'll center the paragraph that will contain the text links.

6   Press Enter twice, press Tab, and type <P ALIGN="CENTER">.

7   Press Enter, press Tab, and type:

```
<A HREF="index.html">Home Page</A> |
```

In the preceding link, the words *Home Page* will display as hyper-text on the Web page. If users click the words Home Page, the index.html file will display. Also notice the pipe symbol (|). You type this symbol between each text link to make differentiating the links easier. The symbol is optional but popular. You're now ready to add the remaining text links.

Tip   You don't have to press Enter and Tab between each of the text link entries in steps 8 through 14. Browsers will show the links in a row regardless of the space you add in the HTML document. We chose to format the text links in the described way to make working with the information easier.

---

8 Press Enter, press Tab, and type:

```
<A HREF="lessons.html">Lessons</A> |
```

9 Press Enter, press Tab, and type:

```
<A HREF="recitals.html">Recitals</A> |
```

10 Press Enter, press Tab, and type:

```
<A HREF="competitions.html">Competitions<A> |
```

11 Press Enter, press Tab, and type:

```
<A HREF="performances.html">Performances</A> |
```

12 Press Enter, press Tab, and type:

```
<A HREF="background.html">Background</A> |
```

13 Press Enter, press Tab, and type:

```
<A HREF="contact.html">Contact Information</A> |
```

The final text link entry is the text equivalent of the Send Us A Note icon you inserted earlier. Thus, this text link uses the `mailto:` compo-nent in the `HREF` attribute. Remember to replace `mm@creationguide.com` with your own e-mail address in the following step.

14 Press Enter, press Tab, and type:

```
<A HREF="mailto:mm@creationguide.com">E-mail Chris</A>
```

15 To complete the text link paragraph, press Enter, press Tab, and type `</P>`.

The final component of the footer is the copyright information. In this section, you create a centered paragraph and enter the copyright information. One interesting twist here is that you can use a special character entity reference to create a copyright symbol.

Tip   A character entity reference is a special key combination that includes the
ampersand (&) symbol and enables you to display nonstandard characters—such as
accent marks, registered trademarks, and so forth—in Web pages. For a list of common character entity references, see *www.creationguide.com/characters*.

---

16 Press Enter twice, press Tab, and type:

```
<P ALIGN="CENTER">&copy 2002 Chris Soll. All Rights Reserved</P>
```

17 Save index.html. Your HTML code should look similar to the code
shown in Figure 8-18.

18 Open index.html in your browser. The footer in the index.html file
should look similar to the footer information in the page shown in
Figure 8-19.

```
index.html - Notepad
File  Edit  Format  View  Help
<TABLE BORDER="1" WIDTH="100%" CELLPADDING="5" CELLSPACING="0">
<TR>
        <TD VALIGN="top" WIDTH="170">
        <A HREF="index.html"><IMG SRC="images/logo.gif" ALT="Chris's Music Instruction"
WIDTH="170" HEIGHT="68" BORDER="0"></A>

        </TD>

        <TD VALIGN="top" WIDTH="*">
        <CENTER><IMG SRC="images/t_home.gif" ALT="Chris Soll's Music Instruction" WIDTH="415"
HEIGHT="62" BORDER="0" ALIGN="middle"></CENTER>

        </TD>
</TR>
<TR>
        <TD VALIGN="top">
        <P ALIGN="CENTER"><IMG SRC="images/footer.gif" ALT="Chris Soll's Music Instruction"
WIDTH="415" HEIGHT="62" BORDER="0" ALIGN="middle"></P>

        <P ALIGN="CENTER">1234 Songbird Alley, Mesa, AZ 85201<BR> 555 555-5555</P>

        <P ALIGN="CENTER">
        <A HREF="index.html">Home Page</A>  |
        <A HREF="lessons.html">Lessons</A>  |
        <A HREF="recitals.html">Recitals</A>  |
        <A HREF="competitions.html">Competitions<A>  |
        <A HREF="performances.html">Performances</A>  |
        <A HREF="background.html">Background</A>  |
        <A HREF="contact.html">Contact Information</A>  |
        <A HREF="mailto:mm@creationguide.com">E-mail Chris</A>
        </P>

        <P ALIGN="CENTER">&copy 2002 Chris Soll. All Rights Reserved</P>

        </TD>

        <TD VALIGN="top">

        </TD>
</TR>
<TR>
```

Figure 8-18   For the music site, the footer information is added to the last cell in the table.

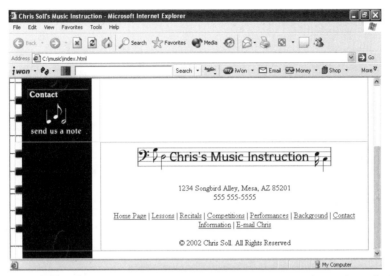

Figure 8-19   You can see how the HTML footer code is interpreted by a browser by previewing the music site's index.html page.

You might have noticed that you've designed everything on the home page except the main content. You'll be happy to hear that there's a method to our madness. Now that you have the basic structure of the home page created, and because you're planning to mimic the home page structure on the subpages, you can use the index.html file to quickly create the foundation pages for the subpages, as described in the next section.

Copying the Home Page Framework to Subpages

By now you've probably realized that we need to make some pages for the navigation bar and text links to link to. Namely, the music site calls for the following pages:

- index.html (which you're already in the process of creating)
- lessons.html
- recitals.html
- competitions.html
- performances.html
- background.html
- contact.html

In this section, you're going to create the six additional HTML pages that make up the music site. You could copy all the code from index.html, paste it into a blank text document, and then save the text document as an HTML file, but we're much lazier than that! Here's how we went about creating most of the code for the subpages:

1 Open the C:\music folder.

2 Right-click the index.html file and click Copy on the shortcut menu.

3 Rick-click in the folder and click Paste.

4 Repeat step 3 five times (so that you have six copies of the index.html file). Your music folder should display as shown in Figure 8-20.

5 Right-click the first copy of index.html, click Rename on the shortcut menu, type lessons.html, and press Enter. Ensure that you rename the copied files accurately and using all lowercase letters; if you change the names of the files at this point, the links you created in your HTML code won't work.

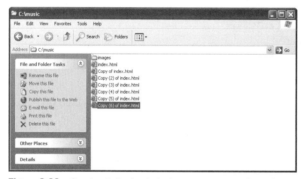

Figure 8-20   Copying index.html six times creates templates for your site's subpages.

6 Using the procedure described in step 5, rename the subsequent files *recitals.html, competitions.html, performances.html, background.html,* and *contact.html.*

7 Open your text editor, open the lessons.html file, and then perform the following six changes, which are highlighted in color in Figure 8-21:

- In the <TITLE> tag, click after the word Instruction and type : Lessons.

- In the <TABLE> tag, change the BORDER attribute to "0".

- In the second cell of the first table row, change t_home.gif to t_lessons.gif.

- Also in the second cell of the first table row, replace the text ALT="Chris Soll's Music Instruction" with the text ALT="Lessons".

● In the navigation bar HTML code, change the b_home2.gif Home button text to b_home.gif.

● Also in the navigation bar HTML code, change the b_lessons.gif Lessons button text to b_lessons2.gif.

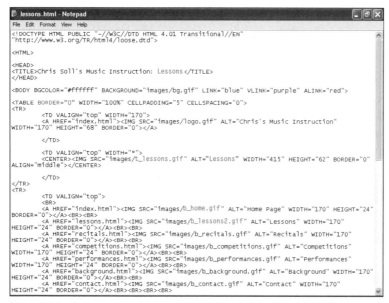

Figure 8-21 To use a copy of index.html as a subpage, you need to slightly modify the HTML code to suit each page.

8 Save lessons.html.

You've just completed the foundation document for the Lessons page. Not too bad! To check your page, double-click lessons.html to view the page in your browser. If everything looks good (as shown in Figure 8-22), you're ready to move on. Your next step is to repeat the short customization process in the remaining subpage documents.

Note Using a completed foundation page to create subpages is fast and promotes consistency throughout your site.

---

9 Open recitals.html in your text editor, and make the following changes:

● In the <TITLE> tag, click after the word Instruction and type : Recitals.

● In the <TABLE> tag, change the BORDER attribute to "0".

● In the second cell of the first table row, change t_home.gif to t_recitals.gif.

- Also in the second cell of the first table row, replace the text ALT="Chris Soll's Music Instruction" with the text ALT="Recitals".

- In the navigation bar HTML code, change the b_home2.gif Home button text to b_home.gif.

- Also in the navigation bar HTML code, change the b_recitals.gif Lessons button text to b_recitals2.gif.

10 Save recitals.html.

11 Open competitions.html in your text editor and make the following changes:

- In the <TITLE> tag, click after the word Instruction and type : Competitions.

- In the <TABLE> tag, change the BORDER attribute to "0".

- In the second cell of the first table row, change t_home.gif to t_competitions.gif.

- Also in the second cell of the first table row, replace the text ALT="Chris Soll's Music Instruction" with the text ALT="Competitions".

- In the navigation bar HTML code, change the b_home2.gif Home button text to b_home.gif.

- Also in the navigation bar HTML code, change the b_competitions.gif Lessons button text to b_competitions2.gif.

12 Save competitions.html.

13 Open performances.html in your text editor and make the following changes:

- In the <TITLE> tag, click after the word Instruction and type : Performances.

- In the <TABLE> tag, change the BORDER attribute to "0".

- In the second cell of the first table row, change t_home.gif to t_performances.gif.

- Also in the second cell of the first table row, replace the text ALT="Chris Soll's Music Instruction" with the text ALT="Performances".

- In the navigation bar HTML code, change the b_home2.gif Home button text to b_home.gif.

- Also in the navigation bar HTML code, change the b_performances.gif Lessons button text to b_performances2.gif.

14 Save performances.html.

15 Open background.html in your text editor and make the following changes:

- In the <TITLE> tag, click after the word Instruction and type : Background.

- In the <TABLE> tag, change the BORDER attribute to "0".

- In the second cell of the first table row, change t_home.gif to t_background.gif.

- Also in the second cell of the first table row, replace the text ALT="Chris Soll's Music Instruction" with the text ALT="Background".

- In the navigation bar HTML code, change the b_home2.gif Home button text to b_home.gif.

- Also in the navigation bar HTML code, change the b_background.gif Lessons button text to b_background2.gif.

16 Save background.html.

17 Open contact.html in your text editor and make the following changes:

- In the <TITLE> tag, click after the word Instruction and type : Contact.

- In the <TABLE> tag, change the BORDER attribute to "0".

- In the second cell of the first table row, change t_home.gif to t_contact.gif.

- Also in the second cell of the first table row, replace the text ALT="Chris Soll's Music Instruction" with the text ALT="Contact".

- In the navigation bar HTML code, change the b_home2.gif Home button text to b_home.gif.

- Also in the navigation bar HTML code, change the b_contact.gif Lessons button text to b_contact2.gif.

18 Save contact.html.

19 Open index.html in your browser. Click each navigation bar button to check your work. A foundation page should display after you click each button; each subpage should include the current page title bar text, a custom title banner graphic, and a current page (black) navigation bar button that corresponds to the displayed page. Also, the table border lines shouldn't display on the subpages (because you changed the BORDER attribute in the <TABLE> tag to "0" on each subpage). Figure 8-22 shows how the Lessons page should display in your browser window.

Figure 8-22   Each subpage now displays a custom title banner and "active" black button.

Congratulations! You've created the structure for the entire music site. Now we'll insert some content on the home page.

Inserting Body Text on the Home Page

In this section, you're going to insert some body text into the music site's home page. What this endeavor actually boils down to is a practice in formatting text. The main content of the home page consists of a couple headings, paragraph text, colored block quotes, and a linked unnumbered list. So as you can imagine, we'll be discussing how to create these types of elements over the next couple pages.

Creating Headings

In HTML coding, you can define six heading levels by using <H1></H1>, <H2></H2>, and so on through <H6></H6> tag sets, with the size 1 heading being the largest and size 6 being the smallest. Figure 8-23 shows a sample of the various heading sizes, and you can see the headings online at *www.creationguide.com/headings.*

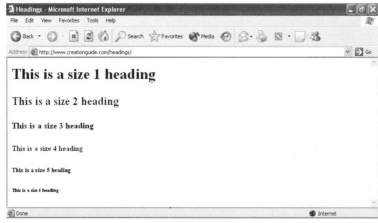

Figure 8-23   Standard HTML headings come in six default sizes.

The music site uses one heading tag on the home page, which formats the welcome message at the top of the page:

1   Open your text editor, and then open C:\music\index.html.

2   In the second row and second cell of the table (the cell after the navigation bar information), click after <TD VALIGN="top">, press Enter, and press Tab.

First you'll define the font style for the cell's body text:

3   Type the following:

```
<FONT FACE="verdana, arial, sans-serif">
```

Notice in step 3 the three font names in the FACE attribute. Because you never know what fonts users will have installed on their systems, you should provide a backup plan when you define font styles. In step 3, if a user's computer has the Verdana font installed, the browser will display upcoming body text in the Verdana font style. If Verdana isn't installed on the user's computer, the browser will look for the Arial font family. If neither Verdana nor Arial is installed on the user's system, the browser will display the body text in a sans serif style (for more information about serif and sans serif fonts, see Chapter 4). If fonts listed in the font tag can't be found on the user's computer, the browser will display the text in the browser's default font style.

Next you'll add a line break and insert a "welcome" heading on the music home page.

4 Press Enter, press Tab, type `<BR>` to add a line break, press Enter, press Tab, and then type the following size 3 heading information:

```
<H3>Welcome to Chris Soll's Online Resource for Music Instruction
and Performance Information!</H3>
```

5 Save index.html. Your code should appear as shown in Figure 8-24.

```
index.html - Notepad
File  Edit  Format  View  Help
        <CENTER><IMG SRC="images/t_home.gif" ALT="Chris Soll's Music Instruction" WIDTH="415"
HEIGHT="62" BORDER="0" ALIGN="middle"></CENTER>

        </TD>
</TR>
<TR>
        <TD VALIGN="top">
        <BR>
        <A HREF="index.html"><IMG SRC="images/b_home2.gif" ALT="Home Page" WIDTH="170"
HEIGHT="24" BORDER="0"></A><BR><BR>
        <A HREF="lessons.html"><IMG SRC="images/b_lessons.gif" ALT="Lessons" WIDTH="170"
HEIGHT="24" BORDER="0"></A><BR><BR>
        <A HREF="recitals.html"><IMG SRC="images/b_recitals.gif" ALT="Recitals" WIDTH="170"
HEIGHT="24" BORDER="0"></A><BR><BR>
        <A HREF="competitions.html"><IMG SRC="images/b_competitions.gif" ALT="Competitions"
WIDTH="170" HEIGHT="24" BORDER="0"></A><BR><BR>
        <A HREF="performances.html"><IMG SRC="images/b_performances.gif" ALT="Performances"
WIDTH="170" HEIGHT="24" BORDER="0"></A><BR><BR>
        <A HREF="background.html"><IMG SRC="images/b_background.gif" ALT="Background" WIDTH="170"
HEIGHT="24" BORDER="0"></A><BR><BR>
        <A HREF="contact.html"><IMG SRC="images/b_contact.gif" ALT="Contact" WIDTH="170"
HEIGHT="24" BORDER="0"></A><BR><BR><BR>

        <A HREF="mailto:mm@creationguide.com"><IMG SRC="images/sendnote.gif" ALT="E-mail Chris"
WIDTH="170" HEIGHT="77" BORDER="0"></A>

        </TD>

        <TD VALIGN="top">
        <FONT FACE="verdana, arial, sans-serif">
        <BR>
        <H3>Welcome to Chris Soll's Online Resource for Music Instruction and Performance
Information!</H3>

        </TD>
</TR>
<TR>
        <TD VALIGN="top">

        </TD>

        <TD VALIGN="top">
```

Figure 8-24   The added code specifies a font style and inserts a size 3 heading.

Adding Paragraph Text

Below the welcome heading you created in the previous section, you'll add some body text. The `<P></P>` tags are the main tags you'll use when entering paragraph text, which you'll do next.

1 Click after the `</H3>` tag you created in the previous section, press Enter, press Tab, and type `<P>Meet Chris!</P>`.

2 Press Enter, press Tab, and type the following:

```
<P>She's an internationally certified senior music instructor who
teaches piano and flute to budding musicians, hobbyists, and
professionals.</P>
```

3 Press Enter, press Tab, and type the following:

```
<P>Chris complements her highly regarded instructional program by
regularly performing throughout the world as well as orchestrating
annual student recitals and competitions.</P>
```

4 Finally, press Enter, press Tab, and type the following:

```
<P>Student testimonials sum up Chris's teaching success best:</P>
```

5 Save index.html.

Your HTML code should appear as shown in Figure 8-25. Furthermore, if
you preview index.html in your browser, your home page should look similar to
the page shown in Figure 8-26. Your page is all set up except for adding a block
quote or two, which is the topic of the next section.

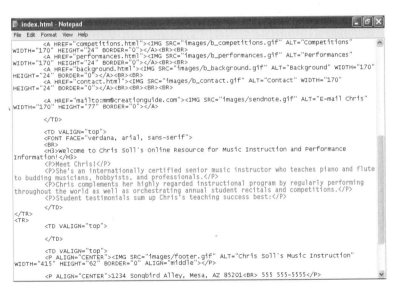

Figure 8-25   This code shows the paragraph text added to the music site's home page.

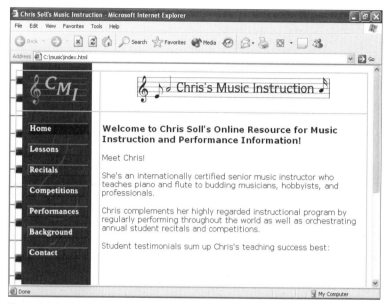

Figure 8-26 At this point, heading and paragraph text should display on your home page.

Formatting Block Quotes and Coloring Text

You can format text as a block quote to set off the text from the surrounding body text. Generally, browsers interpret the <BLOCKQUOTE></BLOCKQUOTE> tag set by indenting the enclosed text's left and right margins. If you really want to indent your paragraph, you can nest block quote commands inside one another, as here: <BLOCKQUOTE><BLOCKQUOTE></BLOCKQUOTE></BLOCKQUOTE>. In this section, you'll create block quotes with maroon text:

1 Open index.html in a text editor if necessary, click after best:</P> in the second cell of the table's second row, press Enter twice, and press Tab.

2 Type <BLOCKQUOTE><BLOCKQUOTE> to create a block quote nested within a block quote.

3 Press Enter, press Tab, and type the following:

```
<FONT COLOR="maroon"><P><I>Chris is by far the best music teacher
I've ever had! She taught me more than I could have learned in a
lifetime from Viktor McTonedeaf, the Royal Music Instructor!</I></P>
```

   Notice that the COLOR attribute in the FONT tag is used to modify the color of the paragraph text.

4 Press Enter twice, press Tab, and type the following:

```
<P ALIGN="RIGHT"><I>- Moe Zart</I></P>
```

This inserts a right-aligned, italicized name, which is associated with the block quote entered in step 3.

5 Press Enter twice, press Tab, and type the following:

```
<P><I>Chris Soll is the best teacher I had before "the incident"
that ended my professional music career--she's a true master!</I></P>
```

6 Press Enter twice, press Tab, and type:

```
<P ALIGN="RIGHT"><I>- Vincent Vanngo</I></P>
```

7 Press Enter, press tab, and type `</FONT>` to end the maroon font color formatting.

8 Press Enter twice, press Tab, and type `</BLOCKQUOTE></BLOCKQUOTE>` to end the block quote formatting setting.

9 Save index.html.

Your block quote text should display in your HTML document as shown in Figure 8-27. Figure 8-28 shows the block quote text when it's viewed in a browser.

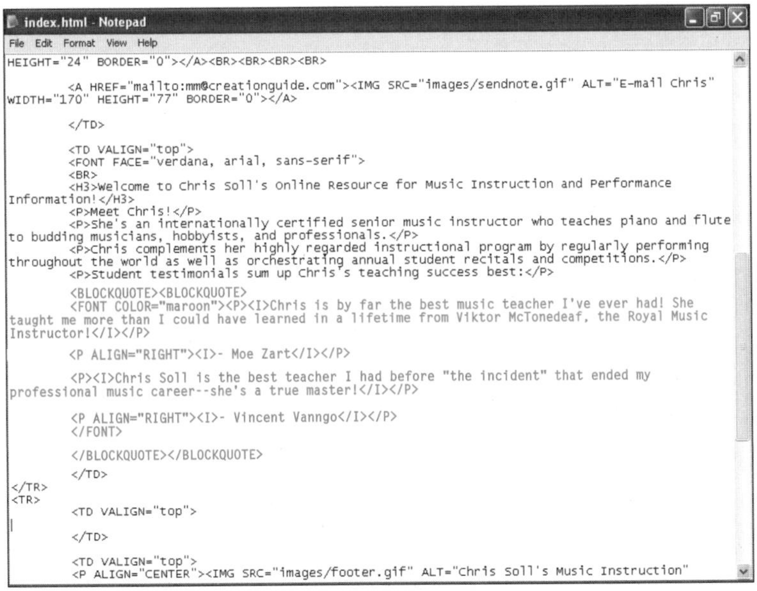

Figure 8-27 You add block quotes to Web pages to offset text.

Figure 8-28   Internet Explorer displays block quotes by indenting the text on the left and right margins.

Creating a Linked Unnumbered List

The final type of body text you'll create on the music home page is an unnumbered list. An unnumbered list appears as a bulleted list on a Web page, as shown in Figure 8-29.

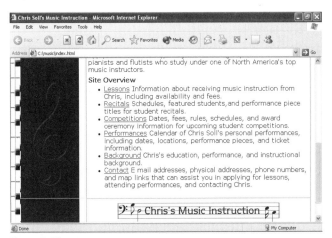

Figure 8-29   By default, unnumbered lists display with bullets.

Note   You can use <OL></OL> HTML commands to create numbered (ordered) lists, or you can use <UL></UL> commands to create unnumbered (bulleted) lists. Each list item within either type of list is identified by the <LI></LI> tag set.

In this section, you'll first add a small amount of text that introduces the unnumbered list, and then you'll create the list (which includes links to appropriate pages):

1   Open index.html in a text editor if necessary, click after the final </BLOCKQUOTE> in the second cell in the second table row, press Enter twice, press Tab, and then enter the following paragraph:

```
<P>Apply for lessons today, and join the elite group of world-class
pianists and flutists who study under one of North America's top
music instructors.</P>
```

2   Press Enter twice, press Tab, and then type the following:

```
<P><B>Site Overview</B></P>
```

In step 3, you'll begin the unnumbered list by inserting the <UL> tag.

3   Press Enter twice, press Tab, and type <UL>.

In steps 4 through 9, you'll create list items by surrounding each list item with the <LI></LI> tag set. Furthermore, you'll format the first word of each list entry as a hyperlink to another page in the site.

4   Press Enter, press Tab, and type the following:

```
<LI><A HREF="lessons.html">Lessons</A> Information about receiving
music instruction from Chris, including availability and fees.</LI>
```

5   Press Enter, press Tab, and type the following:

```
<LI><A HREF="recitals.html">Recitals</A> Schedules, featured
students,and performance piece titles for student recitals.</LI>
```

6 Press Enter, press Tab, and type the following:

```
<LI><A HREF="competitions.html">Competitions</A> Dates, fees,
rules, schedules, and award ceremony information for upcoming
student competitions.</LI>
```

7 Press Enter, press Tab, and type the following:

```
<LI><A HREF="performances.html">Performances</A> Calendar of
Chris Soll's personal performances, including dates, locations,
performance pieces, and ticket information.</LI>
```

8 Press Enter, press Tab, and type the following:

```
<LI><A HREF="background.html">Background</A> Chris's education,
performance, and instructional background.</LI>
```

9 Press Enter, press Tab, and type the following:

```
<LI><A HREF="contact.html">Contact</A> E mail addresses, physical
addresses, phone numbers, and map links that can assist you in
applying for lessons, attending performances, and contacting
Chris.</LI>
```

10 Press Enter, press Tab, and type `</UL>` to end the unnumbered list.

11 Press Enter, press Tab, and type `</FONT>` to complete the body text and end the font family specification.

12 Save index.html.

Your unnumbered list code should display as shown in Figure 8-30 (and your index.html page should display as shown earlier in Figure 8-29).

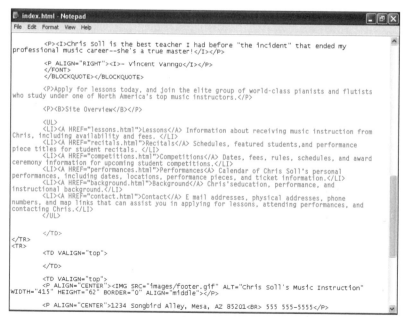

Figure 8-30   The highlighted HTML code includes paragraph text and an unnumbered list, which contains hyperlinks.

Last but not least, you'll insert a linked photograph into the body area of the music site's home page.

Inserting and Linking a Picture

By now, you should be very comfortable with inserting and linking graphics. (You had a lot of practice just a little while ago when you were creating the navigation bar!) For this page, we opted to display the picture below the size 3 heading and along the right side of the page. Furthermore, because the photograph is a picture of Chris, we linked the photograph to the Background page.

To insert a linked picture within your page's body text, follow these steps:

1 Open index.html in a text editor if necessary, click after the </H3> tag in the second cell in the second row of the table, press Enter, and press Tab.

2 Type the following link and image information:

```
<A HREF="background.html"><IMG SRC="images/p_chris.jpg"
ALT="pic: Chris Soll" WIDTH="170" HEIGHT="250" BORDER="0"
HSPACE="25" VSPACE="10" ALIGN="right"></A>
```

In this step, you can see some added attributes to the <IMG> tag, which are defined as follows:

- HSPACE enables you to specify extra space (in pixels) between the image and text on the left and right sides of the image.

- VSPACE enables you to specify extra space (in pixels) between the image and text above and below the image.

- ALIGN indicates to align the picture on the page, and text wraps accordingly. In this example, the picture is aligned to the right side of the page.

3 Save index.html.

Finalizing the Home Page

Finally, you need to remove the table borders on the home page before you can proclaim your project complete. In addition, you should check your links and view all your pages to ensure that you've entered accurate HTML code. First let's get rid of those borders on the home page:

1 Open index.html in a text editor.

2 In the <TABLE> tag, change the BORDER attribute from "1" to "0".

3 Save index.html.

Now let's click around and check your links, graphics, ALT text, and other page elements. For example, you need to make sure that none of your pages display with two black buttons.

4   Open your browser, display index.html (or if the document is already open in your browser, click Refresh), and then click every link (including the linked picture, logo, Send Us A Note icon, and text links) to verify that your links work properly and your pages display correctly. If any links don't respond as expected, open the proper HTML document in your text editor and check the HTML code carefully. Check your banner graphics and button graphics to ensure that you've included the proper graphics on each page.

Your completed home page should look like our sample online version of the music site at *www.creationguide.com/music*. You can use the Source command on the View menu in your browser to display the online Web site's source code. The source code might come in handy if you want to check your own code or if you need some assistance.

Note   You might have noticed that we provided content only for the home page. At this point, we think you're well enough prepared to enter content into the other pages if you desire more practice using HTML.

Using the Music Site's Framework as a Template

After all your hard work creating the music site, we wanted you to have a useful HTML template that you can easily customize. Therefore, we're going to let you in on a little secret. You can create a Web site using the music template even if you don't have any graphics. You don't have to have a background image, banner graphics, or buttons. Instead, you can create an entire Web site using text links and color backgrounds by replacing the content elements in the music site's Web pages. Figure 8-31 illustrates a Web page that uses the music Web site without graphics. You can visit the sample site at *www.creationguide.com/ projects/chapter8/sample*.

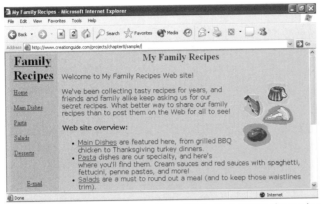

Figure 8-31   You can create a text-based Web site that uses the music site as a template.

Tip   The small graphics on the sample page in Figure 8-35 are clip-art images downloaded and pasted together to create a simple picture. If you prefer not to include a graphic on your page, simply delete the `<IMG>` tag in your HTML document.

After you surf around the sample text site for a bit, visit the template page we created and posted at *www.creationguide.com/projects/chapter8/sample/ template.html*. Figure 8-32 shows the template page, and Figure 8-33 shows some of the template's source code. To speed along your progress when using the template to build a custom page, display the template's source code by clicking the View menu and then Source. Then in the source code window, click the File menu, click Save As, and save the source code to your computer. At that point, you're free to modify your local version of the template by replacing the placeholder text with your custom content. After you're finished creating a page using the template, turn to Chapter 11 to see how you go about uploading your pages to the Internet.

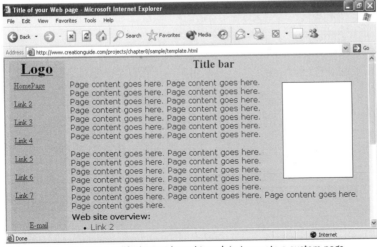

Figure 8-32   You can modify the text-based template to create a custom page.

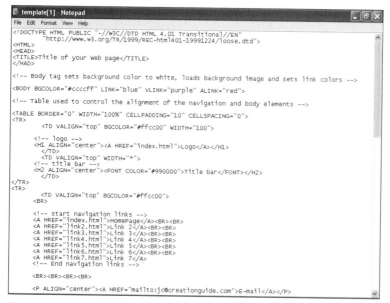

Figure 8-33   You can copy the template's source code to get a good start on the code for your custom page.

Tip   In Figure 8-33, you can see HTML code entries that begin with an exclamation point and two dashes: <!-- logo -->. These types of entries are called *comments*. Comments don't display on a Web page; they're used as notes to developers to help label parts of the HTML document. Comments have been added to the sample template to help you identify HTML components when you customize the source code.

Finally, notice in Figure 8-33 that the <BODY> tag's BGCOLOR attribute has been changed from white (#ffffff) to purple (#ccccff), and that the first <TD> tag in each table row contains a BGCOLOR attribute set to gold (#ffcc00). You can use the BGCOLOR attribute to color your page's background as well as to color your table's cells if you're not using a background image. You can get fairly creative with color by coloring the background one color and then selectively coloring table cells various other colors. (You don't have to color all your table cells the same color.) Refer to the hexadecimal color chart on *www.creationguide.com/ colorchart* if you'd like to experiment with various colors on your Web page.

Additional Resources

As we mentioned, HTML books and Web pages abound. Here are a few of our favorite HTML resources:

■ Castro, Elizabeth. *HTML for the World Wide Web*. 4th ed. Berkeley, CA: Peachpit Press, 2000. (ISBN: 0-201-35493-4) This book does a nice job of visually showing how to use most HTML commands. The textual explanations are brief yet helpful when used in conjunction with the visual references.

■ Morrison, Michael. *Faster Smarter HTML & XML*. Redmond, WA: Microsoft Press, 2002. (ISBN: 0-7356-1861-5) This book targets interested but inexperienced users who want to develop Web pages by using HTML. A nice feature of this book is that it offers numerous opportunities for hands-on learning.

■ Creation Guide Resource page (*www.creationguide.com/resources*) is continually updated to include current Web development resources.

■ World Wide Web Consortium (*www.w3.org*) Web site is the online home for the official most current HTML specifications. As of this writing, HTML 4.01 is the currently accepted specification. Use the Table of Contents, Elements, and Attributes links along the top of the page to find HTML commands and command descriptions. You can find a helpful list of HTML elements at *www.w3.org/TR/1999/REC-html401-19991224/index/elements.html*.

■ Web Developer's Virtual Library (*www.wdvl.com*) provides resources, sample code, and tutorials for Web developers.

■ webmonkey (*www.webmonkey.com*) provides numerous resources for online developers.

Key Points

■ HTML commands serve as instructions that tell a browser how to display a Web page's content.

■ HTML commands appear between < > marks, usually come in pairs, and are not case-sensitive.

■ Opening HTML tags frequently contain attributes to further refine the tag's instructions.

■ The standard tags for HTML documents consist of the following:

```
<!DOCTYPE...>
<HTML>
<HEAD>
<TITLE></TITLE>
</HEAD>
<BODY>
</BODY>
</HTML>
```

■ If possible, store all your Web site documents and graphics within the same master folder. Create an images folder for your Web site's images within the master folder.

■ To make life easier, devise a graphics naming system to help differentiate various image types, such as buttons, banners, pictures, and so forth.

■ When creating Web pages, save your HTML documents and preview your pages in a browser frequently.

■ Always verify that you've included all angle brackets (<>) and quotation marks ("") in your code. Missing small elements or misspelling HTML commands can cause your page to display incorrectly (or not at all) in a browser.

Chapter 9

Creating Web Pages with Microsoft Word

Most of us are creatures of habit—we like to eat at favorite restaurants, hang out with customary friends, and so on. Sometimes, life is more enjoyable (and easier) when we're surrounded by the familiar. Thus, you might feel most comfortable creating Web pages in an "old" standby application such as Microsoft Word. Most people have used Word to create standard documents, so this application easily serves as a widely recognized comfort-zone interface. If you're among the "at least slightly familiar with Word" users, you'll be pleased to find that creating Web pages in Word is very similar to creating standard documents.

In this chapter you'll be able to put all your Word and word-processing knowledge to work, as well as pick up a few Word tricks. By the way, if you generally use another word-processing application, don't be overly concerned at this point; you'll soon see that Word offers the standard fare of word-processing features and commands, so following along in this chapter won't take you much more than knee-deep into new waters.

Gathering Project "Supplies"

To create the Web pages described in this chapter, you'll need the following "supplies":

■ Microsoft Word 2002

■ A browser and an Internet connection (An Internet connection is necessary only to download the project's text file from the Creation Guide Web site.)

■ The following three figures downloaded from *www.creationguide.com/projects/chapter9/images*:
> animated_speaker.gif
> bg_ear.gif
> headphones.gif

■ The following three audio files downloaded from *www.creationguide.com/projects/chapter9/sounds*:
> bone_break.wav
> kiss.wav (optional)
> slap.wav (optional)

■ The following three text files downloaded from *www.creationguide.com/projects/chapter9/text*:
> info.doc
> resume.doc
> soundtips.doc

To obtain the images, sound, and text files, create a folder named *foley* on your computer's hard disk drive, and create three subfolders named *images*, *sounds*, and *text*. (For convenience, we'll refer to your hard disk drive as the C:\ drive throughout this chapter, although your drive letter may vary.) After you create the three folders, connect to the Internet, open your browser, display *www.creationguide.com/projects/chapter9/images*, right-click the animated_speaker.gif filename, and select Save Target As to save a copy of the file to the C:\foley\images folder on your computer, as shown in Figure 9-1. Repeat the "right-click Save Target As" process until you've saved all the images to the C:\foley\images folder, and then repeat the process to download the three sound files to C:\foley\sounds folder and the three text files to C:\foley\text folder.

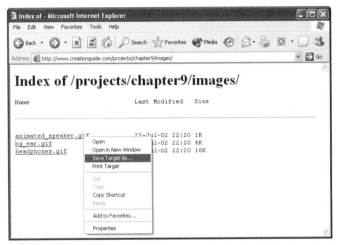

Figure 9-1   To complete this project, you need to download three images, three sounds, and three text files to C:\foley\images, C:\foley\sounds, and C:\foley\text folders, respectively.

Introducing the Web Capabilities of Word 2002

In Chapter 7, we introduce creating an online presence by using free online resources (such as MSN groups). Then in Chapter 8, we show how to use a text editor and some HTML commands to create Web pages from scratch. In this chapter we explain how you can create a Web site using an application that many people already have installed on their computers—Word 2002.

Over the past few years, we've been watching as Word has evolved, with each version incorporating increasing levels of Internet and networking functionality. Word 2002 continues the networking-integration trend of Word by continuing to supply you with a number of ways in which you can interact with the Internet:

■ **View Web pages**   You can click View, choose Toolbars, and then click Web to display the Web toolbar. The Web toolbar provides basic Web navigation buttons similar to the toolbar buttons found in Microsoft Internet Explorer.

■ **E-mail messages**   To create an e-mail interface within Word, you can click the E-mail button on Word's Standard toolbar or click Blank E-mail Message in the New Task pane. Clicking the E-mail button in the Standard toolbar opens the E-mail header pane within the current document view. After the E-mail pane displays, you can enter e-mail addresses in the address text boxes, add text in the Subject text box, and then click Send to send the currently displayed Word document to another person connected to your network or the Internet.

Tip   To close the E-mail pane without sending an e-mail message, simply click the E-mail button in the Standard toolbar.

■ **Create Web pages**   Using the Save As or Save As Web Page feature, Web page templates, Blank Web Page link in the New Document Task Pane, or the Web Page Wizard, you can convert any Word document to a Web page or create Web pages from scratch. When you create a Web page in Word, Word automatically generates the HTML source code necessary to display your document as a Web page. In essence, Word acts as a midrange HTML editor. Keep in mind that although Word isn't a bare-bones HTML editor like Notepad, it isn't as comprehensive as a full-scale HTML editor like Microsoft FrontPage. To help differentiate, Table 9-1 shows the built-in Web page editing capabilities available in Word 2002 compared to the capabilities available in FrontPage 2002 (and in case you'd like to research this issue further, we verified Table 9-1's information through Microsoft's Knowledge Base article Q291149). The main point of Table 9-1 is to show you that you can perform a good number of Web page creation tasks in Word 2002, but you should turn to a true HTML editor like FrontPage to meet more comprehensive and advanced Web site creation needs.

Note   If you're interested in learning more about the e-mail features and Web browsing capabilities of Word 2002, thumb through the resources mentioned near the end of this chapter in the section "Additional Resources."

Table 9-1   Built-In Web Page Editing Capabilities in Word 2002 and FrontPage 2002

Feature	Word 2002	FrontPage 2002
Application, document, and Web object models	Yes	Yes
Authoring and management	No	Yes
Automatic repair of hyperlinks	Yes	Yes
Cascading style sheets	Yes	Yes
Cross-browser Dynamic HTML (DHTML) animation effects	No	Yes
Editing of HTML, DHTML, Script, Active Server Pages (ASP), and Extensible Markup Language (XML)	Yes	Yes
Enhanced color tools	Yes	Yes
HTML source preservation	Yes	Yes
HTML tags revealed on a page	Yes	Yes

Table 9-1   Built-In Web Page Editing Capabilities in Word 2002 and
FrontPage 2002   *(continued)*

Feature	Word 2002	FrontPage 2002
Integration with design-time and ActiveX controls	Yes	Yes
International functionality	Yes	Yes
Microsoft Script Editor	Yes	Yes
Nested subwebs	No	Yes
Personalized HTML formatting	Yes	Yes
Pre-built Web components	Yes	Yes
Quick insertion of code	Yes	Yes
Source control	No	Yes
Targeting of specific browsers and features	Yes	Yes
Themes	Yes	Yes
Visual Basic for Applications	Yes	Yes
Web server administration	No	Yes
Workflow reports	No	Yes

As you can see in Table 9-1, Word offers quite a few basic Web page development capabilities, and you can expand on those capabilities by building up your store of Web page development knowledge. In this chapter you'll gain experience using a number of Word's Web development features. For some people, learning how to create Web pages and Web sites in Word can fulfill their Web publishing needs and they don't need to look further for a Web page development application. So let's get busy.

As we just mentioned, you can create Web pages in Word in three main ways:

- Execute the Save As or the Save As Web Page command to save a document as an HTML file

- Create a Web page by using Web page templates or clicking the Blank Web Page link in the New Document Task Pane

- Create a Web site using the Web Page Wizard in Word

In the next few pages we take a brief look at the preceding three ways of creating Web pages. Then in this chapter's project, we focus on how you can use the Web Page Wizard in Word 2002 to create a Web site, use a Web page template to create a Web page, and modify existing Web pages so you can build custom Web pages and tweak pages based on templates. We also provide hints, instructions, and pointers regarding formatting any HTML document while you're in Word. Throughout the project, we'll explain how to tweak Word-generated Web pages as well as create and add design elements—such as WordArt, clip art, and multimedia files. That's our preamble. Now let's look at how to use Word to create Web pages. First, let's use the quickest method of converting a Word document into a Web page—saving a document as a Web page.

Saving a File as an HTML Document

As you might know, you can save Word documents in various file formats (with various filename extensions, such as .txt, .doc, .rtf, and so forth). Among the file-type options, Word includes a couple options that enable you to save your Word document as a Web page (with an .htm extension). You can save any Word document as an HTML document through the Save As dialog box. When you save a Word document as an HTML document, Word generates the Web page's HTML source code automatically.

Try This!   Before you save a document as a Web page, you should preview how the document will display as a Web page. To preview a document as a Web page, open any Word document (such as the C:\foley\resume.doc file, if you downloaded it for this chapter's project) and then use the following steps to try various methods of previewing Web documents:

1   After opening a Word document, click View on the menu bar and then click Web Layout. The view changes to Web Layout view within the Word application.

2   Click View, and then click Normal to revert to Normal view.

3   Click the Web Layout View button, located in the lower-left corner of the document window. Word's view changes to Web Layout view within the Word application.

4   Click the Normal View button in the lower-left corner of the window.

5   Click File, and then click Web Page Preview. When you use the Web Page Preview command, Word displays the current document in your browser (instead of within Word).

6   Close your browser. Your Word document should still be displayed within Word in Normal view. Close the Word document.

After you preview your Word document as a Web page, you're ready to save the document as a Web page. To do so, you access the Save As dialog box, as described here:

1   Open an existing Word document (such as the C:\foley\resume.doc file you downloaded for this chapter's project), or create a new document and enter some miscellaneous text. Then click File, and click Save As Web Page. The Save As dialog box opens with *Web Page (*.htm; *.html)* already specified in the Save As Type list box along with a Change Title button, as shown in Figure 9-2.

Change Title button

Figure 9-2 To quickly configure the Save As dialog box to save a document as a Web page, choose Save As Web Page on the File menu instead of Save As.

2 Click the Change Title button. The Set Page Title dialog box opens. You can use the Set Page Title dialog box to provide custom text, as shown in Figure 9-3, that displays in a browser's title bar.

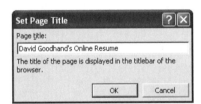

Figure 9-3 Title text displays in a Web browser's title bar.

3 In the Set Page Title dialog box, enter some text that you want to display in the title bar of the viewer's browser whenever your Web page is viewed (for instance, if you're working with resume.doc, you could insert *David Goodhand's Online Resume*), and then click OK.

Tip The Save In pane of the Save As dialog box includes a My Network Places icon (in Microsoft Windows Me, Windows NT, and Windows XP) and a Web Folders icon (in Windows 98). Using the My Network Places or Web Folders feature, you can save Web pages directly to your server if your server supports Web folders. See Chapter 11 for details about creating and using network places and Web folders to upload and manage Web pages.

Click the Save button to save the document as an HTML document (with an .htm extension).

After you save a document as a Web page, you'll see that the file is saved with an .htm filename extension instead of .doc. You can now edit and upload the Web page document just as you would any HTML file you created using a text editor or another HTML editing program.

Furthermore, in addition to creating a Web page using the standard Save As Web Page procedure, Word 2002 also enables you to save Word documents in two other types of formats:

■ **Web Archive**   Saves all the elements of a Web site or Web page—including text and graphics—as a single file, called a single MIME encapsulated aggregate HTML document (MHTML) file. Internet Explorer 4 and later supports this format, but Netscape doesn't.

■ **Web Page, Filtered**   Saves a document as a Web page and removes Microsoft Office-specific tags from the source code. After you save a file using the Web Page, Filtered option, your text and the general appearance of the document will be preserved when you open the document in Office programs, but some features might work differently.

By default, when Word 2002 saves a document as a Web page, the file includes code that enables you to properly display (and edit) the page in Word and online. When you're ready to upload your file to the Web and want to streamline your source code, you can save your Web page using the Web Page, Filtered setting in the Save As Type list box in the Save As dialog box.

On the other hand, if you want to store a copy of a Web page without saving all the related files (such as images) as separate files, or if you want to upload or send your Web page as a single file, you can select the Web Archive setting in the Save As Type list box. Basically, the Web Archive option creates a file similar to the type of file you receive in your e-mail application if someone sends you a copy of a Web page in an e-mail message.

Viewing a Document's HTML Source Code

After you save a Word document as a Web page, you can view the Web page's HTML source code in Word. You can freely edit a document's source code within the Word interface. Keep in mind, however, that the autogenerated code in Word is more complex than the basic HTML commands you worked with in Chapter 8. That's because the Word code includes embedded CSS and commands that enable you to work in the Web page in Word. To view a Web document's HTML source code in Word, follow these steps:

1   Open an .htm document in Word. For simplicity's sake, you'll want to open Word, click File, and then click Open to open your .htm document, or you'll need to drag the .htm document from a folder view into Word. If you double-click an .htm icon name in a folder, you'll open the document in your browser window.

> **Note** If you click the filename of a Word document saved as a Web page and the page opens in Internet Explorer, you can open the document in Word by clicking the Edit button in Internet Explorer. To do so, click the Edit button's drop-down list and then select the Edit With Microsoft Word command. Selecting this option opens the .htm document in Word.

2 After you open an .htm document in Word, click View and then choose HTML Source. The Microsoft Script Editor window opens and displays the page's source code, as shown in Figure 9-4.

> **Note** If this is the first time you're viewing source code in an Office application, you might have to install the Script Editor. If you need to install the Script Editor, Word displays a message box when you choose HTML Source on the View menu. To install the Script Editor, simply insert your Office XP CD into your disk drive and click OK—Word takes care of the remaining installation tasks.

Notice in Figure 9-4 that you can see a document's title text in the document's source code. The title text should match the text you entered in the Set Page Title dialog box. You can modify the Web page's title text directly in the source code within the Microsoft Script Editor window by using standard editing techniques (deleting, inserting text, and so forth).

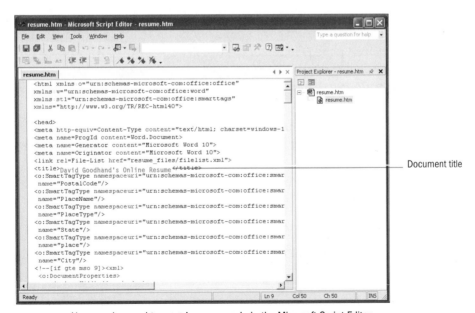

Figure 9-4 You can view an .htm page's source code in the Microsoft Script Editor.

Try This! You can add or change an HTML document's title text without opening the Script Editor by adding or modifying the title text in the document's Properties dialog box. To do so, follow these steps:

1   Open an HTML document in Word.

2   Click File, click Properties, and then click the Summary tab.

3   Type the title text in the Title text box and click OK.

After you peruse the source code, close the Script Editor window and the Word document to prepare for the next section. As you can see, you can create fairly advanced Web pages by simply creating a Word document and then saving the document as a Web page. Furthermore, you can also easily modify Web pages by using standard Word tools and procedures. Finally, you can truly do some Web wading by editing a Word document's HTML source code directly in the Script Editor.

Later in this chapter, when we're well into the project, we show you some ways in which you can edit and modify Web pages by using other tools and features in Word. We don't want to spoil any surprises at this point, but you'll be happy to see that editing Web pages in Word is a whole lot like editing regular documents in Word.

Now let's take a look at some Web page templates that Word provides to assist you in your Web page creation endeavors.

Creating a Web Page with a Template

As you just saw, saving a Word document as a Web page is pretty straightforward, so you might be wondering why you'd want to bother with Web page templates. But as you'll soon see firsthand, templates provide a few advantages and shortcuts over the "save a Word document as a Web page" technique.

Templates can speed up your Web page creation process if you plan to use any of the following elements:

- Headings
- Columns
- Frames
- Hyperlinks that point to areas on the same page
- Common Web page layouts, such as Frequently Asked Questions (FAQ) pages

Tip To open a new blank Web page template, display the File menu, click New, and then click Blank Web Page in the New Document task pane.

The biggest advantage of using a Web page template is that it enables you to jump-start your Web page creation process. When you use a Web page template, you can almost instantaneously add and arrange quite a few elements on your Web page with just a couple clicks. For example, using a template, you can quickly format a two-column Web page containing placeholder headers, hyperlinks, and body text as well as a graphics placeholder. To experiment with Web page templates, perform the following four simple steps:

1 Open Word.

2 Click File and choose New.

3 In the New Document task pane, click the General Templates link in the New From Template section. The default templates available in Word 2002 display in the Templates dialog box.

4 Click the Web Pages tab to view the Web page templates, as shown in Figure 9-5.

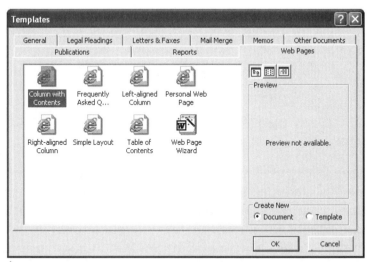

Figure 9-5 A number of Web page templates and the Web Page Wizard are available in the Templates dialog box.

5 Click a template, ensure that the Document option is selected (it's selected by default), and click OK. A new document is created with preformatted elements you can customize to create your Web page. For example, Figure 9-6 shows the result of selecting the Right-Aligned Column Web page template in Word 2002.

Figure 9-6   The Right-Aligned Column Web page template creates a Web page containing placeholder text and a placeholder graphic.

After you create a document based on a Web page template, you can modify the page's text, layout, background, formatting, hyperlink properties, and so forth just as if you were editing any other Word document. You can use the page editing procedures we describe in the project for this chapter on template pages and custom pages as well as on the pages generated by the Web Page Wizard.

When you save a document based on a Web page template, the Save As dialog box automatically selects the Web Page file-type format for you. Before you click the Save button, don't forget to add a title to your Web page by clicking the Change Title button and entering custom title text.

Deleting Files and Folders Generated by Templates   If you practice creating and saving Web pages using templates, you'll want to delete the documents that you created during your practice session. So be sure that you remember where you save the template documents before you click the Save button (in fact, we recommend that you create a temporary folder to hold your practice files). Then ensure that you delete the .htm document as well as the associated folder that's automatically generated to hold the figures used on the template.

When you save a Web page based on a template that includes a graphic (such as the Right-Aligned Column Web page template), Word saves the .htm file and automatically creates a similarly named subfolder without even telling you. The subfolder contains the graphic images used on the Web page. For example, if you save the Right-Aligned Column Web page template with its default filename to a folder, such as C:\website, your C:\website folder will contain a file named Right.htm along with a folder named Right_files, as shown below. To delete all your practice files in this case, you would need to delete both the Right.htm file and the Right_files folder.

Building a Web Page with the Web Page Wizard

In addition to the Save As feature and Web page templates, Word 2002 comes equipped with a Web Page Wizard tool (as we pointed out in Figure 9-5). The Web Page Wizard enables you to generate a foundation Web site by working through a series of dialog boxes. For example, you can use the wizard to generate a home page along with any number of additional pages. After you run the wizard, you can customize each page to create an entire Web site—the wizard gets you started by linking your subpages to your home page. One of the most useful benefits of the Web Page Wizard is that you can apply Web templates to existing documents, as we show you in the upcoming project.

If you plan to follow along in the upcoming project—and we strongly recommend that you do—you're about to become very familiar with the Web Page Wizard. So we won't dillydally here with an overly long description of the tool—you'll see it in action in just a moment.

Planning Your Word 2002 Web Page

In this chapter's project, you'll learn how to create a personal page and an online resume, which is a convenient resource to have on hand these days. Like most people, we're pretty familiar with personal pages and resumes. Therefore, the planning stage merely required us to consider the typical types of information to include on our fictitious site and resume as well as how we wanted to organize the site's information.

For this project, we chose to create a site for a foley artist. A foley artist is a person who creates or alters sounds for use in films, videos, and other electronically produced works. The word *foley* originated with Jack Foley (1891–1967), who was the pioneering sound effects editor at Universal Studios in the 1930s. Foley artists are skilled professionals in a creative field, so we anticipated that the site should be professional yet somewhat "fun," easy to navigate, and straightforward. Of course, we could've also taken a different approach altogether for such a creative character, but creating an avant-garde foley Web site and online resume didn't seem to be the most useful approach for this book.

At this point in the planning process, we knew the type of information we wanted to include (typical home page introductory data, resume data, contact information, and a casual-toned sound tips page) and the stylistic approach we wanted to take (creative yet simple). We were also planning to use the Web Page Wizard in Word. Therefore, our next step was to streamline the process by entering the information into Word documents. (We'll talk about creating foundation documents in just a bit.) As you'll soon see, the Web Page Wizard can automatically format headings and text in your Web site if you format your Word document using the default *styles* in Word. So we formatted the documents' information by using the default styles in Word, as described later.

Note   A *style* is a set of formats (such as Arial, bold, 24 point) saved as a group and given a name (such as Heading 1) that can be applied to text or paragraphs.

Next, we made a rough sketch of how we wanted to display the foley artist's home page and a simple site map indicating the various pages we wanted to include. Figure 9-7 shows the home page sketch, and Figure 9-8 shows the site map.

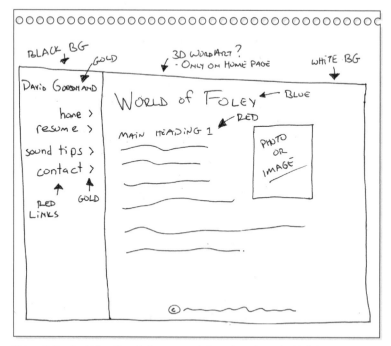

Figure 9-7   David Goodhand's home page is based on the typical left-frame navigation bar scheme.

After we created the Word documents, snooped around the formatting options in Word, sketched our home page, and outlined the site's structure, we were ready to proceed with the Web Page Wizard. But before we start creating the Web page, let's take a few moments to go over our document preparation steps.

> **Note**   As you'll see later in this project, we planned to include a *Print Version* link on the Resume page. Although online resumes are convenient, many employers also request a printable version of a resume so that they can "pass it around the table" during the hiring process.

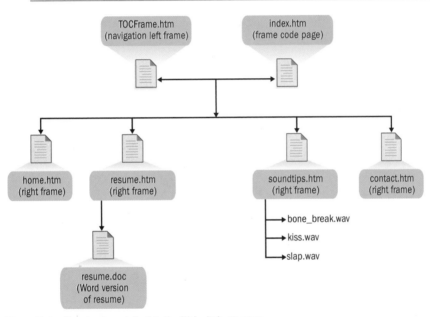

Figure 9-8   The storyboard depicts the Web site's structure.

Formatting a Text Document

As we mentioned, before we clicked our way into the Web Page Wizard, we created Word documents containing the site's main information to use as our foundation documents (including info.doc, resume.doc, and soundtips.doc). You don't have to create foundation documents, but the Web page creation process can be greatly simplified with just a little foresight and planning. The key to preparing a document that the Web Page Wizard can easily format is to enter text in a Word document and then apply standard Word styles to page elements.

Whether or not you know it, you use styles every time you create a Word document. Every time you create a new Word document, you open a blank document based on the Normal template, which includes style definitions, such as Normal (for normal text), Heading 1, Heading 2, and so forth. When you click within text in a document, the applied style name displays in the Style drop-down list in the Formatting toolbar and in the Styles And Formatting task pane (if you have your Styles And Formatting task pane opened), as described in the following Try This!

You can apply styles to text while you're entering it by selecting the style you want to use in the Style drop-down list box on the Formatting toolbar or in the Styles And Formatting task pane before you type. Or you can format text after you've entered it by selecting existing text and then choosing a style in the Style drop-down list or Styles And Formatting task pane.

Styles are handy tools—you can use them to create custom styles, including your own naming schemes and formatting preferences. But for our purposes—using the Web Page Wizard—you just need to know the bare essentials of the Styles feature in Word. Simply knowing how to format your future Web page's text using Word's basic three or four default styles is a good start. If you're interested in a more complete discussion of Word styles, refer to the references listed in the "Additional Resources" section near the end of this chapter.

Note   The documents for this project use the Normal, Heading 1, Heading 2, Heading 3, and Bull List styles.

If you preformat your text document, the Web Page Wizard will format your text based on the typical styles included in the default Normal template in Word. You'll see what we mean after you work through the wizard. If you're working on your own resume instead of the sample resume, we suggest that as you enter your information, you style your Word document using the Normal, Heading 1, Heading 2, Heading 3, and possibly the Bull List styles for now. (You can apply the Bull List style by selecting text and clicking the Bullets button in the Formatting toolbar.) After you work through the Web Page Wizard, you'll have additional styles available that you can use to format your Web page's text manually.

Try This!   To view all the styles used in the C:\foley\resume.doc file, follow these steps:

1   Open C:\foley\resume.doc.

2   Click Tools on the menu bar, click Options, and then click the View tab.

3   On the View tab, type **1** in the Style Area Width text box, and then click OK. The view will change to include a Style Area pane that shows the name of each style applied to each element in the document, as shown here:

Style drop-down list

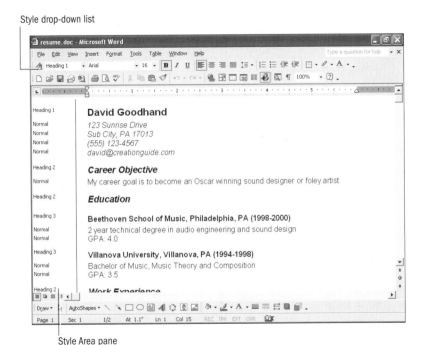

Style Area pane

4   You can resize or hide the Style Area pane by dragging the pane's right-side rule line or by replacing the 1 with a 0 or another measurement in the Style Area Width text box on the View tab of the Options dialog box.

Try This!   To practice applying styles, try reformatting David Goodhand's name using the Heading 2 style instead of Heading 1. To do so, take these steps:

1   Open C:\foley\resume.doc if it's not open already.

2   Click the Styles And Formatting button on the Formatting toolbar, and click anywhere in the David Goodhand text, as shown here.

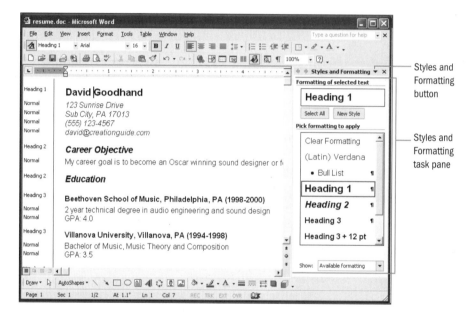

3   To change the style, you can click a style in the Pick Formatting To Apply area in the Styles And Formatting task pane, or you can click a style in the Style drop-down list on the Formatting toolbar. In the Styles And Formatting task pane, click Heading 2.

4   To change the text back to the Heading 1 style, ensure that your cursor is in the David Goodhand text, click the Style drop-down list, and click Heading 1.

5   Click the Styles And Formatting button to close the Styles And Formatting task pane (or simply click the close button in the upper-right corner of the task pane).

In addition to formatting entire paragraphs of text, you can apply styles to selected text. To do this, simply select the text you want to format, and then click a style in the Styles And Formatting task pane or on the Style drop-down list.

At this point, you can close the resume.doc file if it's open. As mentioned earlier, the upcoming project assumes that you created the C:\foley directory on your computer and you've download the info.doc, resume.doc, and soundtips.doc files to the directory. But if you'd like, you can use your own files in place of David Goodhand's documents throughout the upcoming procedures. Regardless of which foundation documents you use, ensure that your folder and files are properly set up.

Following the Wizard's Lead

Finally, we've arrived at the fun part—creating a Web site using the Web Page Wizard. So let's not spend any more time philosophizing; let's get started:

1 Open Word, click File, and then click New.

2 In the New Document task pane, click the General Templates link in the New From Template section.

3 In the Templates dialog box, click the Web Pages tab, and then choose the Web Page Wizard icon.

4 Ensure that the Document option is selected in Create New section, and then click OK. The Web Page Wizard opens, as shown in Figure 9-9.

Figure 9-9 The Web Page Wizard's opening page briefly outlines the upcoming steps.

5 Click Next. The Title And Location page appears. In the Web Site Title text box, type **David Goodhand's World of Foley** and display (or type) **C:\foley** in the Web Site Location text box.

6 Click Next. The Navigation page appears, as shown in Figure 9-10.

7 In the Navigation dialog box, ensure that the Vertical Frame option is selected, and then click Next. The Add Pages page appears.

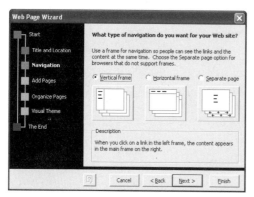

Figure 9-10   During the Navigation step, you select where you want to display your Web site's navigation links.

David Goodhand's Web site includes a home page and his resume, sound tips, and contact pages. Thus, his site incorporates four pages. You use the Add Pages dialog box to create the number of pages you want to include in your Web site.

8   In the Add Pages page, click the Remove Page button three times. The Personal Web Page, Blank Page 1, and Blank Page 2 items are removed.

9   Click the Add Existing File button.

10   In the Open dialog box, specify that you want to use the info.doc file as your home page. To do this, navigate to C:\foley\text and then double-click the info.doc file. The info file is added to the Current Pages In Web Site list box on the Add Pages screen.

11   Repeat steps 9 and 10 to add the resume.doc and soundtips.doc files.
    At this point, you should have the info, resume, and soundtips files listed in the Current Pages In Web Site list box. We determined earlier that David's site needs four pages. Therefore, we need to add one more page to the Web site.

12   On the Add Pages page, click Add New Blank Page. Your modified Add Pages dialog box should look similar to Figure 9-11.

13   Click Next. Use the Organize Pages page to create a hierarchy for your Web pages and to rename the blank pages. The names you supply here are also the hyperlinks that display on your home page that link to the subpages.

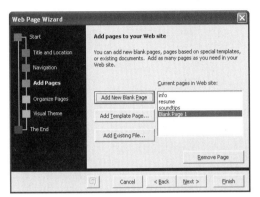

Figure 9-11   The Add Pages page shows that David Goodhand's Web site will include four pages.

14 In the list box, select info, and then click the Rename button.

> **Tip**   In the Organize Pages page, you can select a page name and click Move Up or Move Down to reposition the file in the list. The list reflects how the wizard creates your navigation bar, so organizing the page names here saves you from having to reorganize the links in your navigation bar later.

15 In the Rename Hyperlink dialog box, type **home**, as shown in Figure 9-12, and then click OK.

Figure 9-12   You use the Rename Hyperlink dialog box to rename a page and specify the hyperlink text in the navigation bar.

16 Select Blank Page 1, click Rename, type **contact**, and then click OK. Your modified Organize Pages page should look similar to the dialog box shown in Figure 9-13.

> **Caution**   *Don't use spaces and capital letters in page names.* Some servers don't support filenames and folder names with spaces, and some servers are case-sensitive. While working through the wizard, your best bet is to enter page names in all lowercase letters and without spaces. After you complete the wizard, you can adjust the appearance of display text by adding spaces and capital letters in your Web site without affecting the actual page names. The goal of the wizard is to make Web page creation easier for you; therefore, don't complicate your life by including spaces and capital letters in filenames.

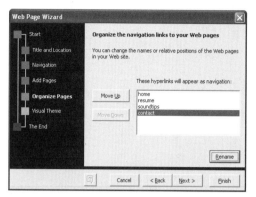

Figure 9-13   The modified Organize Pages page shows the Web site's pages.

17 Click Next to access the Visual Theme page.

At this point, you can pick from a variety of formatting *themes* to automatically style your Web pages. You can also choose not to use a theme. In this project, we'll select a theme so that you can experiment with the types of formatting offered by the Visual Theme feature. Keep in mind that when you select a theme, you aren't married to it. You can easily add, change, and modify themes after you complete the wizard. In fact, later in this chapter, you'll be modifying the theme you select in this procedure.

> **Lingo**   A *theme* is a coordinated set of fonts, colors, and graphics that are used to add visual appeal to a page or group of pages.

18 In the Visual Theme dialog box, ensure that Add A Visual Theme is selected, and click the Browse Themes button.

19 In the Theme dialog box, scroll down and select the Modern Shapes theme. (You might receive a dialog box prompting you to install the theme; if so, ensure that your CD is in your disk drive and follow the simple directions in the installation dialog box.) Next, ensure that the Active Graphics and Background Image check boxes are cleared and that Vivid Colors is selected, as shown in Figure 9-14.

> **Tip**   If the Modern Shapes theme isn't listed in your Theme dialog box, you can use another theme, such as the Capsules theme. Later in this project, you can color the headings in your Web site maroon if you'd like to have your pages match the sample project Web site shown on *www.creationguide.com/foley*.

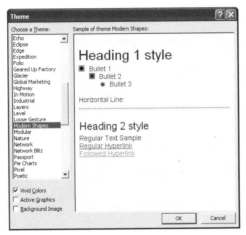

Figure 9-14   For this project you should select Modern Shapes with Vivid Colors selected. If Modern Shapes isn't listed, choose another theme such as Capsules with Vivid Colors selected.

20 Click OK.

21 Click Next on the Visual Theme page, and then click Finish.

After a few seconds (and some windows flashing up on your monitor), Word generates your Web site and displays your home page. At this point, your home page should look similar to the home page shown in Figure 9-15.

Notice that the Frames toolbar opens automatically because the page is divided into two frames (one frame for the navigator bar and the other for page content). Also notice that when you click the hyperlinks (in Word, you have to press Ctrl+hyperlink to follow a link) in the navigation bar, they will display the page created to serve as each hyperlink's target page.

Note   After Word generates your Web site, you can close the Frames toolbar. You won't need it in this project to customize your Web site.

At this point the Web Page Wizard's job is done—you're now fully in charge of formatting the remainder of your Web page. Fortunately, because you have this text, you're not alone in your endeavor. Throughout the remainder of the chapter, we explain various ways that you can customize, format, clean up, smooth out, and generally add a more professional look to your Web pages.

Tip   When you work on Web sites in Word, you'll frequently find that you have a number of windows opened at once. To save all your files in a single step, press and hold the Shift key, and then choose Save All on the File menu. Similarly, to close all open files after you save them, press and hold the Shift key and then choose Close All on the File menu.

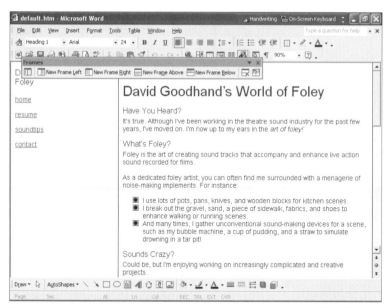

Figure 9-15   You're now ready to customize the final product of the Web Page Wizard.

Changing Background Colors

At this point in the Web site's development, you might be thinking that we've suddenly lost all design sense; otherwise, why would we have you create an entire Web site with a boring yellow (or other plain colored) background? Well, we won't leave you hanging with butter-flavored pages. You have yellow pages at the moment because we didn't want to use the Modern Shapes background image on David Goodhand's Web site. Instead, we're going to color the backgrounds to look a little more professional. Coloring a Web page's background is a snap. The only "tricky" part about this process is that you have to color the background for each page in the Web site. Here are the steps you need to complete to accomplish this:

1 Click in the navigation bar area, display the Format menu, choose Background, and click the black color square.

2 Click anywhere in the right frame, display the Format menu, choose Background, and click the white color square.

   Next, you need to change the background color to white in the resume, soundtips, and contact pages, which are set to display in the Web site's right frame.

3 In the navigation bar, hold Ctrl and click resume. The right frame changes and displays David Goodhand's resume.

4   Click anywhere in the right frame, display the Format menu, choose
Background, and click the white color square.

5   Hold Ctrl, click soundtips, click the right frame, and change the background color to white.

6   Hold Ctrl, click contact, click the right frame, and change the background color to white.

7   Hold Ctrl and click home. At this point, your navigation bar should
have a black background, and every content page that displays in the
right frame should have a white background.

8   Hold Shift, open the File menu, and select Save All, as shown in
Figure 9-16.

Figure 9-16   You can press Shift and select Save on the File menu to save all open documents
at once.

Tweaking the Navigation Bar Settings

Now that the background looks a little sleeker, you're ready to perform a couple
small tweaks to modify the navigation bar. When we initially created David's
Web site, we weren't too happy with the navigation bar's width, title text, and
text alignment, so we adjusted those elements. In addition, we modified the
hyperlink font styles, as described later in this chapter. You can follow the next
few steps to modify the navigation bar's width, replace the navigation bar's title
text, and realign the links.

Tip   You can display a ruler while you design your Web page by clicking View and choosing Ruler.

---

1 To make the navigation bar narrower, display the ruler (choose Ruler on the View menu), click on the ruler between the two gray boxes that specify the right edge of the black area, and drag the frame's edge left to the 1.5-inch mark.

2 Select all the text in the navigation bar (drag to select or press Ctrl+A), click Align Right in the Formatting toolbar, and then click in a blank area to deselect the text.

3 Select the *David Goodhand's World of Foley* text, click the Font Size drop-down arrow on the Formatting toolbar, choose 10, click the Bold button, click the Font Color button's drop-down arrow, click the gold color square, and then type **David Goodhand** (to replace the existing text).

4 To position David's name, ensure that the cursor is inserted after the *d* in *Goodhand*, hold Shift, and press Enter.

5 Next, place the cursor's insertion point before the *D* in *David*, hold Shift, and press Enter.

Now you're going to add a small artistic touch to the navigation bar to help draw attention to the text links in the navigation bar and differentiate navigation bar hyperlinks from the main body text.

6 Click after the home hyperlink, click Bold on the Formatting toolbar, click the gold color square on the Font Color drop-down menu, press your space bar once, and type >.

7 Click after the resume hyperlink, click Bold, click the gold color square on the Font Color drop-down menu, press your space bar once, and type >.

8 Click after the sound tips hyperlink, click Bold, click the gold color square on the Font Color drop-down menu, press your space bar once, and type >.

9 Click after the contact hyperlink, click Bold, click the gold color square on the Font Color drop-down menu, press your space bar once, and type >.

10 Finally, one more minor tweak—click between the *d* and *t* in *soundtips*, and press the spacebar.

Your home page should now be shaping up to look a little more professional, as shown in Figure 9-17.

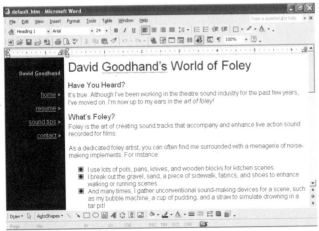

Figure 9-17 Although the wizard does a bulk of your Web site creation work, you have plenty of opportunity to modify and customize your site, including sprucing up the navigation bar.

Saving, Closing, and Reopening Your Site

Now that you have the foundation of your Web site in place, we think it's a good time to address saving, closing, and reopening your files. When you create a Web site using the Web Page Wizard in Word, you'll find that you have quite a few open files in your taskbar. Therefore, just to streamline activities and to ensure that you'll know how to save, quit, and reopen your Web site files, we're interrupting your regularly scheduled formatting tasks with some mundane workaday tasks:

1 To save all open files at once, hold Shift, display the File menu, and click Save All.

2 To close all open files, hold Shift, and click Close All on the File menu.

Note The Web Page Wizard saves your home page as *default.htm* instead of *index.htm* or *index.html*. Some servers will recognize either filename as a home page. Verify with your hosting service (if you have one) that the server recognizes default.htm as the page it will show if no filename is specified in a Web address. (For example, when you type *www.domain-name.com* in your browser's address bar, the domain's server assumes that you want to see the default.htm page.) Most likely, *default.htm* will work fine. In our case, as if to illustrate our point, the *www.creationguide.com* hosting service required us to rename the default.htm file to index.html. Fortunately, you don't have to worry about renaming the default.htm file until you're ready to upload your site to the Web. Then it's a simply matter of renaming default.htm to either index.htm or index.html and moving on from there.

---

3 After all your files are saved and closed, you can reopen your home page in Word. Keep in mind that if you attempt to open default.htm (or any other .htm file) by clicking it within the foley folder view, you'll display the .htm file in your browser window. To open an .htm file so you can work on it in Word, use either of the following methods:

- Open the foley folder, right-click default.htm, choose Open With, and click Microsoft Word, or

- Open Word, click Open on the File menu, navigate to C:\foley, select default.htm, and then click Open.

Granted, the saving, closing, and reopening tasks aren't that thrilling, but following this routine is smart, especially if you decide to spread out this project over a couple days. Plus, by closing the wizard-created pages, you'll reduce the number of windows you have open while you work.

Creating and Inserting WordArt

You might recall in Part One of this book that we promised to show you how to use the WordArt tool in Word to create text graphics for your Web pages. Well, WordArt time is upon us. When we created David's foley artist Web site, we felt it needed some spicing up graphically. We thought the best way to incorporate some graphical elements would be to add a WordArt element along with a couple images and some links to sound files. In this section we'll show you how to use WordArt to add an image to the home page. Then later in this chapter, we talk about adding an image and linking sound files.

An obvious way to use WordArt on David's Web site is to create a graphical heading on his home page, which we did. Just follow these steps to achieve a result similar to ours:

1 Open C:\foley\default.htm in Word.

2 Click in the right frame, and ensure that paragraph marks are showing in the right frame. (If they aren't showing, click the Show/Hide ¶ button in the Standard toolbar after you click in the right frame.)

3 Click before the *D* in *David*, and press Backspace to delete the paragraph marker above David's name.

4 Select the *David Goodhand's World of Foley* text without selecting the following paragraph marker, as shown in Figure 9-18.

Figure 9-18   To replace existing text with WordArt, select the text without selecting the following paragraph marker.

5   On the menu bar, click Insert, point to Picture, and then click WordArt.

For this project, we'll use the fourth WordArt style in the third row down (as shown in Figure 9-19; on the screen you can see that it's the rainbow-colored text casting a shadow). If you want to choose another style, simply click on the square within the WordArt Gallery dialog box.

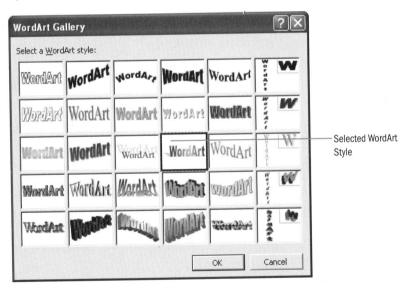

Figure 9-19   The WordArt Gallery dialog box shows thumbnails of available WordArt styles.

6   Select the rainbow WordArt sample, and then click OK.

7   In the Edit WordArt Text dialog box, type **World of Foley**, as shown in Figure 9-20, and ensure that the font is Arial Black and the size is 24. Then click OK. The WordArt displays on your home page as shown in Figure 9-21—but clearly, the graphic needs some added attention. Click the WordArt item—notice that the WordArt toolbar opens automatically. You'll see that the WordArt toolbar comes and goes depending on whether the WordArt element is selected.

Figure 9-20   The text you enter in the Edit WordArt Text dialog box serves as the foundation of your WordArt image.

Figure 9-21   The first phase of adding WordArt shows a promising start, but you need to do some tweaking to make the WordArt blend into your page.

8   In the Formatting toolbar, click the Show/Hide ¶ button to hide the paragraph markers.

> **Tip**   In this project, you insert WordArt inline—that is, within a line in your document just as text is inserted within a line. If you'd like your WordArt to float and display in front of or behind text, you can do so. Formatting a WordArt item (or other image, for that matter) as a floating element enables you to drag the element to different areas on your page without aligning it along text lines. To change the manner in which WordArt can be positioned in relation to text, click the WordArt item, click the Text Wrapping button on the WordArt toolbar, and then choose a Text Wrapping option other than In Line With Text.

9   Right-click the WordArt element and then select Format WordArt to access the Format WordArt dialog box.

> **Note**   You can also open the Format WordArt dialog box by clicking the Format WordArt button in the WordArt toolbar.

10   On the Colors And Lines tab in the Fill section, click the Color drop-down list and then select the dark blue color square (first row, third-to-the-last color square).

11   On the Colors And Lines tab in the Line section, ensure that 1 appears in the Weight text box, click the Color drop-down list, and then select the blue-gray color square (second row, second-to-the-last color square).

12 Click OK, and then display the Drawing toolbar if necessary (choose Toolbars on the View menu and select Drawing).

13 On the Drawing toolbar, click the Shadow Style button, and choose Shadow Style 6 as shown in Figure 9-22.

Figure 9-22   You can use the tools on the Drawing toolbar to format WordArt, clip art, and other types of images.

14 Click in a blank area on your Web page. Your WordArt element should now appear as shown in Figure 9-23.

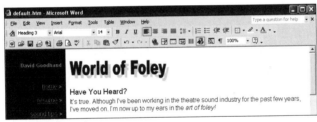

Figure 9-23   Your custom WordArt image should now display with the colors you specified and a modified shadow style.

15 Click the Save button on the Standard toolbar to save your Web page with the WordArt element.

Working with Text and Adding Copyright Information

At this point we should start to pay some attention to the Web site's body text and subpages. Namely, we want to add some white space around the text to create a clean, open feeling and we need to add some standard footer information, including copyright text. First, we'll use Word's Reveal Formatting feature to indent the text by .25 inches on the left and right sides, as described here:

1 In the Formatting toolbar, click the Styles And Formatting button.

2 Click the drop-down arrow in the Styles And Formatting task pane titlebar, and choose Reveal Formatting. The Reveal Formatting task pane opens, as shown in Figure 9-24.

> **Tip**   You can also open the Reveal Formatting task pane by opening the Formatting
> menu and choosing Reveal Formatting.

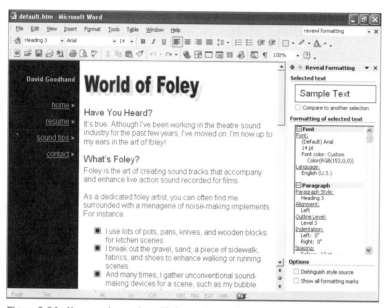

Figure 9-24   You can view and modify formatting settings using Word's Reveal Formatting task
pane.

3   In your Web page, click in the right frame, press Ctrl+A to select all the
text, and then click the Indentation setting in the Reveal Formatting
task pane.

4   On the Indents And Spacing tab in the Paragraphs dialog box, enter .25
in the Left text box in the Indentation section, enter .25 in the Right text
box, click the Special drop-down arrow, choose (none), click OK, and
then close the Reveal Formatting task pane.

> **Note**   As mentioned earlier in the chapter, you have to press and hold the Ctrl key
> whenever you click a hyperlink in Word if you want to follow the hyperlink to its desti-
> nation file or location. At this point, we might as well warn you up front that you'll
> need to cultivate some patience for Ctrl+hyperlink clicks. When you press Ctrl and
> click a link in Word, the associated page eventually displays, but you won't get the
> quick response you're accustomed to.

5   Hold Ctrl and click the resume link in the navigation bar, display the
Reveal Formatting task pane (as described in steps 1 and 2), and then
repeat steps 3 and 4 to format the text on the Resume page.

6   Hold Ctrl and click the sound tips hyperlink, display the Reveal Formatting task pane, and then repeat steps 3 and 4 to format the text on
the Sound Tips Web page.

Notice on the Sound Tips page that a quotation follows each sub-
heading. For this page, you'll want to indent and color the quotations
to help make them stand out against the sound tip text.

7   Select the quotation text (you can easily identify the text because it's
italic) below the *Breaking Bones* heading, click Heading 5 in the Style
drop-down list in the Formatting toolbar, click Italic, click Increase Indent
twice, press the Right Arrow key once, and hold Shift and press Enter.

8   Select the quotation below the *Kissing* heading, click Heading 5 in the
Style drop-down list in the Formatting toolbar, click Italic, click
Increase Indent twice, press the Right Arrow key once, and hold Shift
and press Enter.

9   Select the quotation below the *Slap or Punch* heading, click Heading 5
in the Style drop-down list in the Formatting toolbar, click Italic, click
Increase Indent twice, press the Right Arrow key once, and hold Shift and
press Enter. Your sound tips page should look similar to the page shown
in Figure 9-25.

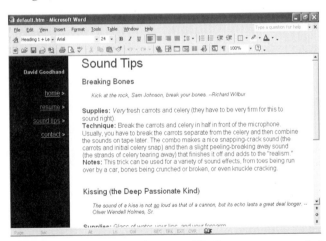

Figure 9-25   By making just a few text modifications, you can ensure that your text displays in an
easy-to-read format.

10   Hold Ctrl and click the contact hyperlink.

11   Select the *This Web Page is contact* text, click the Style drop-down arrow
in the Formatting toolbar, choose Heading 1, and then type **Contact**.

12 Press Enter, and then type the following contact information:

> **123 Sunrise Drive**
> **Sub City, PA 17013**
> **(555) 123-4567**
> **david@creationguide.com**

Tip   By default, Word formats e-mail and Web page addresses as hyperlinks as soon as you press the spacebar or Enter key after you type the address. If you'd like to remove the automatic formatting while you're typing, position your cursor at the end of the hyperlink, and press your Backspace key once.

---

13 Display the Reveal Formatting task pane, and repeat steps 3 and 4 to format the text on the contact Web page.

While we're working with your Web site's body text, let's add copyright information to each Web page in the site.

14 Hold Ctrl and click the home hyperlink, scroll to the bottom of the home page's text, and click after the last paragraph (after *...in no time!*).

15 Press Enter three times, click 10 pt in the Font Size drop-down list on the Formatting toolbar, and click Center.

16 Now that your cursor is in position, press Ctrl+Alt+C to insert a copy-right symbol (©), press your spacebar, enter the year followed by your name and a period, press your spacebar, and then type **All rights reserved**. For example, your copyright information should display similar to the following:

© Copyright 2002 Mary Millhollon and Jeff Castrina. All rights reserved.

17 Triple-click the copyright text to select it, and press Ctrl+C to copy the line to your Clipboard.

Tip   Triple-clicking enables you to quickly select all text in a paragraph.

---

18 Hold Ctrl and click the resume hyperlink.

19 Scroll to the bottom of the Resume page's text, click after the last para-graph (after *...sound effect stages*), press Enter three times, and press Ctrl+V to paste the copyright information into the document.

20 Use the Ctrl+V keyboard combination to paste the copyright information to the bottom of the sound tips and contact pages in the same manner you pasted the information in the Resume page, as described in step 19.

21 Press Shift, and choose Save All on the File menu.

22 Press Shift, and choose Close All on the File menu.

You should now have copyright information on each page of your Web site, your Contact page should contain basic information, and the body text throughout your site should display with an eye-pleasing .25-inch margin on both sides of the body text (for instance, see Figure 9-27 a little later in this chapter). With your text nicely under control, you're ready to add a couple images.

Inserting Images

As you know (and as we discuss in Chapter 3), images serve a number of purposes on Web sites, including presenting buttons, displaying banners, providing visual appeal, promoting logos, customizing backgrounds, and more. In the upcoming sections we show you how to insert a basic image, add clip art using the Insert Clip Art task pane, insert a horizontal rule, and include a background image on a page.

Inserting a Basic Image

The first image-related procedure on the agenda is to simply insert a picture. For this exercise, you'll insert an image onto the home page to create some visual appeal:

1 Open C:\foley\default.htm in Word and position your insertion point to the left of the *World of Foley* WordArt component.

2 On the menu bar, click Insert, point to Picture, and then click From File.

3 In the Insert Picture dialog box, click the headphones.gif image stored in the C:\foley\images folder, as shown in Figure 9-26.

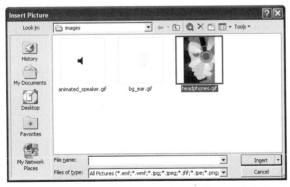

Figure 9-26   The Insert Picture dialog box enables you to find and insert pictures you have stored on your computer, disk, network, or other storage medium.

4   Click Insert. The image displays inline and to the left of the WordArt component.

> **Tip**   Keep in mind that we advocate inserting images that are already sized properly for your Web page (see Chapter 3). If you're unsure about how to size your image, you can use Word to help set your image's size. To do so, insert your image into your Word document and resize the image using the Format Picture dialog box. Then delete the image from your Word document, open your original image in your paint program, create a new version of your image using the new dimension settings (remember to save the resized image with a new name), and insert the resized version of your image into your Word document.

5   Double-click the picture to open the Format Picture dialog box.

6   In the Format Picture dialog box, click the Layout tab, select Square in the Wrapping Style section, click Right in the Horizontal Alignment section, and click Advanced.

7   In the Advanced Layout dialog box, click the Text Wrapping tab, click in the Right text box in the Distance From Text section, enter 0, and click OK twice to close the open dialog boxes.

8   Click in the Web page's body text to deselect the image, click Save, open the File menu, and choose Web Page Preview. Your default.htm page should now include an image in the upper-right corner of the Web page, as shown in Figure 9-27.

9   Close your browser window so you can continue working in the Word version of your Web site.

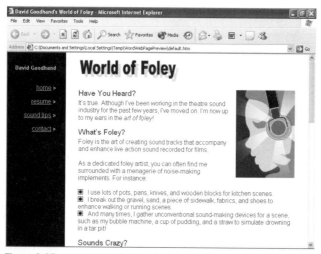

Figure 9-27   Adding an image to the home page helps create visual appeal and keeps the reader's focus from straying off the edge of your page.

Inserting and Customizing Clip Art

In some cases you might want to add a graphic but you don't have an image on hand. In those instances, Microsoft's Clip Art task pane, along with your Microsoft Office 2002 Media CD, might be able to come to your rescue. Therefore, with that in mind and to ensure that you're fully prepared to create your own Web sites in Word, we decided that this project should include the steps required to insert and customize clip art, as presented here:

1 Hold Ctrl and click *contact* in the navigation bar to display the Contact page.

2 On the Contact page, click to position your insertion point before the *C* in the *Contact* heading.

3 On the Menu bar, click Insert, point to Picture, and then click Clip Art.

Tip To make adding clip art as seamless as possible, insert your Office 2002 Media CD into your disk drive before you search for clip art. Furthermore, if this is the first time you're using clip art in Word, you might receive a dialog box asking if you want to install your clip art (which you'll want to do, so you'll need to have your Office 2002 Media CD in your disk drive to continue).

---

4 In the Search Text box of the Clip Art task pane, type **memorandum**, display the Search In list in the Other Search Options section, and ensure that only Office Collections icon appears as a stack of check boxes containing a check mark (this indicates that all categories are selected with Office Collections), as shown in Figure 9-28.

Figure 9-28 You can tell Word where to search for clip art; if you're connected to the Web, Word can search for free clips available in Web Collections during your search.

Tip   If the Office Collections check box appears empty or as a single check box in the Selected Collections drop-down menu, click the check box until the selected stacked check box icon displays.

---

5   Click Search.

6   Click the yellow memo notes in the Results list to insert the clip art, as shown in Figure 9-29.

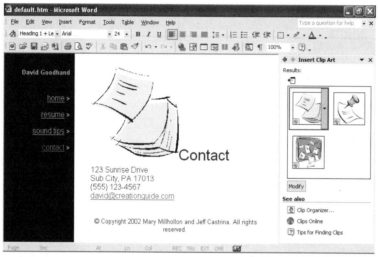

Figure 9-29   After you insert a clip art image, you can format and position the image on your Web page.

At this point you can start to customize the clip art image. For this project, you'll recolor the image to blend into your Web site's color scheme.

7   Right-click the image and choose Edit Picture.

8   Double-click a yellow portion of the picture to open the Format AutoShape text. Box, and then click the Colors And Lines tab.

9   In the Fill section, click the Color drop-down arrow, choose the gold color square, and click OK.

10   Right-click in a white area of the clip art image (or on the image's selection box), and choose Format Drawing Canvas.

11   In the Format Drawing Canvas dialog box, click the Colors And Lines tab, click the Color drop-down arrow in the Fill section, and choose dark blue.

Now you're ready to resize and reposition the clip art image, which you can do from within the Format Drawing Canvas dialog box.

12 Click the Size tab, ensure that the Lock Aspect Ratio check box is selected (it's selected by default), and enter .75 in the Height text box in the Size And Rotation section.

13 Click the Layout tab, choose Square in the Wrapping Style section, choose Right in the Horizontal Alignment section, and click Advanced.

14 In the Advanced Layout dialog box, click the Text Wrapping tab, locate the Distance From Text section, enter 0 in the Right text box, and click OK twice to close the open dialog boxes.

15 With the clip art selected, choose Toolbars on the View menu, and select Drawing.

16 On the Drawing toolbar, click the Shadow Style button, and click Shadow Style 6, as shown earlier in this chapter in Figure 9-22.

17 Click in a blank area on your Web page to deselect the clip art image, close the Clip Art task pane, and then click the Save button. Your Contact page should look similar to the page shown in Figure 9-30.

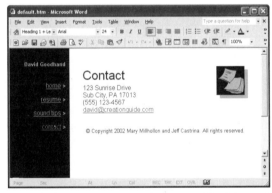

Figure 9-30 Judiciously used, clip art can add subtle creative touches to a Web page and provide information about the page's purpose.

Adding a Horizontal Rule

Before you put your Office 2002 Media CD back into its jewel case, let's add a horizontal rule to David's Resume page:

1 Hold Ctrl and click *resume* in the navigation bar to display the Resume page.

2 On the Resume page, click before the *123* in *123 Sunrise Drive*, click Insert on the menu bar, point to Picture, and then click Clip Art.

3 In the Clip Art task pane, enter **Web divider** in the Search Text box, click Search, click the first line in the first row of the search results, and close the Clip Art task pane.

4 Right-click the line, choose Format Horizontal Line.

5 In the Format Horizontal Line dialog box, change the Measured In drop-down list box to Percent, ensure that 100 appears in the Width text box, change the Height setting to 2 pt as shown in Figure 9-31, and click OK.

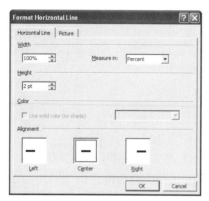

Figure 9-31   Formatting a line using the Percent setting enables the line to expand and contract to fit users' browser windows.

6 Click in a blank area of the document to deselect the horizontal rule, click the Save button, choose Web Page Preview on the File menu, and click the resume link in your browser window to view the Resume page. Your Web page should look similar to the page shown in Figure 9-32.

Figure 9-32   A simple horizontal rule adds a professional touch to the Resume page.

7 Close your browser window.

Including a Background Image

Before you move on to configuring hyperlinks in the next section (we thought we'd mention that to give you something to look forward to if you're getting a little tired of inserting images), we want to show you how to add a background image to David Goodhand's home page. In this case, you're going to add a very light image to emulate a watermark, but you can follow these same steps to add any image to a Web page's background:

1   In Word, hold Ctrl and click *home* in the navigation bar to display David's home page, and then ensure that your insertion point is located somewhere in the main area of the page (in the right frame).

2   On the menu bar, click Format, choose Background, and click Fill Effects.

3   In the Fill Effects dialog box, click the Picture tab, and click the Select Picture button.

4   In the Select Picture dialog box, navigate to the C:\foley\images folder, double-click the bg_ear.gif image, and click OK in the Fill Effects dialog box.

5   Click Save, and then choose Web Page Preview on the File menu. A light gray image representing sound and an ear should display on your page's background, as shown in Figure 9-33.

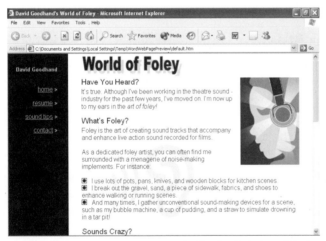

Figure 9-33   You can create a watermark effect by displaying a light image as your Web page's background.

6   Close your browser window, and then close Word.

Working with Hyperlinks

Last but not least, we're going to show you how to work a little magic with hyperlinks. Namely, you're going to undertake the following hyperlink-related tasks to help finalize David's Web site:

■   Reformat the existing hyperlinks in the navigation bar and change the color of followed hyperlinks

■ Add a Print Version hyperlink to the Resume page so that viewers can easily view and print David's resume as a Word document

■ Customize the ScreenTip text associated with each hyperlink in the navigation bar

■ Reformat the e-mail address on the Resume page as a Mail To hyperlink

■ Link an animated GIF image to a sound clip

■ Add a Go To Top link at the bottom of the Sound Tips page

Knowing how to accomplish these tasks will give you a better-than-average grounding for mastering the art of working with hyperlinks. You'll need to know how to work with hyperlinks when you create your own custom Web pages, so this information will come in handy down the road. As usual, we'll start you off with the most basic task and work toward more complex tasks (although rest assured, none of this gets too convoluted). Our first hyperlinking escapade entails simply reformatting the existing hyperlink and followed hyperlink styles.

Modifying Hyperlink Styles

As discussed earlier, Word uses styles and templates to create pages. While you were working through the Web Page Wizard to create your template-based Web pages, you applied the Modern Shapes (or another) theme to your Web site's templates. (That's how the headings in your text document ended up being dark red on your Web pages.) The template the Web Page Wizard applied includes *Hyperlink* and *FollowedHyperlink* styles (which are defined in the document's embedded cascading style sheet). So if you want to change the properties of all hyperlinks within a frame, you're better off changing the Hyperlink and Followed-Hyperlink styles instead of formatting each hyperlink individually. In this section we'll show you how to edit the Hyperlink and FollowedHyperlink styles so that you can change the hyperlinks in your navigation bar from anemic-looking red underlined links to strong red nonunderlined links, and you can display visited hyperlinks in a darker shade of red instead of gray:

1 Open C:\foley\default.htm in Word.

2 Click within the text of the home link in the navigation bar, click Format in the menu bar, and then click Styles And Formatting.

   Notice that the Styles And Formatting task pane displays the Hyperlink style in the Formatting Of Selected Text text box. Because you positioned the cursor within text formatted with the Hyperlink style before you opened the Styles And Formatting task pane, Word displays the Hyperlink style in the Styles And Formatting task pane.

Tip   You can also open the Styles And Formatting task pane by clicking the Styles And Formatting button in the Formatting toolbar.

---

3   In the Styles And Formatting task pane, position your cursor over the word *Hyperlink* in the Formatting Of Selected Text text box, and then click the down arrow that appears.

4   Click Modify on the drop-down list.

5   In the Modify Style dialog box, click the Format button, and then click Font on the pop-up menu, as shown in Figure 9-34.

Figure 9-34   The Font dialog box provides access to the full range of font properties available for a style.

6   In the Font dialog box, click the Font Color drop-down list and click More Colors.

7   In the Colors dialog box, click the Custom tab, ensure that 204 displays in the Red text box, enter 0 in the Green text box, and ensure that 0 displays in the Blue text box.

8   Click OK to close the Colors dialog box.

9   In the Font dialog box, display the Underline Style drop-down list, choose (none), select Bold in the Font Style list box, and click OK twice to close the open dialog boxes.

     At this point, the hyperlinks in your navigation bar should display a little brighter, a lot bolder, and free from underlines. Next, you need to pay some attention to followed hyperlinks. To help speed up this process, we'll show you a couple formatting shortcuts this time:

10 In the Styles And Formatting task pane, point to FollowedHyperlink in the Pick Formatting To Apply list box.

11 After the down arrow appears, click Modify.

12 In the Formatting section of the Modify Styles dialog box, click the Bold button, click Underline to turn off underlining, click the Font Color drop-down arrow, and choose More Colors.

13 In the Colors dialog box, click the Custom tab, enter 153 in the Red text box, enter 0 in the Green text box, and ensure that 0 displays in the Blue text box.

14 Click OK twice, and then close the Styles And Formatting task pane.

15 Click Save, choose Web Page Preview on the File menu, click a couple links in your navigation bar to see the effects of your style formatting changes, and then close your browser window.

Tip   To refresh your Web site's view in your browser, you might need to first clear your history. To do this in Internet Explorer, choose Internet Options on the Tools menu, display the General tab in the Internet Options dialog box, click the Clear History button, click Yes, wait a couple seconds while your browser works, and then click OK. After you clear your history, click Refresh in your browser window's toolbar. Your navigation bar should display as if you haven't yet visited any pages in your Web site.

Adding Hyperlinks

Our next task is to add a hyperlink that provides a link to a text version of David's resume. Basically, we'll add a hyperlink that points to the resume.doc file that's stored in the C:\foley\text folder. When you upload your Web site, you'll also need to upload the text folder containing the resume.doc file to your server so viewers can access the resume's text file online. To create a link pointing to resume.doc, follow these steps:

1 Hold Ctrl and click the resume hyperlink in the navigation bar to display the Resume page.

2 Ensure that the insertion point is located at the top of the Resume page in the main frame.

3 In the menu bar, click Insert and then click Hyperlink. The Insert Hyperlink dialog box displays. Figure 9-35 shows the Insert Hyperlink dialog box after the proper information is inserted.

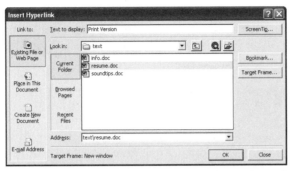

Figure 9-35 The Insert Hyperlink dialog box assists you in creating and configuring hyperlinks.

Tip You can also press Ctrl+K to display the Insert Hyperlink dialog box.

---

4 In the Address text box, type **text\resume.doc** (or double-click the text folder in the files and folder list box, and then select resume.doc).

Tip Keep in mind that whenever you create hyperlinks you must enter uppercase and lowercase letters in filenames accurately. Some servers are case-sensitive. If you enter the name of a linked page inaccurately, you'll end up with broken links on your Web site. Therefore, if you're unsure of a file's path and name, the easiest way to accurately specify a target file in Word is to navigate to the resource by clicking folders and files in the Insert Hyperlink dialog box.

---

5 In the Text To Display text box, type **Print Version**. This text will display at the top of the Resume page (because that's where your cursor is located), and it will serve as the hyperlink text that links to the non-HTML version of David's resume.

6 Click the Target Frame button, select New Window in the drop-down list in the Set Target Frame dialog box (see Figure 9-36), and then click OK. Selecting the New Window option specifies that you want resume.doc to open in a new window when users click the Print Version link.

Figure 9-36 A hyperlink can open a linked resource in the current browser window, a specified frame, or a new window.

7   Click OK to close the Set Target Frame dialog box, and then click the ScreenTip button. The Set Hyperlink ScreenTip dialog box opens. In the ScreenTip Text box, type **Open an easy-to-print version of David's resume**, as shown in Figure 9-37.

Figure 9-37   The text you type in the ScreenTip Text box displays as pop-up text when users point to the hyperlink.

Lingo   A *ScreenTip* is descriptive text that pops up when the mouse cursor hovers over a hyperlink.

---

8   Click OK to close the Set Hyperlink ScreenTip dialog box.

9   Click OK in the Insert Hyperlink dialog box. Then save the Web page. The Resume page should now contain a Print Version link at the top of the page, as shown in Figure 9-38.

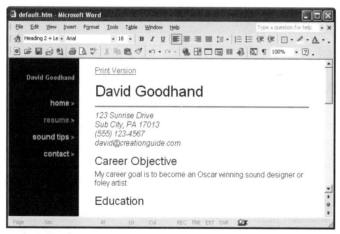

Figure 9-38   When users click the new Print Version hyperlink, the resume.doc file opens as a Word document in a separate window.

10   Press Ctrl and click the Print Version hyperlink to see how the text document opens in a new window. Then close the text document.

Adding ScreenTips to Existing Hyperlinks

As you just saw, you can customize the ScreenTip text that pops up when viewers hold their mouse cursor over a hyperlink. By default, the Web Page Wizard doesn't display any ScreenTip text for a hyperlink online and shows the hyperlink's filename in a ScreenTip while you're working in Word. You should add Screen-Tip text to make your page more user-friendly (or at least more entertaining). To do so, follow these steps:

1 Right-click the home hyperlink in the navigation bar, click Hyperlink, and then click Edit Hyperlink. The Edit Hyperlink dialog box opens, which looks very much like the Insert Hyperlink dialog box shown in Figure 9-35.

2 Click the ScreenTip button, type **Home Page** in the Set Hyperlink ScreenTip dialog box, and then click OK twice.

3 Right-click the resume hyperlink in the navigation bar, click Hyperlink, and then click Edit Hyperlink.

4 Click the ScreenTip button, type **David Goodhand's resume** in the Set Hyperlink ScreenTip dialog box, and then click OK twice.

5 Right-click the sound tips hyperlink in the navigation bar, click Hyper-link, and then click Edit Hyperlink.

6 Click the ScreenTip button, type **Tips for making top quality noise** in the Set Hyperlink ScreenTip dialog box, and then click OK twice.

7 Right-click the contact hyperlink in the navigation bar, click Hyperlink, and then click Edit Hyperlink.

8 Click the ScreenTip button, type **Contact David** in the Set Hyperlink ScreenTip dialog box, and then click OK.

9 Click Save in the Standard toolbar, choose Web Page Preview on the File menu, and then place your cursor over each hyperlink to view each link's ScreenTip text.

10 Close your browser window.

> **Tip**   If your browser doesn't show your Web page properly at first when you preview, click the home link in the navigation bar. After you preview the home page, you should be able to click the other links in the navigation bar normally to display the associated pages.

Creating a Mail To Hyperlink

Next on our agenda is to show you how to format David's e-mail address on the Resume page as a Mail To hyperlink. If you'd like, you can copy the Mail To link to each subpage (such as including the link in the footer text) so the link is easily accessible to viewers.

Lingo   A *Mail To* hyperlink is a link that automatically opens a preaddressed blank e-mail message form when a user clicks the link.

As you're about to see, formatting a Mail To hyperlink is very similar to inserting any other type of hyperlink:

1 On David Goodhand's home page, select the *david@creationguide.com* e-mail address, right-click the selected text, and click Hyperlink.

2 In the Link To pane of the Insert Hyperlink dialog box, click the E-mail Address icon. The Insert Hyperlink dialog box alters its contents so that you can specify e-mail settings, as shown in Figure 9-39. Notice that the Mail To options enable you to automatically provide Subject line text in the message as well as your e-mail address.

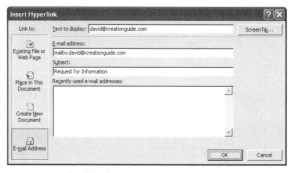

Figure 9-39   The Mail To options in the Insert Hyperlink dialog box contains the information that appears in a preformatted e-mail message window after a user clicks the Mail To hyperlink.

3 In the E-mail Address text box, type your e-mail address or *david@creationguide.com*, ensure that the e-mail address displays properly (without the *mailto:* prefix) in the Text To Display text box, and type **Request for Information** in the Subject text box.

4 Click the ScreenTip button and type **Please send your comments to David** in the Set Hyperlink ScreenTip dialog box. Click OK twice to close the dialog boxes. The e-mail address now displays as a hyperlink on the Resume page.

> **Note**   Notice that the *Mail To* and *Print Version* hyperlinks display in regular red text instead of bold text. The hyperlinks display in the theme's default color scheme because earlier in this chapter, you customized the Hyperlink and FollowedHyperlink styles only in the navigation bar frame, not in the main fame.

5   Save the file, and choose Web Page Preview on the File menu.

6   Click the Mail To link to ensure that a blank e-mail message form opens when the Mail To link is clicked. Close the message form after it opens, and close the browser window.

> **Note**   Always check hyperlinks after you create them to ensure that you formatted the hyperlink's properties properly and that the hyperlink responds in the way you intended.

Linking Images

Our next-to-last task will be to show you how to format a graphical element as a hyperlink. You should remember this technique when you want to link graphical buttons to subpages. For David's Web site, you'll insert an animated GIF file on the Sound Tips page and link the animated GIF to a sound file. Of course, you can link any resource to an image (such as another page on the Web or in your Web site). In this project we chose to link a sound file to an animated GIF to introduce a way in which you can include audio on your custom Web pages. Further, we wanted to show you that inserting an animated GIF entails the same steps as inserting a standard image, as you can see here:

1   In Word, click Ctrl+sound tips to display the Sound Tips page.

2   Click after the *Breaking Bones* heading, press the spacebar twice, click Insert, choose Picture, and click From File.

3   In the Insert Picture dialog box, display C:\foley\images\ animated_speaker.gif, and then double-click the animated_speaker.gif file.

> **Note**   Animated GIFs don't appear animated until you view the image in a browser. Therefore, animated GIFs won't be animated while you're working in Word. However, when you preview your Web page in your browser, you'll see the animated GIF image in action.

4   Press the spacebar twice, and type **sound clip**. To conform to good design practices, you'll be including a text link to the sound file along with the animated GIF link.

5   Click the speaker image and click the Insert Hyperlink button in the Standard toolbar.

6   In the Link To section of the Insert Hyperlink dialog box, click Existing File Or Web page, click the ScreenTip button, add the following ScreenTip text: **Listen to breaking bones**, and click OK.

7   In the files and folders list box, double-click the sounds folder, select the bone_break.wav file, and click OK.

8   Select the sound clip text, choose 10 pt in the Font Size drop-down list on the Formatting toolbar, and click the Insert Hyperlink button on the Standard toolbar.

9   In the Insert Hyperlink dialog box, ensure that Existing File Or Web Page is selected in the Link To section, click the ScreenTip button, add the following ScreenTip text: **Listen to breaking bones**, and click OK.

10 In the files and folders list box, double-click the sounds folder, select the bone_break.wav file, and click OK.

11 Save your changes, and then choose Web Page Preview on the File menu. Your Web page should display with two new links—the small animated speaker image and the sound clip hypertext—as shown in Figure 9-40.

12 Click each sound link to test the links (make sure your speakers are on so you can hear the sound effects), then close the browser window.

Note   We included extra sound files in the Chapter 9 sounds folder in case you'd like to include sound clips for the kiss and slap or punch sound tips. To quickly add sound links after subsequent headings, simply copy the speaker and hyperlink text following the *Breaking Bones* heading (select the speaker image and text, and press Ctrl+C), click after another heading, and paste the information (press Ctrl+V). Then, simply edit each components hyperlink settings (right-click and choose Edit Hyperlink) to point to the proper sound file.

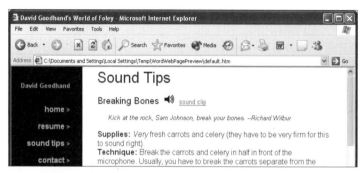

Figure 9-40   On the Sound Tips page, users can click either the animated GIF or the sound clip hyperlink to listen to a sample of the described sound effect.

Creating Links to Other Areas on the Current Page

Finally, we get to "last but not least." In this section we show you how to include a hyperlink that points to another area on the same page. This technique is especially useful on long pages or pages that are clearly divided into blocks of information, such as FAQ pages. For this project's Web site, we envision David adding quite a bit of entertaining information to the Sound Tips page, so we thought we'd show you how to add a Go to Top link at the bottom of that page. As David adds more information to the page, he might want to include a menu of links at the top of the page with Go to Top links after each sound tip entry (similar to the same-page links shown on *www.creationguide.com/resources*).

The key to creating a same-page hyperlink is to insert *bookmarks* at the locations you want to jump to. After you insert bookmarks, you simply format a hyperlink to display the bookmarked location, as described here:

Lingo   A *bookmark* is a hidden component that identifies a location or text selection. You give each bookmark a unique name so you can easily refer to it in the future.

---

1   In Word on the Sound Tips page, click at the top of the page (on the line above the Sound Tips heading), click Insert on the menu bar, and choose Bookmark.

2   In the Bookmark dialog box, type **top** in the Bookmark Name text box (as shown in Figure 9-41), and click Add.

Figure 9-41   You can define bookmarks to serve as hyperlink targets.

3   Scroll to the end of the last sound tip entry, press Enter three times, click Center on the Formatting toolbar, click Insert Hyperlink on the Standard toolbar, and click the Bookmark button.

4   In the Select Place In Document dialog box, click the top bookmark, as
shown in Figure 9-42.

Tip   In addition to bookmarks, you can use headings as hyperlink targets in Word.
Notice in Figure 9-42 that because the text in your Web site uses standard Word heading styles, you can also target a hyperlink to locations on the page by clicking a heading.

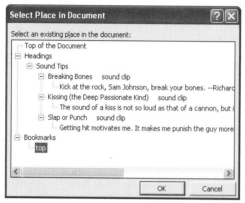

Figure 9-42   In Word, hyperlinks can target bookmarks or headings.

5   Click OK, and then replace the #top text in the Text To Display text
box with Go to Top.

6   Click the ScreenTip button, type **Return to the top of the page**, and
click OK twice to close the dialog boxes.

7   Select the Go to Top hyperlink and choose 10 pt on the Font Size drop-
down list on the Formatting toolbar.

8   Click Save, choose Web Page Preview on the File menu, click sound
tips in the navigation bar, test your Go to Top link, and then close your
browser window.

If you're feeling somewhat spunky, you could copy and paste the Go to
Top hyperlink so that the link appears below each sound tip file. This type of
setup would be ideal if David creates an extensive list of sound effect samples
and explanations.

Previewing Your Word-Generated Web Page

Congratulations! You've completed the Word 2002 Web site project. In the process, you've learned how to use the Web Page Wizard and you've gotten quite a
bit of hands-on experience in modifying Web pages, including adding components and working with hyperlinks, WordArt, clip art, and styles. Now you can sit
back, click around, and preview all your hard work.

Note   If you opted to read through this chapter without creating the Web site or if you want to compare your site to the Web pages we developed for this project, you can view David Goodhand's completed Web site at *www.creationguide.com/foley*.

As mentioned toward the beginning of this chapter, you can preview your Web pages in a number of ways. Furthermore, we encouraged you to preview your pages while you worked through this chapter's steps. At this point you might as well look at the pages in your Web browser as a whole, so that you can see how the pages will display and how well your hyperlinks work. By now you should be familiar with the process—choose Web Page Preview on the File menu to open your Web site pages in your browser. Figure 9-43 shows thumbnails of the completed Web site's pages. As a finalization step, remember to click your hyperlinks to ensure that your Web page responds properly to users' requests.

After you preview and test your Web site on your computer, your site will be ready for uploading to a server.

See Also   *Chapter 11 describes how you can go about uploading your Web site to a server when you're ready for your site to go live.*

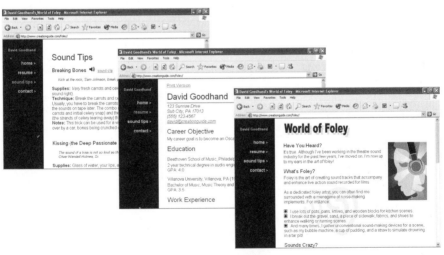

Figure 9-43   After paying attention to all the little details during Web site creation, you can sit back and click through your completed work.

Additional Resources

As you might know, numerous Word 2002 books and resources exist, and they all cover much more than Web page creation features. To help narrow the field, we've listed a few of our favorite Word 2002 resources:

■ Millhollon, Mary and Katherine Murray. *Microsoft Word Version 2002 Inside Out.* Redmond, WA: Microsoft Press, 2001. ISBN: 0-7356-1278-1. This book provides comprehensive coverage of the features in Word and serves as a good Word 2002 documentation guide (plus you're already familiar with one of the authors, and we think you'll appreciate Katherine Murray's wealth of knowledge as well).

■ Perspection, Inc. *Microsoft Word Version 2002 Step By Step.* Redmond, WA: Microsoft Press, 2001. ISBN: 0-7356-1295-1. This book serves as a hands-on guide designed to teach you Word 2002's full range of features (and you'll find that many of Word's features can assist you in building effective Web pages).

■ Microsoft's official home page for Word users (*www.microsoft.com/office/word*) shows you new tricks and allows you to access support and stay on top of possible software updates.

Key Points

■ You can use Word 2002 to create Web pages by using the Save As Web Page feature, Web page templates, the New Document task pane, or the Web Page Wizard.

■ After you save a document as an HTML page in Word, you can edit the Web page in Word view or you can access the HTML source code to edit the HTML commands directly.

■ Word 2002 provides a number of Web page templates on the Web Pages tab of the Templates dialog box.

■ Templates help you to quickly add headings, hyperlinks, columns, frames, and other Web page features to a blank document.

■ The Web Page Wizard can assist you in formulating entire Web sites, including home pages, subpages, themes, and other common Web site components.

■ Applying styles to your text before you import it into a Web page template simplifies your task when you apply themes to your Web pages.

■ After you create Web pages, you can customize and modify Web page text and components using many of the standard features and tools in Word.

Chapter 10

Creating Web Sites with FrontPage

When you watch the news on TV, the only "equipment" you need is the TV and a place to sit. But what about when you rent a video or order a pay-per-view movie that's filled with cool special effects and has an awesome soundtrack? Instead of turning to grandma's 13-inch hand-me-down TV, you'd probably prefer the ultimate in home entertainment systems: You know, the rare setup that can be easily controlled by a *single* remote control and has an ultra-clear big-screen TV, digital cable, Dolby stereo, and surround sound components artfully blending into the shadows—all strategically placed for optimal viewing and listening pleasure from the comfortable folds of an enormous leather couch. Granted, these "extras" aren't strictly necessary, but they sure can make a big difference sometimes. The same can be said of HTML editors. Notepad (a basic text editor) can be likened to the "TV, seat, and remote control" way of creating Web pages, whereas FrontPage provides the "luxury home entertainment system" approach to Web site development. In this chapter, we're going for the "extras."

To create the Web pages described in this chapter, you'll need the following "supplies":

- Microsoft FrontPage (preferably version 2002)

- An Internet connection (An Internet connection is necessary to download the sample project's graphics and text files from the Creation Guide Web site.)

- The mars.doc and thankyou.htm files downloaded from *www.creationguide.com/projects/chapter10/text*
  To download these files, create a folder named "sky" on your computer's hard drive. (For convenience, we refer to your hard drive as the C:\ drive throughout this chapter.) Then connect to *www.creationguide.com/projects/chapter10/text*, right-click mars.doc, select Save Target As, and save the file to the C:\sky folder on your computer. Repeat the process to save thankyou.htm to your C:\sky folder.

- The following 36 figures downloaded from *www.creationguide.com/projects/chapter10/images* into a folder named C:\sky\images (as described after the figure list):

b_aboutus.gif	bg.gif	mars.jpg
b_aboutus2.gif	bigdip1.gif	neptune.jpg
b_contact.gif	bigdip2.gif	saturn.jpg
b_contact2.gif	bigdip3.gif	solarsystem.gif
b_gallery.gif	bigdip4.gif	t_aboutus.gif
b_gallery2.gif	bigdip5.gif	t_contact.gif
b_links.gif	bullet_star.gif	t_gallery.gif
b_links2.gif	corner_botm_left.gif	t_links.gif
b_meetings.gif	corner_botm_right.gif	t_meetings.gif
b_meetings2.gif	corner_top_left.gif	t_skyguide.gif
b_skyguide.gif	corner_top_right.gif	titlebar-home.gif
b_skyguide2.gif	logo.gif	titlebar.gif

Tip   If you're Zip savvy, you can download the file zip_images10.zip and extract the images locally.

To obtain these figures, first create an images folder in C:\sky. Then connect to *www.creationguide.com/projects/chapter10/images*, right-click an image's filename (or the Zip file if your computer is set up to open Zip files), choose Save Target As, and save a copy of the file to the C:\sky\images folder on your computer, as shown in Figure 10-1. Repeat the process for each image.

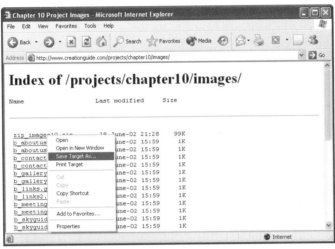

Figure 10-1   Before you can complete this project, you need to download the image files from the Internet.

Introducing FrontPage: A Full-Featured HTML Editor

For this book's final project, we show you how to use FrontPage to create a fairly advanced Web site. FrontPage is a full-featured HTML editor that you can purchase as a stand-alone application or as part of Microsoft Office XP Developer. As you'll see in this chapter, using a true HTML editor such as FrontPage opens numerous doors to Web page design for beginning designers. Full-scale HTML editors also provide some handy shortcuts for more seasoned designers. Our goal is to give you firsthand experience in creating a Web site that uses a number of Web page elements that are easily implemented using full-fledged HTML editors. These elements include (but are not limited to) the following:

- **Button rollover effects**   Buttons that seem to glow or change appearance in other ways when users place their cursors over the buttons. (By the way, when a user places a mouse cursor over a button or hyperlink, this action is called *hovering*.)

- **Cascading style sheets (CSS)**   Code that defines attributes and layout settings for HTML tags in one location. Style sheets reduce (and oftentimes eliminate) the need to repeatedly insert and define attributes in HTML tags. Style sheet definitions can be contained in linked CSS documents or embedded in Web pages' source code.

■   **Counter** A component that displays the number of times users have
    accessed a Web page. The counter number increments (increases) by 1
    each time a visitor accesses the page.

■   **Image map** A picture with clickable areas that link to related pages
    or other areas on the current page. The image serves as a directory, and
    users access information by clicking areas of the picture, such as click-
    ing New York on a U.S. map to display a Web page about New York.

■   **Marquee text** Text that slides in from the edge of the page (left or
    right) like ticker tape. You can create marquee text that slides in once
    and then stays put, repeats a specified number of times, or repeats
    continuously.

■   **Thumbnails** Small images that link to larger images. Thumbnails
    enable users to decide whether they want to view a larger version of
    an image (which might take extra time to download).

Before you see how easily you can use FrontPage to create the preceding
elements, let's give the FrontPage interface a quick once-over to preview where
you're headed.

Strolling Past the FrontPage Window

Much of the FrontPage interface is similar to that of other Office applications. In
other words, when you first open FrontPage, you'll probably feel that it looks
quite familiar—that is, if you're used to working in Office. In fact, at first glance,
you'll see the Standard and Formatting toolbars across the top, menu bar
options, a workspace area, and a status bar along the bottom. But in addition to
the standard fare, FrontPage offers a couple key interface options to assist you
in creating Web pages. Namely, the FrontPage interface includes a Views bar
and three view options—Normal, HTML, and Preview—as shown on the left in
Figure 10-2. These elements will help you track the multiple files and folders of
your Web site, preview Web pages during development, edit HTML source code,
manage hyperlinks, and more. For example, you can use the HTML view to
access a Web page's source code, as shown on the right in Figure 10-2, and the
Preview view to preview Web pages as you build them. You'll be using all three
views in this chapter's project.

As you'll soon see, taking advantage of many of the features in FrontPage
requires you merely to select menu options, click toolbar buttons, and complete
dialog boxes—activities you should be accustomed to if you're a veteran of other

Office programs, such as Microsoft Word. Therefore, although FrontPage is considered a high-end HTML editor with advanced Web development capabilities, you should feel comfortable working within its interface pretty quickly—even if you've never composed so much as a single text-based Web page in an HTML editor. Regardless of any predevelopment jitters, we're confident that if you work through this chapter's project, you'll have a strong grasp of FrontPage's capabilities.

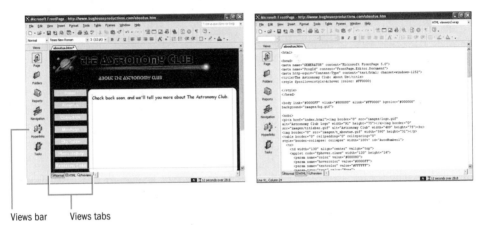

Views bar   Views tabs

Figure 10-2 For the most part, you'll design a FrontPage Web page in Normal viewing. At times, you might need to view and edit a FrontPage Web page's source code in HTML view.

The Advantages of Using FrontPage

Like all full-service HTML editors, FrontPage sports some definite advantages. FrontPage is fairly easy to use (after you know where to look and what you're looking for), it provides many advanced design features, and it creates HTML code automatically. Using FrontPage, you can easily create professional-looking Web pages with just a few clicks. Throughout the project in this chapter, we highlight a lot of FrontPage's functionality. Our reasoning for covering a wide range of FrontPage capabilities also includes a hidden benefit: *You'll learn how to create Web pages in FrontPage, and you'll also learn about HTML editors in general.*

Mastering applications (such as HTML editors and word processors) entails knowing the typical functions available in the application. For example, you know that most word-processing applications have a Find feature. Thus, regardless of the word-processing application you're using, if you need to find text, you probably look automatically for the application's Find or Search tool. Similarly, with HTML editors, if you learn some of the capabilities of FrontPage—and it has a lot of them—you can benefit from that knowledge when you work in similar environments. So using FrontPage as a model, you'll be introduced to a selection of tasks that most HTML editors offer. That way, if you later decide to design Web pages using another HTML editor, you'll have a good idea of the types of features to look for. Or if you decide to design your Web pages in FrontPage, you'll be way ahead of the game.

FrontPage Server Extensions

The final issue we need to touch on before we get going on the chapter project is *FrontPage Server Extensions*, which are specific to FrontPage. Before the onset of advanced HTML editors, developers had to write, buy, or copy code to enable certain Web page features, such as forms, counters, Java programs, and so forth. FrontPage provides the code for many of these features, enabling designers to easily include functionality that requires some coding—without having to manually insert code or acquire the code in some other way. The catch is that your server (or your hosting service) needs to support FrontPage Server Extensions. So before you go crazy using the advanced design features of FrontPage, check with your Web hosting service to verify that they support FrontPage Server Extensions.

Lingo   *FrontPage Server Extensions* are installed on servers to enable additional functionality in Web pages created or imported in FrontPage.

You can control whether a Web page you're building includes components that require FrontPage Server Extensions. The easiest way to avoid extension-reliant features is to configure FrontPage to deactivate (and dim) features that require extensions. When you do this, you avoid including components that rely on your server's capabilities (because FrontPage won't allow you to insert extension-reliant components). To control the availability of features requiring FrontPage Server Extensions, do the following:

1   Display the Tools menu, click Page Options, and click the Compatibility tab.

2   Clear the Enabled With Microsoft FrontPage Server Extensions check box in the Servers section to deactivate features requiring extensions, and click OK.

After you complete the preceding steps, all features that require extensions appear as dimmed options in menus and dialog boxes, and any components already installed on the page are disabled and the related HTML code displays as gray text.

Editing Existing FrontPage Sites One of the convenient features of FrontPage is its online editing capabilities. When you install FrontPage, the Edit With Microsoft FrontPage command is automatically added to the Microsoft Internet Explorer toolbar, with the Edit button, as shown here:

You can quickly edit your online Web pages by displaying your Web page in Internet Explorer, clicking the Edit button drop-down arrow, and clicking FrontPage. After you select FrontPage on the Edit button's drop-down list, FrontPage opens automatically, asks for your user ID and password if required, and then displays the page for editing.

When you're satisfied with your changes, you can click Save in FrontPage to automatically save the changes as a local copy of the Web page, or you can save and upload the changed version of your Web page to your server if you're editing your own site. This quick-access editing feature is great for making small tweaks and fixing typos. But be careful when you're making major changes to your Web page and uploading them directly from FrontPage. By default, after you've made changes to a down-loaded Web page, clicking Save in FrontPage and saving a file to your server (instead of using Save As to save the changes to your local machine) overwrites your existing online Web page; reverting to your "old" Web page might be tricky or nearly impossible after you save the modified version online directly from FrontPage. (See Chapter 12 for more information about saving and archiving Web information.)

In this day and age, most hosting services support FrontPage Server Extensions. You'll definitely find some exceptions, including hosting services that support some but not all of the FrontPage Server Extensions. So if you're shopping for a hosting service and think you'll be using FrontPage extensions (such as for a FrontPage page hit counter), you'll want to ensure that your hosting service supports FrontPage Server Extensions before you plunk down any cash and commit to the hosting service's plan. For our purposes in this chapter, however, you don't need to have server space to create the project. For the most part, you build the site locally on your computer, so you won't need to worry about server space and FrontPage Server Extensions until you're ready to publish your Web site online (that is, "go live") or if you want to test the publishing feature in FrontPage by publishing the project site. We talk a little about publishing FrontPage sites later in this chapter, but you'll need to consult one of the references in the section "Additional Resources" for a full discussion of this topic as well as turn to Chapter 11 for some Web publishing tips.

At this point, you know enough to get started on the project. So let's forge ahead to our final frontier in this book's Web-site-development section and have some fun creating a Web site in FrontPage!

Planning Your FrontPage Web Site

When we initially planned this chapter's project site, we intended to create a team page featuring a fictitious softball team. Unfortunately, we couldn't bribe enough of our friends to pose for the team picture, so we opted to create a Web site for an astronomy club instead. We ended up incorporating many of the functionalities we had originally planned for the softball site into the astronomy site. For example, instead of making an image map out of a team picture, in which you could click each person's head to access a stats or personal page, we used a solar system image map in which you can click each planet to access a page of information about that planet. We hope that as you experiment with the techniques we present in this project, you'll begin to think of ways you can vary them to create custom Web sites.

After determining that an astronomy club site would suit our purposes, we decided that the site should consist of a custom home page linking to standard-format subpages. Using a nonstandard home page is a common Web site design technique used to make the home page stand out from the subpages. Because FrontPage offers so many options, we felt that showing a nonstandard home page made good design sense and would also enable us to show you a few additional features of FrontPage. To see our planning process, take a look at Figures 10-3 through 10-5. Figure 10-3 shows a sketch of the Big Dipper design we came up with for the home page. Figure 10-4 shows the sketch of the standard subpage layout. And finally, Figure 10-5 shows the astronomy club site's storyboard.

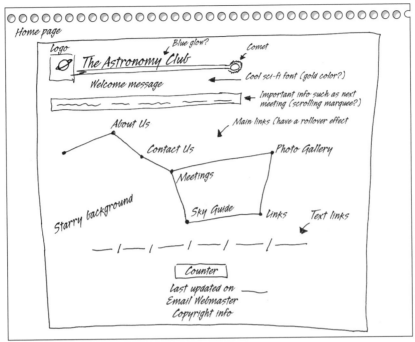

Figure 10-3 A sketch of the astronomy club's home page shows the big dipper containing links to the site's main subpages.

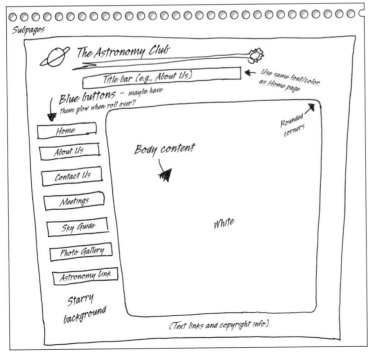

Figure 10-4 A sketch of a typical astronomy club subpage shows that the subpages will be structured differently from the home page.

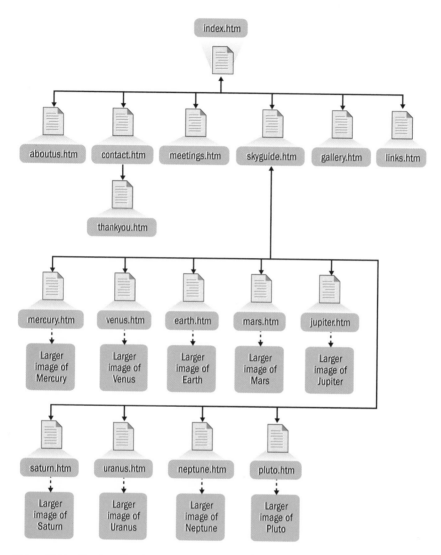

Figure 10-5   Storyboarding the astronomy club's Web site clarifies the Web site's hierarchy.

Because of the relative complexity of the home page, you're going to create that page last. In this project, you'll start the design process by solidifying the site's standard layout for subpages by creating a subpage.htm document that you can use as a template to create the site's pages. But first, before you begin building Web pages, you need to tell FrontPage that you want to create a new Web.

Creating a New Web

As we just mentioned, the first step to designing a Web site is to express your Web-page-building intentions to FrontPage by creating a new Web. To do so, follow these steps:

Note   FrontPage refers to Web sites as *Webs*.

---

1   Ensure that you've created a folder named C:\sky\images in which you've stored the images you downloaded from *www.creationguide.com/projects/chapter10/images*. Also be sure that you've downloaded mars.doc and thankyou.htm from *www.creationguide.com/projects/chapter10/text* and stored the files in C:\sky.

2   Open FrontPage, and close the blank document if a blank document displays.

3   If the Page Or Web task pane isn't displaying, open the File menu, select New and then click Page Or Web.

4   In the New section, click the Empty Web option and the Web Site Templates dialog box opens. Click in the Specify The Location Of The New Web text box, highlight the existing text, type **C:\sky** or click Browse and navigate to C:\sky, and then click OK. After some brief processing in which FrontPage adds FrontPage Server Extensions to your Web folder (C:\sky), you'll see the FrontPage title bar change to Microsoft FrontPage - C:\sky, which means you're ready for action.

5   In the Views bar along the left side of the FrontPage window, click the Reports icon. A site summary appears. This report displays because you have graphics stored in C:\sky\images and mars.doc and thankyou.htm stored in C:\sky.

Note   Although having all the images you plan to use on your Web site ready up front is convenient, it's not necessary. But because the astronomy club's graphics are readily available (and because this book is about creating Web pages, not Web graphics), you can simplify creating the Web in this project (or any project for that matter) by organizing the graphics for the site before you start creating it.

---

6   Click the Page icon in the Views bar and click Create A New Normal Page button in the Standard toolbar to open a blank page (notice

the title bar text in FrontPage changes to Microsoft FrontPage -
C:\sky\new_page_1.htm).

You're now ready to create a standard subpage that you can use as a template for the astronomy club's Web site.

Creating the Subpage Layout

In this section you'll create a standard subpage layout that you'll be able to copy
and use to create foundation pages for each subpage in the site. First you'll
set the subpage's page properties.

Setting Page Properties

To begin, ensure that you have a blank workspace displaying in FrontPage. If
you followed the steps in the preceding section, you should be set. Here are the
steps to create a basic subpage:

1   Right-click a blank area on the page and select Page Properties. The
Page Properties dialog box opens.

2   In the Title text box on the General tab, type **The Astronomy Club**, as
shown in Figure 10-6.

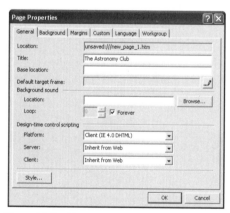

Figure 10-6   You can enter title text in the Page Properties dialog box.

3   Click the Background tab, select the Background Picture check box to
specify that you want the page to use a background picture, and then
click Browse.

4   In the Select Background Picture dialog box, double-click the images
folder in C:\sky and then click bg.gif, as shown in Figure 10-7.

Tip   To see a thumbnail of a selected image in the Select Background Picture dialog box, click the Views drop-down arrow in the dialog box's toolbar and select Preview.

---

5   Click Open to select the background image and return to the Page Properties dialog box.

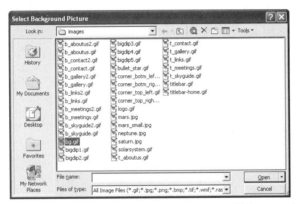

Figure 10-7   To assign a background image to your Web page, select bg.gif in the Select Background Picture dialog box.

6   Continuing on the Background tab, click the Enable Hyperlink Roll-over Effects check box, and then click the Rollover Style button. The Font dialog box opens. In the Font area, retain the (Default Font) selection, and in the Font Style text box, select Normal.

7   Click the Color drop-down box, click the red color square (red's the default color), and click OK. This setting specifies to display text links in red whenever a user's mouse cursor hovers over the text link.

8   Next on the Background tab, click the Background drop-down arrow and click the black color box; then click the Text drop-down arrow and click the black color box.

Note   Step 8 doesn't contain a mistake—you *should* set both the background and the text colors to black. For this project, most of the text you enter will display in white table cells, so to save yourself time later on, you should set the default text color to black at this point even though the background is set to black as well.

---

9   Click the Hyperlink drop-down arrow and click the blue color box; click the Visited Hyperlink drop-down arrow and click the purple color box; then click the Active Hyperlink drop-down arrow and click the

red color box. The Background tab should now look like the one
shown in Figure 10-8.

Lingo   An *active hyperlink* refers to a hyperlink that's being clicked. If you set an
active hyperlink color property to red, the hyperlink will appear red while the user
clicks the link.

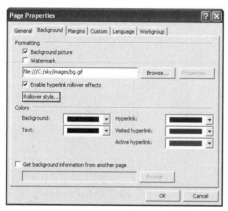

Figure 10-8   The completed Background tab shows the default colors you selected for the
current Web page.

Even though the project uses the default hyperlink colors, you
should click each component's color boxes to replace the "automatic"
color setting for each element. If you don't replace the automatic colors with specified colors, some browsers might insert custom hyperlink
colors that might not work well with your site—for example, if a user's
"visiting" hyperlinks are set to black, the links will disappear into the
black background after the user clicks them.

10 Click OK to implement the Page Property settings and close the Page
Properties dialog box.

Saving Your Work

Before you get too far along, you should save your work. You'll be able to use
the same basic settings for all subpages, so you'll save the page you're currently
creating as a generic template that you can copy to create all the site's subpages.
To save the current file, follow these steps:

1   On the File menu, click Save.

2   In the Save As dialog box, click the Change Title button (located in the
lower-right portion of the dialog box) to open the Set Page Title dialog

box, and change the text to The Astronomy Club: Generic Page, as shown in Figure 10-9. Then click OK.

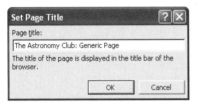

Figure 10-9   You configure the Set Page Title dialog box to modify a page's title text.

3 In the File Name text box, type **subpage**, and then click Save.

Adding the Logo and the Title Banner Graphic

In this section you'll continue to configure the subpage template by inserting the astronomy club's logo and title banner graphic, which appears along the top of every page:

1 In the C:\sky\subpage.htm document (which should be opened in FrontPage if you're continuing the project from the previous section), click the Insert menu, point to Picture, and then choose From File.

> **Tip**   If you closed subpage.htm, you can reopen the document by opening FrontPage, clicking the Open icon (or clicking Open on the File menu), navigating to C:\sky in the Open dialog box, and double-clicking subpage.htm.

2 In the Picture dialog box, display the contents of the images folder in the C:\sky\images folder, select the logo.gif file, and click Insert (or, simply double-click the logo.gif file). The logo (which is Saturn and a few miscellaneous moons) displays on the page.

3 On the Standard toolbar, click the Insert Picture From File button, and double-click the titlebar.gif file. The title bar image is inserted next to the logo.

4 Right-click the logo.gif image (the Saturn image), select Picture Properties, click the General tab, click in the Text box in the Alternative Representations section, type **Astronomy Club Logo**, and then click OK.

5 Right-click the titlebar.gif image, select Picture Properties, click the General tab, click in the Text box in the Alternative Representations section, type **Astronomy Club**, and then click OK.

6   Right-click the logo image again, select Hyperlink, type **index.htm** in the Address text box, and then click OK.

At this point, the logo is linked to the (future) home page, and both graphics are inserted and left-aligned by default. In most browsers, the left alignment will help keep the graphics side by side, but because two images span the top of your page, the title bar could feasibly wrap to the next line in some browsers if users resized their browser windows to a very small size (in which case the logo would display on the top line and the title bar would display flush-left below the logo graphic on the next line—not the effect you're after for this Web site). Just to be safe, you can add the "no break" (`<NOBR></NOBR>`) HTML tags to your page's source code to specify that the two graphics should be kept together regardless of the browser's window size.

7   In FrontPage, click the HTML view option. The HTML source code displays in FrontPage's workspace window.

Before you add the `<NOBR></NOBR>` tags, let's make working in FrontPage easier by enabling FrontPage to wrap the code text.

8   Click Tools, click Page Options, and display the HTML Source tab.

9   In the General section, click Reformat Using the Rules Below, select the Allow Line Breaks Within Tags check box in the Formatting section, and click OK.

Now you'll be able to view your HTML code without having to scroll left and right as much, which means you're ready to add the `<NOBR></NOBR>` tags.

10 In the source code, click after the opening paragraph tag (`<p>`), type `<NOBR>`, click before the closing paragraph tag (`</p>`), and type `<NOBR>`. Figure 10-10 shows the newly added HTML tags (in orange) that will ensure that the graphics will always display next to each other.

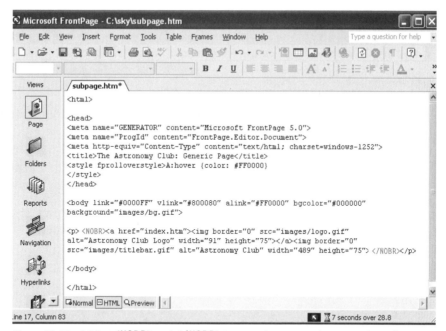

Figure 10-10 Adding <NOBR> and </NOBR> to a page's source code ensures that a line break won't separate particular elements.

11 Click Save (your capped code will automatically change to all lower-case code), and then click the Normal view tab to redisplay the graphical representation of subpage.htm in your working area. Your page should display as shown in Figure 10-11.

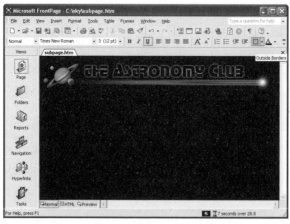

Figure 10-11 At this point the subpage.htm includes background, logo, and title bar images.

Inserting a Table

In this section you'll create the foundation table used to contain the body text of each subpage in the astronomy club's Web site. Take your time going through the upcoming steps—it's easier to configure your table correctly the first time around instead of trying to find an erroneous setting. Furthermore, although this section might seem to include a few too many steps, the steps throughout are fairly repetitive, so the process isn't overly complex. (In other words, don't let the number of steps get to you.) When you create your own tables, you'll probably have to experiment with a few settings before you get your table just right—which is exactly what we do, too. To create your table for this project, follow these steps:

1   Press your down arrow key once to position your cursor below the graphics, and press Shift+Enter to position your cursor where you want to insert the table.

2   In the Standard toolbar, click the Table button, drag to select two rows and five columns worth of boxes on the pop-up window, and then release to insert the table into your page. Figure 10-12 illustrates the table creation process. As you can see, the table borders display when you first insert a table. In effect, the table's borders are set to display as 1-pixel wide. Later, after you fill the table with content, you'll change the table's borders setting to 0 to hide the table's lines.

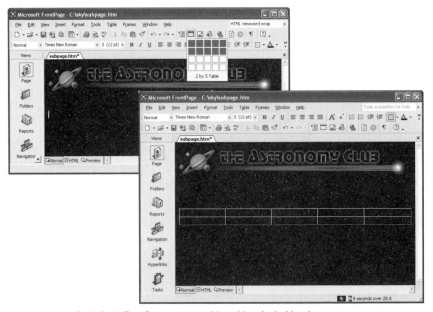

Figure 10-12   By default, FrontPage creates tables with a 1-pixel border.

3   Right-click anywhere on the table, choose Table Properties, ensure that Cell Padding is set to 0, Cell Spacing is set to 0, Specify Width is set to 100 percent, the Size setting under Borders is set to 1, and click OK.

4   Right-click the cell in row 1, column 1. On the shortcut menu, select Cell Properties.

5   In the Cell Properties dialog box, set the Horizontal Alignment option to Center, set Vertical Alignment to Top, ensure that the Specify Width check box is selected, enter 130 in the Specify Width text box, and select the In Pixels option, as shown in Figure 10-13.

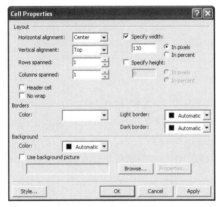

Figure 10-13   You use the Cell Properties dialog box to configure a table cell.

6   Click OK to activate the settings.

Tip   Don't forget to save often while you work!

---

7   Right-click the cell in row 2, column 1. On the shortcut menu, select Cell Properties.

8   In the Cell Properties dialog box, set the Horizontal Alignment Option to Center, set Vertical Alignment to Bottom, set the Specify Width setting to 130 pixels, select the Specify Height check box, set the Specify Height setting to 15 pixels, and click OK.

9   Right-click the cell in row 1, column 2. Select Cell Properties. Set the Horizontal Alignment Option to Left, set Vertical Alignment to Top, set the Specify Width setting to 1 pixel, and click OK (don't worry if you don't see a change in your table just yet—the cell won't resize until you format the cell below it as well).

10 Right-click the cell in row 2, column 2. Select Cell Properties. Set the Horizontal Alignment Option to Left, set Vertical Alignment to Bottom, set the Specify Width setting to 1 pixel, select the Specify Height check box, set the Specify Height setting to 15 pixels, and click OK. (Now the second column in your table should be 1-pixel wide.)

11 Right-click the cell in row 1, column 3. On the shortcut menu, select Cell Properties, set Horizontal Alignment to Left, set Vertical Alignment to Top, set the Specify Width setting to 15 pixels, specify the Background Color as White, and click OK.

12 Right-click the cell in row 2, column 3. On the shortcut menu, select Cell Properties, set Horizontal Alignment to Left, set Vertical Alignment to Bottom, set the Specify Width setting to 15 pixels, click the Specify Height check box, set the Specify Height setting to 15 pixels, specify the Background Color as White, and click OK.

13 Right-click the cell in row 1, column 4. On the shortcut menu, select Cell Properties, set Horizontal Alignment to Left, set Vertical Alignment to Top, clear the Specify Width check box (don't set a width for this column because you'll want it to resize to fit each user's browser window), specify the Background Color as White, and click OK.

14 Right-click the cell in row 2, column 4. On the shortcut menu, select Cell Properties, set Horizontal Alignment to Left, set Vertical Alignment to Bottom, clear the Specify Width check box, select the Specify Height check box, set the Specify Height settings to 15 pixels, specify the Background Color as White, and click OK.

15 Right-click the cell in row 1, column 5. On the shortcut menu, select Cell Properties, set Horizontal Alignment to Right, set Vertical Alignment to Top, set the Specify Width setting to 15 pixels, specify the Background Color as White, and click OK.

16 Right-click the cell in row 2, column 5. On the shortcut menu, select Cell Properties, set Horizontal Alignment to Right, set Vertical Alignment to Bottom, set the Specify Width setting to 15 pixels, set the Specify Height setting to 15 pixels, specify the Background Color as White, and click OK. Your table should now display as shown in Figure 10-14.

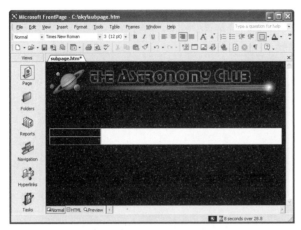

Figure 10-14   You can modify the internal layout of a table by adjusting cell properties.

Notice in Figure 10-14 that the right set of table cells displays as a white rectangular area. You're now going to add small graphics to the white area's corner cells to create the illusion that the table has rounded corners:

17 Click in the cell in row 1, column 3. On the Insert menu, point to Picture and choose From File. Select the corner_top_left.gif image in the C:\sky\images folder, and then click OK.

> **Tip**   To get an idea of how the corner graphics work, view the small curved graphics in a paint program or preview the image in the Insert Picture dialog box. You can easily imagine how the small curve can create the illusion of a rounded corner when it's inserted into a table cell.

18 Click in the cell in row 2, column 3. Click Insert Picture From File on the Standard toolbar, and double-click corner_botm_left.gif image in the C:\sky\images folder.

19 Right-click the newly inserted corner_botm_left.gif image. On the shortcut menu, click Picture Properties, click the Appearance tab if necessary, select Bottom in the Alignment drop-down list, and click OK.

20 Click in the cell in row 1, column 5 (because you formatted the cell to align information to the right, your cursor will appear to the far right of the cell). Click Insert Picture From File on the Standard toolbar, and double-click corner_top_right.gif image in the C:\sky\images folder.

21 Click in the cell in row 2, column 5. Click Insert Picture From File, and double-click corner_botm_right.gif image in the C:\sky\images folder.

22 Right-click the newly inserted corner_botm_right.gif image. On the shortcut menu, click Picture Properties, click the Appearance tab if necessary, select Bottom in the Alignment drop-down list, and click OK.

23 Click Save on the toolbar. At this point, your table should display as shown in Figure 10-15.

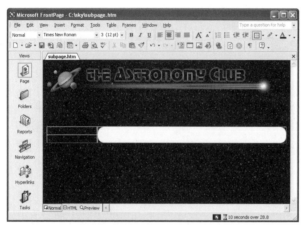

Figure 10-15   Small graphics added to table cells create the appearance of rounded table corners.

Adding Navigation Buttons

Now that the table is created, you're ready to start filling the table's cells. First on the agenda is to add some navigation buttons to the first column in the table. FrontPage offers some nice special-effects buttons, which you'll use in this project:

1 Click in the cell in row 1, column 1.

2 On the Insert menu, point to Web Component, select Dynamic Effects in the Component Type section, choose Hover Button in the Choose An Effect section (notice the component's description displays below the list boxes in the Insert Web Component dialog box; as you click effects, the description changes), and click Finish.

3 Configure the Hover Button Properties dialog box, as shown in Figure 10-16, using the following settings:

Option	Setting
Button Text	Home
Link To	index.htm
Button Color	Navy
Effect	Glow
Width	120
Background Color	Automatic
Effect Color	Blue
Height	24

Figure 10-16   FrontPage enables you to create hover buttons by configuring the Hover Button Properties dialog box.

4 Click OK.

5 Press Enter. On the Standard toolbar, click Web Component, ensure that Dynamic Effects and Hover Button are selected, and click Finish. Type **About Us** in the Button Text text box, type **aboutus.htm** in the Link To text box, specify the remaining settings as outlined in step 3, and then click OK.

6 Press Enter. Click Web Component, ensure that Dynamic Effects and Hover Button are selected, and click Finish. Type **Contact Us** in the Button Text text box, type **contact.htm** in the Link To text box, specify the remaining settings as outlined in step 3 (which are the default settings), and then click OK.

7 Press Enter. Click Web Component, ensure Dynamic Effects and Hover Button are selected, and click Finish. Type **Meetings** in the Button Text text box, type **meetings.htm** in the Link To text box, specify the remaining settings as outlined in step 3, and then click OK.

8 Press Enter. On the Insert menu, click Web Component, ensure that Dynamic Effects and Hover Button are selected, and click Finish. Type **Sky Guide** in the Button Text text box, type **skyguide.htm** in the Link To text box, specify the remaining settings as outlined in step 3, and then click OK.

9 Press Enter. Click Web Component, ensure that Dynamic Effects and Hover Button are selected, and click Finish. Type **Photo Gallery** in the Button Text text box, type **gallery.htm** in the Link To text box, specify the remaining settings as outlined in step 3, and then click OK.

10 Press Enter. Click Web Component, ensure that Dynamic Effects and Hover Button are selected, and click Finish. Type **Astronomy Links** in the Button Text text box, type **links.htm** in the Link To text box, specify the remaining settings as outlined in step 3, and then click OK.

11 Click Save. Your subpage should display in Normal view and Preview view as shown in Figure 10-17.

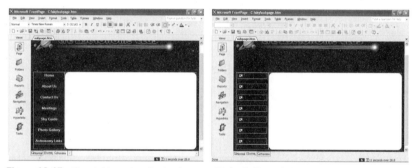

Figure 10-17   Your table and navigation buttons display in Normal view but not yet in Preview view.

As you can see in Figure 10-17, FrontPage 2002 encounters a little glitch when you insert hover buttons; basically, you can't preview your hover buttons in Preview view automatically (notice the broken link images in the Preview screen shown in Figure 10-17). In time, Microsoft might offer a patch to correct this, but for now you have two workaround choices:

● Preview your pages in your browser by selecting Preview In Browser on the File menu, choosing the browser you want to use, and clicking Preview.

● Modify each hover button's code to correct the problem.

If you choose to preview your Web pages in your browser throughout the remainder of this exercise, go ahead and skip to the next section and choose Preview In Browser on the File menu or click the Preview In Browser button on the Standard toolbar each time we suggest that you preview your Web page. If you prefer to tweak your HTML code a little to avoid opening your browser throughout the chapter, we present the steps here. The steps are manageable, and this is a prime example of how knowing a little HTML coding can help when you're working with HTML editors.

12 Click HTML at the bottom of the window to display your page's HTML code.

The code for each hover button appears between an `<applet>` `</applet>` tag set, so you should see seven `<applet></applet>` tag sets in HTML. You can tell which button an applet applies to by looking at the `value` attribute for the parameter that defines the button's text. For example, following is the entire applet code for one button; notice that the fifth line indicates that this applet applies to the Home button:

```
<applet code="fphover.class" codebase="./" width="120" height="24">

    <param name="color" value="#000080">

    <param name="hovercolor" value="#0000FF">

    <param name="textcolor" value="#FFFFFF">

    <param name="text" value="Home">

    <param name="effect" value="glow">

    <param name="url" valuetype="ref" value="index.htm">

</applet><p>
```

The problem in the current hover button code lies in the `codebase="./"` attribute in the first line of each `<applet>` tag. This attribute tells FrontPage to look in a subdirectory for the file `fphover.class`. In actuality, FrontPage stores the class file in the same folder as your Web page, so there's no need for browsers to look in a subdirectory for the class file. Although this explanation might sound a tad obtuse, the fix is simple—you just need to delete `codebase="./"` in each `<applet>` tag (see Figure 10-18, where we've highlighted some of the instances of the `codebase="./"` attribute), as described next.

13 In the first `<applet>` tag, select `codebase="./"` as shown in Figure 10-18, and press Backspace (or right-click and choose Delete).

14 Repeat step 13 for each button's applet code (remember—you have seven buttons, so you should delete `codebase="./"` seven times).

15 Save your file and click Preview at the bottom of the FrontPage window. After you save the code changes, your hover buttons should display in Preview mode as expected.

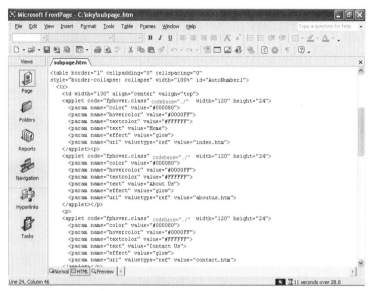

Figure 10-18   If you want to preview your hover buttons in FrontPage's Preview mode, you have to slightly tweak each button's code.

Tip   If you encounter problems while working in FrontPage (or other Microsoft application), a terrific resource to turn to is Microsoft's online Knowledge Base. To access the Knowledge Base, display *http://support.microsoft.com* in your browser, and click the Search The Knowledge Base link.

Adding Footer Information below the Table

The final components you'll add to the subpage template before you begin to create actual site pages are the bottom-of-the-page elements: a text-based navigation bar and copyright information. As we discuss earlier in the book, your Web pages should include text-based navigation links for users who turn off graphics or access the Web with nongraphical browsers. Furthermore, you should include copyright information to protect your creation. To add bottom-of-the-page information to the astronomy club's Web, follow these steps:

1   In Normal view, click in the area below the table, click the drop-down arrow on the Font Color button in the Formatting toolbar, and click the white color box.

2   Type (including the pipe symbols) **Home | About Us | Contact Us | Meetings | Sky Guide | Photo Gallery | Links**

3   Select the line of text you just typed, display the font drop-down list in the Formatting toolbar, and choose Comic Sans (or Comic Sans MS).

4 Click the Center button on the Formatting toolbar to center the text.

5 Click at the end of the line of text, press Enter, and then type **Questions or comments about the Web site? E-mail the Webmaster**.

6 Press Enter, display the Font Size drop-down list in the Formatting toolbar, choose 1 (8 pt), and then type **Copyright 2002 – [*your name or organization's name*]**.

7 Press Enter, and click Save in the Standard toolbar.

You're now ready to link the navigation bar's text and add a Mail To link to the *E-mail the Webmaster* text:

8 Select Home in the text-based navigation bar, right-click the selected text, and click Hyperlink.

9 In the Insert Hyperlink dialog box, ensure that the Look In drop-down list shows *sky*, click in the Address text box, type **index.htm** (be sure to delete the http:// if it displays), as shown in Figure 10-19, and then click OK or press Enter.

Tip   You can also press Ctrl+K to open the Insert Hyperlink dialog box.

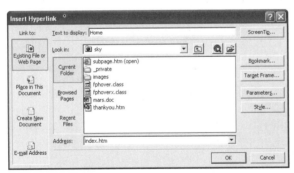

Figure 10-19   The Insert Hyperlink dialog box enables you to easily configure hyperlinks in FrontPage.

Tip   If you want to add a ScreenTip to your text hyperlinks, click the ScreenTip button in the Insert Hyperlink dialog box.

---

10 Repeat steps 8 and 9 using the following parameters:

Select and Right-Click	Enter in the Address Text Box
About Us	aboutus.htm
Contact Us	contact.htm
Meetings	meetings.htm
Sky Guide	skyguide.htm
Photo Gallery	gallery.htm
Links	links.htm

11 Select the *E-mail The Webmaster* text, right-click the selected text, and click Hyperlink to open the Insert Hyperlink dialog box.

12 In the Insert Hyperlink dialog box, click the E-Mail Address button in the Link To section, as shown in Figure 10-20.

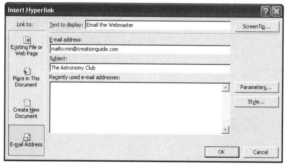

Figure 10-20   You can create hyperlinks that automatically open a preaddressed message form.

13 Enter your e-mail address in the E-mail Address text box, enter The Astronomy Club in the Subject text box (see Figure 10-20), click OK, and then save your work. The lower portion of your subpage template should appear as shown in Figure 10-21, which shows the Preview view (remember, if you didn't modify your hover button's applet code, you need to choose Preview In Browser on the File menu to properly preview your subpage Web page).

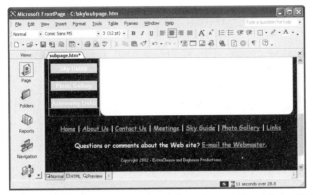

Figure 10-21   The subpage's footer information provides visitors with text links, Webmaster access, and copyright information.

14 Close subpage.htm.

You now have a subpage template ready for use.

Using the Subpage Layout to Build Web Pages

Now you're going to use subpage.htm to create a couple subpages for the astronomy club's Web. The site requires six main subpages:

- aboutus.htm
- contact.htm
- meetings.htm
- skyguide.htm
- gallery.htm
- links.htm

In this section you'll complete the contact.htm and skyguide.htm as well as a subpage (mars.htm) of the skyguide.htm page. Although we don't walk you through the creation of all the subpages, the images you downloaded from *www.creationguide.com/projects/chapter10/images* include title bar text graphics so that you can complete all the subpages on your own if you want to. We chose to show you how to complete mars.htm, skyguide.htm, and contact.htm because creating each of those pages includes information on how to add particular functionality to your Web pages, as follows:

- **mars.htm**   Shows you how to use the thumbnail feature in FrontPage as well as copy text from a Word document and modify cascading style sheets. Furthermore, this page links to the Sky Guide page (skyguide.htm).

- **skyguide.htm**   Teaches you how to create an image map in FrontPage.

- **contact.htm**   Provides a quick overview of how to create a working form in FrontPage.

After you create the three subpages described in this project, you'll be fully prepared to experiment and complete the remaining subpages on your own.

Preparing to Create Subpages

Preparing to create subpages is straightforward now that you've laid such a solid groundwork by creating the subpage.htm template. To use the template, you simply save copies of the subpage.htm file with different names and title text, as follows:

1 Open C:\sky\subpage.htm in FrontPage.

2 Click Save As on the File menu to open the Save As dialog box and ensure that the Save In text box displays the C:\sky folder.

3 In the Page Title section, click the Change Title button, type **The Astronomy Club: About Us** in the Set Page Title dialog box, and click OK.

> **Tip**   You can change a Web page's title text at any time. To do so, click Properties on the File menu, change the Title text, and then click OK. You added title text for each page as you created the pages in the preceding section.

4 In the Filename text box, type **aboutus.htm**, and click Save. Notice that the Web page's tab changes (below the toolbars) to reflect the new name of the current document.

5 Without closing the current document (which is aboutus.htm at this point), repeat steps 2 through 4 using the filenames and title text shown in the following table:

Save As Filename	Page Title Text
contact.htm	*The Astronomy Club: Contact Us*
meetings.htm	*The Astronomy Club: Meetings*
skyguide.htm	*The Astronomy Club: Sky Guide*
gallery.htm	*The Astronomy Club: Gallery*
links.htm	*The Astronomy Club: Links*
mars.htm	*The Astronomy Club: Mars*

Tip   You need to name the subpages in the same way they were referenced when you linked the navigation buttons and hypertext links. For example, the About Us subpage needs to be saved with the name aboutus.htm. Do not alter the file names at this point.

---

6   Close FrontPage, open your C:\sky folder, and verify that the folder contains a file for each Web page in your Web site.

7   After you verify the list of newly created files, close your C:\sky folder.

Adding Text and a Title Bar Graphic

After you create new files based on the subpage.htm file, you can open the new documents in FrontPage and customize the files' contents. The first subpage you'll create is an informational page about the planet Mars. In this section you'll add text and a title bar graphic:

1   Open FrontPage, click the Open button on the toolbar, display the contents of C:\sky in the Open dialog box, and double-click the mars.htm file.

2   Click to the right of the title bar graphic, press Shift+Enter, click Insert Picture From File on the Standard toolbar, display the contents of C:\sky\images, and double-click t_skyguide.gif. The mars.htm page is a subpage of the Sky Guide, so it should display the Sky Guide subtitle bar.

3   With your cursor still located at the end of the Sky Guide graphic, press your Delete key twice to bring the table closer to the t_skyguide.gif image.

4   Right-click the t_skyguide.gif image, select Picture Properties, click the General tab, type **Sky Guide** in the Alternative Representations Text box, and click OK.

   Now you'll add some text to the Web page's table.

5   Open C:\sky, and then double-click mars.doc (*not* mars.htm) to open the Word document.

6   Arrange your desktop so that you can see some portion of the Word document's text as well as mars.htm in FrontPage, similar to the layout shown on the left in Figure 10-22.

7   Click within the Word document, and press Ctrl+A to select the entire contents of the Word document.

Tip   You can type text directly into the table (as you'll see later in this project), but we provided text for this page so that you wouldn't have to retype the information. You can also copy and paste information into FrontPage, or you can use the File command on the Insert menu to import text from another file.

---

8   Drag the selected text in the Word document into the large white portion of the table in mars.htm (which is technically the fourth cell in the first row of the table). The text should fill the table cell, as shown on the right in Figure 10-22.

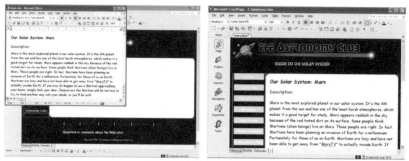

Figure 10-22   For this project you can drag text from a Word document into your Web page. Because you did not enter width or height limitations for the cell, the cell expands to accommodate the copied text.

9   Save your Web page, and close the Word document.

Modifying Cascading Style Sheet (CSS) Settings

To help format your Web pages' contents, you can create external and embedded *cascading style sheets* from within FrontPage. An *external style sheet* means that formatting code is placed in a separate document that your Web page links to, while an *embedded style sheet* places formatting code within the current Web page's source code.

Lingo   A *cascading style sheet* contains code that defines the appearance and formatting of a Web page or group of Web pages.

When you use style sheet settings, you define the style for a particular page element—such as a heading 3 or bulleted list item—and then browsers (and FrontPage) will automatically apply the style settings to all instances of the element. For instance, if you want all heading 3 type headings to display in blue, you only have to modify the style settings for the h3 element. After you save the modified settings, all heading 3s will appear blue.

In this section you'll use FrontPage to customize styles by defining an embedded style sheet. Therefore, the styles you define on the mars.htm page will only apply to the mars.htm page. To define embedded styles in FrontPage, follow these steps:

1   Ensure that mars.htm displays in Normal view in FrontPage, and then click Style on the Format menu.

2   In the Style dialog box, click the List drop-down arrow, and choose HTML tags. A list of HTML tags displays in the Styles list.

    First, you will specify to display all heading 3 elements in blue and 12 point.

3   In the Styles list, choose h3, as shown in Figure 10-23.

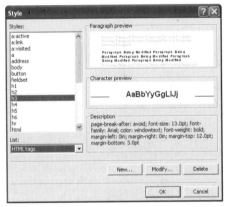

Figure 10-23   You can define HTML styles by selecting the style you want to format from the list of HTML tags in the Style dialog box.

4   Click Modify, click Format in the Modify Style text box, and click Font.

5   In the Font dialog box, click 12 pt in the Size list box, click the Color drop-down arrow, click the blue color square, and click OK three times to close the open dialog boxes.

    Both the *Description:* and the *Planetary Data:* headings should now appear blue and in 12 point. Now, you'll replace the standard black bullets in the bulleted list with custom bullets:

6   Click Style on the Format menu, click HTML tags in the List box, select li in the Syles list, and click Modify.

7   In the Modify Style dialog box, click Format, and click Numbering.

8   In the Bullets And Numbering dialog box, click Browse, display the contents of the C:\sky\images folder in the Select Picture dialog box,

and double-click bullet_star.gif.to complete the Bullets And Number dialog box.

9   Click OK three times to close the open dialog boxes. The bulleted list on your page should display with star images in Normal view as shown in Figure 10-24, and your source code should now include embedded styles as shown in Figure 10-25 (with the orange color high-lighting the formatting information you added in the preceding steps).

10   Save mars.html and ensure that it displays in Normal view in preparation for the next section.

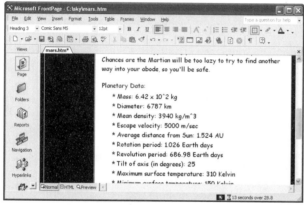

Figure 10-24   The newly defined styles colors heading 3s blue and displays the bulleted list with star bullets.

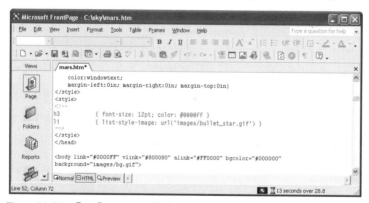

Figure 10-25   FrontPage automatically generates embedded style information.

Inserting a Thumbnail Image

Now that you've imported and formatted text in your Mars Web page, you're ready to add an image. In this section you'll insert a thumbnail image of Mars, which means viewers will be able to click a small image of Mars to view a larger version of the picture. Providing a thumbnail image speeds your page's download time and provides viewers the option to download a larger version of the picture if they desire. To insert a thumbnail image in FrontPage, follow these steps:

1   In FrontPage, click to the right of *Our Solar Sytem: Mars* (the top line of the inserted text), click Insert Picture From File on the Standard toolbar, and double-click the mars.jpg image from the C:\sky\images folder. A very large picture of Mars takes over your view in FrontPage.

2   Click Mars and then display the Pictures toolbar (if the toolbar doesn't display automatically, choose Toolbars on the View menu, and then choose Pictures). Figure 10-26 shows the Mars picture along with the Pictures toolbar.

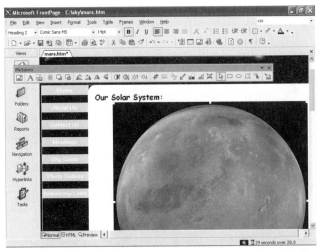

Figure 10-26   You can create a thumbnail image of Mars directly in FrontPage.

3   With the picture of mars still selected, click the Auto Thumbnail button in the Pictures toolbar (it's the third button from the left). A 100-by-100-pixel version of Mars is created from the larger version of mars.jpg. The smaller graphic is automatically named mars_small.jpg.

4   Right-click the thumbnail picture of Mars, choose Picture Properties, select the Appearance tab if necessary, and configure the properties as follows:

Option	Setting
Alignment	Right
Border Thickness	0
Horizontal Spacing	15
Vertical Spacing	10

Tip   If you want your thumbnail to display larger than 100 x 100 pixels, you can select the Specify Size check box in the Picture Properties dialog box and change the size of the thumbnail image.

---

5   Click OK, and then click in the text to deselect the graphic.

6   Right-click anywhere on the table and choose Table Properties. The Table Properties dialog box opens.

7   In the Borders section, type **0** in the Size text box, and then click OK.

8   Click Save, click Change Folder in the Save Embedded Files dialog box, double-click the images folder, click OK twice, and then click the Preview view tab (or choose Preview In Browser on the File menu). Your mars.htm page should now look similar to Figure 10-27, and the small graphic is automatically linked to mars.jpg.

Tip   To test the thumbnail link, click the Preview view tab and then click the thumbnail picture of Mars. Click the Normal view tab to return to working view.

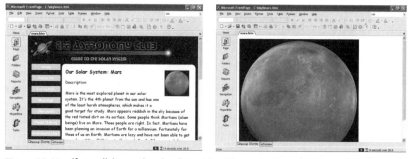

Figure 10-27   If you click your thumbnail graphic while previewing your page, a large image of Mars should display.

9   Close mars.htm.

Note   The project image files you downloaded from *www.creationguide.com/projects/ chapter10/images* include neptune.jpg and saturn.jpg, which are pictures of Neptune and Saturn (respectively) that you can use if you'd like to create additional planet informational pages for extra practice.

Congratulations! You've completed your first subpage for the astronomy club's Web site. No reason to stop now—in the next section, you'll learn how to add an image map.

Creating an Image Map

In this section you'll create an image map on the Sky Guide's main subpage. You'll create the image map from a picture of the solar system. You'll format the solar system image so that when users click the picture of Mars, the mars.htm page you created in the preceding section will display. To accomplish this (it's easier than it sounds), follow these steps:

1   Open FrontPage, click the Folders icon in the Views Bar, and double-click the skyguide.htm file.

2   Click to the right of the title bar graphic, press Shift+Enter, click Insert Picture From File on the Standard toolbar, and double-click t_skyguide.gif.

3   With the cursor still located at the end of the Sky Guide graphic, press your Delete key twice to bring the table closer to the t_skyguide.gif image.

4   Right-click the t_skyguide.gif image, select Picture Properties, click the General tab, type **Sky Guide** in the Alternative Representations Text box, and click OK.

  Now you'll add some content to the Web page's table.

5   Click in the large table cell to the right of the Home button, and type **This Month's Featured Item: Our Solar System.**

6   Select the text, click the Center icon on the Formatting toolbar, and select Comic Sans (or Comic Sans MS) in the Font drop-down list.

7   Click after the word *System*, and press Shift+Enter twice.

8   Type **Click a planet to go to the planet's information page. Note: Only Mars is active at this time.**

9   Click in the blank area between the two text components you added in steps 5 and 8.

10   On the Standard toolbar, click Insert Picture From File, navigate to the C:\sky\images folder if necessary, and double-click solarsystem.gif.

11   Right-click anywhere on the table, choose Table Properties, set the Border Size to 0 in the Table Properties dialog box, and then click OK.

12   Click Save on the toolbar. Then preview your Web page. Your page should appear similar to the Web page shown in Figure 10-28.

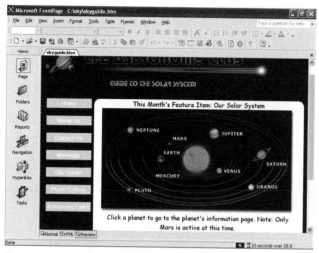

Figure 10-28   You'll use the solar system picture to create an image map.

13 Return to Normal view in FrontPage.

14 Click the solar system image. The Pictures toolbar should open automatically. Notice the Rectangular Hotspot, Circular Hotspot, and Polygonal Hotspot tools located toward the right end of the Pictures toolbar.

Lingo   A *hotspot* is a clickable area on an image that's linked to another Web page or another area on the current page.

---

15 Click the Polygonal Hotspot tool, and then click multiple points around Mars and the Mars label in the solar system graphic to create a polygon, as shown in Figure 10-29. When you complete the polygon, the Insert Hyperlink dialog box opens automatically. If necessary, click Existing File Or Web Page in the *Link To:* section.

Figure 10-29   The Hotspot tools on the Pictures toolbar enable you to draw clickable areas on images.

16 In the Insert Hyperlink dialog box, double-click mars.htm (*not* mars.doc) in the C:\sky file list.

Tip   If you create a line that you don't want to use, right-click to remove the existing lines, and start over.

---

17 Create shapes around the remaining planets (if desired) that point to future pages, such as mercury.htm, venus.htm, earth.htm, jupiter.htm, saturn.htm, uranus.htm, neptune.htm, and pluto.htm.

18 Save skyguide.htm, preview the page in Preview view, move your cursor over Mars (notice that the cursor changes to a hand), and click Mars to see whether your link works.

19 Click the Normal view tab, close skyguide.htm, and close FrontPage.

You're well on your way to creating the astronomy club's Web site. The final subpage you'll create is a form within the contact.htm page.

Creating Forms

At this point you should be getting used to adding elements and configuring settings in FrontPage. As we mentioned at the beginning of the chapter, the trick lies in knowing where to find tools and configuration menus. In this section you'll create an online form. As you might recall from Chapter 2, an online form enables users to enter information into text boxes. Then when users click the form's Submit button, the results will be sent to your e-mail address.

Note   When you use Forms on your Web site, your server must support FrontPage Server Extensions and you must publish the form using the publishing tool in FrontPage.

Caution   *Do not display your form in Preview view before you publish it to the Web.* If you do, FrontPage 2002 adds code that inhibits your page from publishing properly. When you create a form, you must publish it to the Web and then preview the form in either FrontPage or your browser.

Preparing the Contacts Page

The first step to creating a form on the Contacts page is to prepare the page by adding a title bar and inserting title text, as described in the following steps:

1 Open FrontPage, click Folder in the Views Bar, and double-click the contact.htm file.

2 Click to the right of the title bar, press Shift+Enter, click Insert Picture From File, display the contents of C:\sky\images, and double-click t_contact.gif.

3   With the cursor still located at the end of the Contact Information graphic, press your Delete key twice to bring the table closer to the t_contact.gif image.

4   Right-click the t_contact.gif image, select Picture Properties, click the General tab, type **Contact Page** in the Alternative Representations Text box, and click OK.

Inserting a Form Area and Adding Labels

Now that the Contacts page is ready for action, you're set to create an online form. First you'll insert the standard form box and then enter labels for the form's text boxes, option buttons, and selection boxes:

1   Click in the large table cell to the right of the Home button, point to Form on the Insert menu, and choose Form. An outlined area displays within the table that contains Submit and Reset buttons, as shown in Figure 10-30.

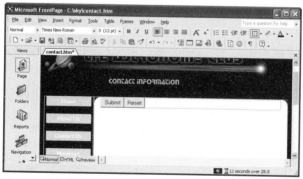

Figure 10-30   The first step toward creating a form is to insert a form component, which automatically includes the Submit and Reset buttons.

2   With the cursor positioned to the left of the Submit button, type **Name:**, and then press Shift+Enter.

3   Type **E-mail Address:** and press Enter.

4   Type **Are you currently a club member?** and press Enter.

5   Type **If so, how often do you attend our monthly meetings?** and press Enter.

6   Type **Please let us know how you found our Web site (check all that apply):**, press Shift+Enter, type **I attended a meeting.**, press Shift+Enter, type **I found it in a search engine.**, press Shift+Enter, type **A friend told me.**, and then press Enter.

7   Type **Please enter comments or questions here:**, press Shift+Enter, and then press Enter. Your form should appear similar to the form in progress shown in Figure 10-31.

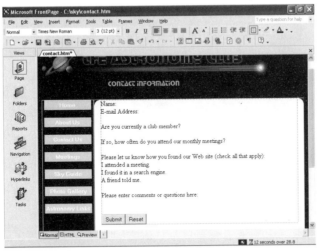

Figure 10-31   The form in progress shows only the form's text and basic buttons.

Creating Form Fields

You're now ready to enter the form fields, the areas in which viewers select or enter text so that they can submit information.

> **Note**   We'll format the form fields in a moment—so don't be concerned if the form fields don't look quite right at this point.

1   Click after Name:, press the spacebar, point to Form on the Insert menu, and choose Textbox.

2   Click after E-mail Address:, press the spacebar, point to Form on the Insert menu, and choose Textbox.

3   Click after Are You Currently A Club Member?, point to Form on the Insert menu, choose Option Button, type **Yes**, press your spacebar, point to Form on the Insert menu, choose Option Button, and then type **No**.

4   Click after If So, How Often Do You Attend Our Monthly Meetings?, press the spacebar, point to Form on the Insert menu, and choose Drop-Down Box.

5   Click before I Attended A Meeting, point to Form on the Insert menu, choose Checkbox, and press your spacebar.

6 Click before I Found It In A Search Engine, point to Form on the Insert menu, choose Checkbox, and press your spacebar.

7 Click before A Friend Told Me, point to Form on the Insert menu, choose Checkbox, and press your spacebar.

8 Click below Please Enter Comments Or Questions Here, point to Form on the Insert menu, and choose Text Area.

9 Click Save. Your form should now display as shown in Figure 10-32.

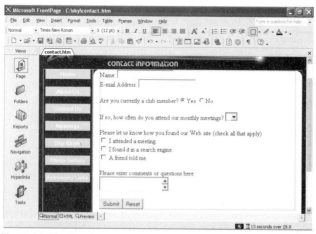

Figure 10-32   Your form should now include labels and unformatted form fields.

Configuring Form Field Properties

You now have the bulk of the form created. The next step is to configure the properties for each form field and specify the form's overall properties. So get your right-click finger ready—you're about to configure some property forms.

1 Right-click the field next to Name and select Form Field Properties.

2 In the Name field of the Text Box Properties dialog box, type **Name**, set the Width In Characters to **25** (as shown in Figure 10-33), enter **1** in the Tab Order text box, and then click OK.

Figure 10-33   You use the Text Box Properties dialog box to set the properties for a text box.

> **Note**   The Tab Order form field property specifies the order the cursor will move
> through a form if a user pressesTab to move from field to field.

3   Right-click the field next to E-mail Address, select Form Field Properties, type **Email**, set the Width In Characters to **30**, enter **2** in the Tab
Order text box, and then click OK.

4   Right-click the Yes button, choose Form Field Properties, type **Member**
in the Group Name text box, type **Yes** in the Value text box, ensure
that Selected is selected in the Initial State section, enter **3** in the Tab
Order text box, and click OK.

5   Right-click the No button, choose Form Field Properties, type **Member**
in the Group Name text box, type **No** in the Value text box, ensure that
Not Selected is selected in the Initial State section, and click OK.

> **Note**   Note that you don't have to set a tab order for both the Yes and No options.
> Because the options are members of the same group, users can move to the group by
> pressing the Tab key. Then they can select an option by using the arrow keys. When
> they're ready to move to the next section of the form, they can pressTab.

6   Right-click the If So, How Often Do You Attend Our Monthly Meetings?
drop-down list box, and choose Form Field Properties. The Drop-
Down Box Properties dialog box opens.

7   Type **Attendance** in the Name text box, enter **4** in the Tab Order text
box, and then click Add. The Add Choice dialog box opens.

8   In the Add Choice dialog box, enter **Every meeting**, choose the
Selected option in the Initial State section, and click OK.

9   Click Add, type **Every other month**, and click OK.

10   Click Add, type **Couple times a year**, and click OK.

11   Click Add, type **Never**, and click OK. Your Drop-Down Box Properties
dialog box should look like the one shown in Figure 10-34.

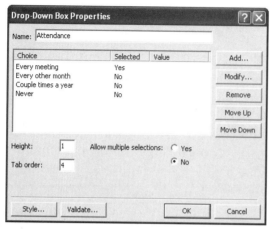

Figure 10-34   The completed Drop-Down Box Properties dialog box shows all the options and which option will be selected by default.

12 Click OK.

13 Right-click the first check box, choose Form Field Properties, enter **FoundWebSite** in the Name text box, enter **Attended a meeting** in the Value text box, enter **5** in the Tab Order text box, and click OK.

14 Right-click the second check box, choose Form Field Properties, enter **FoundWebSite** in the Name text box, enter **Search engine** in the Value text box, enter **6** in the Tab Order text box, and click OK.

15 Right-click the third check box, choose Form Field Properties, enter **FoundWebSite** in the Name text box, enter **Friend** in the Value text box, enter **7** in the Tab Order text box, and click OK.

16 Right-click the scrolling text box, choose Form Field Properties, type **Comments** in the Name text box, enter **40** in the Width In Characters text box, enter **8** in the Tab Order text box, enter **3** in the Number Of Lines text box, and click OK.

17 Right-click the Submit button, choose Form Field Properties, enter **Submit** in the Name text box, enter **9** in the Tab Order text box, and click OK.

18 Right-click the Reset button, choose Form Field Properties, enter **Reset** in the Name text box, enter **Clear Form** in the Value/Label text box, enter **10** in the Tab Order text box, and click OK.

19 Click the Back arrow once and press your spacebar to insert a space between the Submit and Clear Form buttons.

20 Click before the Name: label at the top of the form, and press Shift+Enter. Then save your work without previewing the form

(remember, in order for your form to work properly, you need to publish your form to the Web before you preview the form).

Naming Your Fields   Generally, you should supply a name for every form field. Field names
help identify information after it's submitted to you as well as enable browsers to differentiate like
elements. You can configure your form to display each field's name along with the submitted data.
This setup will help you to quickly see what information was submitted in response to which form
field entries. For example, here's what a filled-in online form and confirmation page might look like:

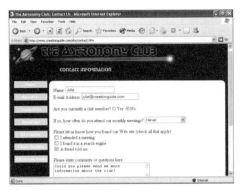

Next, you would receive an e-mail message containing the submitted information similar to
the following message:

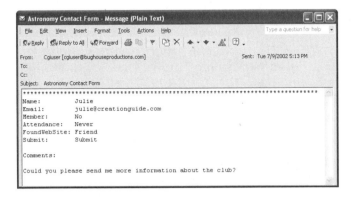

The images displayed here show how the form you're creating in this project will display after
you publish the contact form to a Web server.

Completing the Contacts Page

To complete the Contacts page, you need to hide the table's borders and set the
form's properties.

1   Right-click anywhere on the table, choose Table Properties, enter **0** in the Size text box in the Borders area, and click OK.

2   Right-click the form, and choose Form Properties. The Form Properties dialog box opens.

3   In the Form Properties dialog box, ensure that the Send To option is selected, enter your own e-mail address in the E-mail Address text box, and enter **Astronomy Contact Form** in the Form Name text box.

4   In the Form Properties dialog box, click Options, click the E-mail Results tab, ensure that the Include Field Names check box is selected, and enter **Astronomy Contact Information** in the Subject Line text box. Selecting the Include Field Names option specifies that the field names should accompany the submitted information, and the subject line text will appear in e-mail messages you receive after users click the Submit button.

5   Click the Confirmation Page tab, type **thankyou.htm** in the URL Of Confirmation Page text box (we created a simple thankyou.htm file for you, which you should've downloaded to the C:\sky folder from *www.creationguide.com/projects/chapter10/text*), click OK twice, and then click No.

6   Save and close contact.htm, and then close FrontPage.

Note   To view a published version of the contacts page, visit *www.creationguide.com/sky/contact.htm*.

That's it for your subpage experimentation for this project. You've worked through a number of FrontPage features that you should be able to use when you create your own Web site. But before we wrap up this project, we need to create the astronomy club's home page.

Creating a Home Page in FrontPage

Last but not least, you're ready to create the home page. Creating this page might seem a little tricky at moments, and we'll readily admit that it's probably the most advanced procedure we describe in this book. However challenging, though, we want to give you an inkling of where you can go from here if we've inspired you to continue designing Web sites. (And we hope you do!) Furthermore, we thought you might be interested in seeing how tables and graphics are sometimes used to create advanced page layout designs. Anyway, let's start by setting up the home page's framework.

Setting Up the Home Page Framework

To begin, follow these steps:

1   Open FrontPage, open C:\sky\subpage.htm, choose Save As on the File menu, click the Change Title button, enter **Astronomy Club's Official Web Site** in the Set Page Title dialog box, click OK, enter **index.htm** in the File Name text box, and click Save.

2   Right-click a blank area of the page, click Page Properties, click the Background tab, click the Text color box in the Colors section, choose White, and click OK.

3   Place your cursor before the Home link in the text-based navigation bar, drag to select everything above the text-based navigation bar (including the title bar and logo graphic), right-click the selected elements, and click Cut.

4   Press Enter, and then press the Up arrow button (or click in the space above the text-based navigation bar).

5   Click Insert Picture From File, display the contents of C:\sky\images if necessary, and double-click titlebar-home.gif and press Enter.

6   Click Web Component on the Standard toolbar, choose Dynamic Effects, and double-click Marquee. The Marquee Properties dialog box opens.

7   In the Marquee Properties dialog box, type **Our Next Meeting is February 21. Reserve your space today!** in the Text text box—this is the message that will scroll across the page.

8   Choose the Slide option in the Behavior section, clear the Continuously check box in the Repeat section, and enter **1** in the Repeat text box, as shown in Figure 10-35.

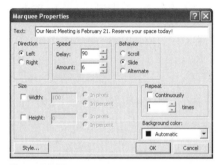

Figure 10-35   Among other properties, you can specify whether marquee text scrolls continuously or scrolls a predetermined number of times.

9 Click the Style button, click Format, click Font, choose Comic Sans (or Comic Sans MS) in the font list box, choose White in the Color box, and click OK three times to close all open dialog boxes.

10 Press the Right arrow to deselect the marquee component, press Enter, click the Table button in the toolbar, and create a 1-row, 5-column table. Your index.htm page should look similar to the page shown in Figure 10-36.

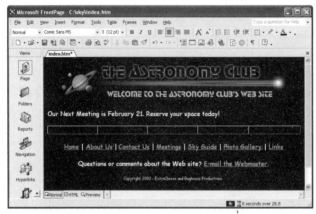

Figure 10-36   The astronomy club's home page is based on a custom table.

11 Right-click the table, choose Table Properties, click the Alignment drop-down list, select Center, ensure the Specify Width check box is selected, enter **580** in the Specify Width text box, choose the In Pixels option, ensure that Cell Padding and Cell Spacing are set to 0, and click OK.

12 Select all five table cells, right-click the selected cells, choose Cell Properties, set Vertical Alignment to Top, and then click OK.

13 Right-click the titlebar-home.gif graphic, choose Picture Properties, click the General tab, type **Welcome to the Astronomy Club Web Site** in the Alternative Representations Text box, and click OK.

14 Click Save.

Assembling the Main Graphic

You're now going to insert pieces of an image that has been cut to fit into the table. The image, before we chopped it into pieces, is shown in Figure 10-37. The reason we divided the image into separate graphics is that we wanted to use *Dynamic HTML (DHTML)* to create a glowing rollover effect whenever users place their cursor over a hyperlinked area. If we hadn't wanted to show the roll-over effect (and demonstrate how you can chop up and reassemble pictures when necessary), we could've created an image map similar to the solar system image map you created on the Sky Guide page earlier in this chapter.

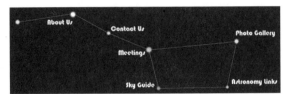

Figure 10-37 The original Big Dipper image shown here was chopped into pieces for this project.

Note *DHTML (Dynamic HTML)* is a technology that provides Web pages with the capability to change and update automatically in response to a user's actions, such as displaying a graphic or additional information in response to a user's mouse movement.

---

1 In index.htm, click in cell 1, click Insert Picture From File on the Standard toolbar, display the contents of C:\sky\images, and double-click bigdip1.gif.

2 Click in cell 2 and insert b_aboutus.gif.

3 Click in cell 3, insert bigdip2.gif (a transparent graphic that will help to align the other graphics), press Shift+Enter, insert b_contact.gif, press Shift+Enter, insert b_meetings.gif, press Shift+Enter, and insert b_skyguide.gif.

4 Click in cell 4 and insert bigdip3.gif.

5 Click in cell 5, and insert bigdip4.gif (another transparent image), press Shift+Enter, insert b_gallery.gif, press Shift+Enter, insert bigdip5.gif, press Shift+Enter, and insert b_links.gif. Your index.htm page should display as shown in Figure 10-38.

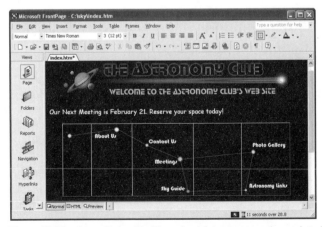

Figure 10-38 After piecing Big Dipper back into shape, you're ready to link the Big Dipper pieces to your subpages.

Creating Links within the Main Graphic

The next step is to link each image that contains a button name in the Big Dipper graphic to the appropriate subpage:

1   Right-click the About Us text, choose Hyperlink, ensure that the sky folder appears in the Look In text box, type **aboutus.htm** in the Address text box (or select the aboutus.htm file in the file list), and click OK.

> **Tip**   To speed up the hyperlinking process, you can double-click file names in the file list in the Insert Hyperlink dialog box instead of typing each file name into the Address text box.

2   Link the remaining graphics as follows:

Graphic	Link To
Contact Us	contact.htm
Meetings	meetings.htm
Sky Guide	skyguide.htm
Photo Gallery	gallery.htm
Astronomy Links	links.htm

3   Click Save.

Adding Dynamic HTML to the Main Graphic

Next you'll add the rollover effect to each hyperlinked area in the table by using the FrontPage DHTML toolbar:

1   Select the About Us button and choose Dynamic HTML Effects on the Format menu. The DHTML Effects toolbar displays. You'll configure the toolbar to display as shown in Figure 10-39.

Figure 10-39   The DHTML Effects toolbar assists you in applying dynamic effects to your Web pages.

2   In the On drop-down list, choose Mouse Over.

3   In the Apply drop-down list, choose Swap Picture, click the Choose Settings drop-down list, select Choose Picture, and then double-click b_aboutus2.gif in the C:\sky\images folder.

4 Repeat steps 1 through 3 for each linked area, linking the secondary graphics as follows:

Link	Picture File
Contact Us	b_contact2.gif
Meetings	b_meetings2.gif
Sky Guide	b_skyguide2.gif
Photo Gallery	b_gallery2.gif
Astronomy Links	b_links2.gif

5 Close the DHTML Effects toolbar.

6 Right-click the table, choose Table Properties, enter **0** in the Size text box in the Borders section, click Apply, and then click OK.

7 Click Save and then preview your work.

8 Click the Normal view tab to return to your working area.

Adding Finishing Touches to the Home Page

Finally, to complete the home page, you'll insert counter and last-modified date elements. To insert a counter, follow these steps:

1 On index.htm, click after the Links hyperlink in the text navigation bar, press Enter, point to Web Component on the Insert menu, and choose Hit Counter in the Component Type list. Click Finish and the Hit Counter Properties dialog box displays.

> **Note** Counter elements won't display until you publish your FrontPage Web.

2 In the Choose A Counter Style list, select the green digital number style (it's the last style on the list), then choose the Fixed Number Of Digits check box, accept the default setting of 5 digits, and click OK.

3 Press Enter, choose Date And Time on the Insert menu, and click OK on the Date And Time dialog box. The date will automatically update each time you edit the page.

4 Save index.htm, and then click Preview. Your page should look similar to the page shown in Figure 10-40. After you publish your sky Web site, your home page will display the counter instead of placeholder text.

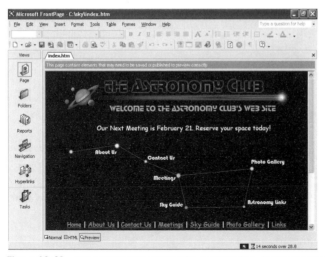

Figure 10-40   The completed index.htm file is shown here in Preview mode.

You've completed the home page and most of the subpages for the astronomy club's Web site. Great work! You should now understand some of the cool capabilities of FrontPage. We hope this newfound knowledge will help you as you design and create your own Web sites.

Tip   To see a live version of the astronomy club Web site created in this project, visit *www.creationguide.com/sky*.

As far as the astronomy club's site, the only remaining step is to publish the C:\sky Web by using the Publish feature in FrontPage. Be sure to read the following section as well as refer to Chapter 11 before you upload your astronomy club Web site to your server space.

A Word about Publishing

When you create Webs in FrontPage, your best bet is to upload the pages using the FrontPage Publish Web feature, especially if you've inserted items that rely on FrontPage Server Extensions (such as forms and counters). To publish your site, select the Publish Web option on the File menu. You should have your server space and address already lined up. Furthermore, you should have ensured with your hosting service that FrontPage Server Extensions are supported. For more information about publishing FrontPage Webs and using FrontPage Server Extensions, contact your Internet service provider (ISP), see Chapter 11, and refer to the help files in FrontPage.

Additional Resources

Here are a couple FrontPage references we've found helpful:

- Buyens, Jim. *Microsoft FrontPage Version 2002 Inside Out.* Redmond, WA: Microsoft Press, 2001. This book is a complete FrontPage documentation source.

- *www.microsoft.com/frontpage* is the definitive online resource for FrontPage.

Key Points

- FrontPage is a full-featured HTML editing program.

- You can use FrontPage to easily create advanced Web page features such as button rollover effects, image maps, thumbnails, forms, counters, and other Web page components.

- The FrontPage interface enables you to display your Web pages in Normal (working) view, HTML view, and Preview view.

- Learning FrontPage opens doors to using other full-service HTML editors because it exemplifies the types of capabilities HTML editors can provide.

- Before you create your Web pages using FrontPage, you should ensure that your Web hosting service supports FrontPage Server Extensions. (These days, most servers support extensions to some degree.)

- Before you start creating Web pages in FrontPage, you should set up a Web, which provides special formatting to a selected folder.

- You can simplify the process of building a Web site by creating a standard template that you can save as subpages.

- The key to creating Webs in FrontPage is keeping your files organized, knowing where to find FrontPage tools and menu options, and experimenting with various settings.

- For best results, upload FrontPage files using the Publish Web feature.

Part III

The Rest: Going Live and Moving On

Ten years ago, a couple friends of ours hatched a plan to build a cabin in the White Mountains. It all started one day when they were chatting over coffee. Their conversation turned to vacations and getaways, and soon they were half-jokingly sketching their "dream" mountain cabin. Not long after their initial conversation, they found themselves talking to an architect. In a few weeks, the blueprints were solidified, and they were gathering supplies and laying the cabin's foundation. Within the year, the cabin was built. But they didn't stop there. Ever since, they've been improving their cabin. They regularly take on "big jobs" (such as building cabinetry and a stone fireplace) as well as "not-so-big" tasks (such as creating a rock garden and hand-sewing drapes). As a result of our friends' hard work, attention to detail, and dedication, even the most casual passerby can see that our friends' cabin is a unique and well-loved mountain escape.

You might be wondering—How in the world does this little story relate to Web site development? Fortunately, the answer's simple, and it serves as a foundation for Part III. Specifically, after you post your Web site (as described in Chapter 11), you should count on providing continuing attention to your Web pages (as discussed in Chapter 12).

Chapter 11

Sending Your Web Pages into the Real World

When you create Web pages, you'll eventually be ready to display your pages online. That's what this chapter is all about—moving your pages off the "for your eyes only" desktop and onto the "for everyone to see" Internet. Most likely, you've built Web pages so that you can create a Web presence—not just as an intellectual exercise—so we'll go with that assumption.

The key to going "live" and getting your pages onto the Web is to copy your HTML documents and image files onto a server. In Chapter 5, we go over server space, domain names, and ISPs in detail, so we won't rehash those subjects here. If you need an in-depth refresher on those topics, refer to Chapter 5. If you feel comfortable moving on, here's a short list of items you'll need to gather before your Web pages can go live:

- HTML and image files, properly named and organized.

- Server space. (You can pay a monthly fee to a hosting service for server space, you can use free server space, or you can use server space your ISP provides as part of your Internet connection account.)

- A software application that enables you to transfer files from your computer to a server. (We discuss this requirement later in this chapter.)

- A Web address. (You need to purchase a domain name and register it with a hosting service, or you need to set up a Web address on a free server, or you need to obtain your Web address from your ISP—ISP server space is usually based on the ISP's domain name followed by your username.)

At this point in the book, the preceding list shouldn't sound too daunting. Furthermore, in just a bit, we describe exactly which file transfer applications you can use and how you can copy files onto a server. So even if you have a few questions about the preceding requirements, hang on—we'll address each requirement shortly.

In addition to transferring your files to a server, you have a couple other tasks to attend to. Namely, you'll need to check your Web pages after you transfer your files to a server, and you'll need to let others know that your site is available for viewing.

These three "post production" tasks—transferring files, checking live Web pages, and getting the word out—are the main points we touch on in this chapter. If you have all your files, an Internet connection, and some server space on hand, your site can be available online by the end of this chapter.

Transferring Your Files to the Internet

Having HTML and image files as well as some server space and an Internet connection means that you're ready to post your Web pages. You can transfer files across the Internet in several ways. Here are some of the methods you can use to transfer files:

- FTP programs
- Web Folders and My Network Places
- Web publishing wizards
- ISP interfaces and HTML editors
- Browsers

There's really no way around it—you're going to have to use some method to post your pages. After all, one of the most common transactions a Web designer has with a server is to *upload* HTML documents, images, and media files. Therefore, read on. Uploading is pretty straightforward as long as you keep in mind the process's main goal, which is moving files from your computer to a server *in an organized manner.*

Lingo   *Uploading* refers to the process of copying files from your computer to a server. *Downloading* refers to copying files from a server to your computer (such as when you downloaded graphics from the Creation Guide Web site to complete the projects in Part II of this book).

Whenever you upload files from your desktop to the Internet, you use FTP. The trick to transferring files using FTP is to use an application or interface that's designed specifically to serve as an FTP agent. Although that "trick" doesn't seem too profound, stating the obvious is well worth the space necessary to clarify what it means to use FTP. We've seen people's eyes glaze over as soon as we've uttered those three mysterious letters—*F-T-P.* Fortunately, as with many other Web page creation technologies, using FTP to upload Web page files isn't at all intimidating after you've gotten up to speed on a few basics.

Lingo   *FTP* is a client/server protocol that enables you to use a computer to transfer files between computers over the Internet.

FTP Applications

We think standard FTP applications provide one of the easiest and most straight-forward methods of uploading files to the Internet. Apparently we're not alone in this thinking because zillions of FTP applications are available as freeware, shareware, and commercial software. For the most part, we use a program named CuteFTP for Microsoft Windows-based PCs and Fetch for Macintosh computers. But you can find numerous other FTP applications online (free for download as well as available for purchase) and at computer software retailers.

Tip   You should be able to buy a good FTP program for a very reasonable price. Generally, purchasing an FTP application means you'll have added functionality compared to most barebones freeware and shareware utilities. Keep in mind that you probably received an FTP application from your ISP with your startup package. If so, contact your provider or leaf through your ISP documentation for application-specific instructions.

Figure 11-1 shows the interface of CuteFTP, which is a fairly typical FTP application interface.

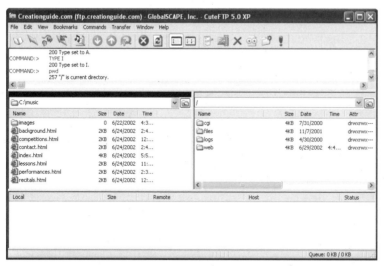

Figure 11-1   Using CuteFTP, you can drag files from your computer into a directory on your server.

The beauty of most newer FTP applications is that you can drag and drop the files you want to upload from one window into another. For example, in CuteFTP, you can display a local folder in the left pane (Figure 11-1 shows the music folder created in the Chapter 8 project) and display your server space in the right pane. To upload your Web page files, you simply select and drag the files or folders from the left pane into the right pane.

We've heard from a number of users that the most intimidating part of using an FTP application is configuring the initial connection. Fortunately, after you initially configure a connection, most FTP applications keep the connection data "on file" for future use.

Caution   Beware—if you're using a shareware program and your allotted trial time runs out, you risk losing the configuration information for your FTP connections. If this happens, you have two options: You can purchase a full-fledged copy of the shareware program, or (in some cases) you can temporarily backdate your system clock so that you can open the shareware application and retrieve your configuration information.

Even though every FTP application has a custom interface for gathering account information, you'll need to provide a few basic types of information to establish an FTP connection to a server no matter which application you use:

■ **FTP site label** A name you provide for the FTP account you're creating. The sole purpose of the site label is to help you remember which FTP account goes with which server. So be sure to name your connections logically.

■ **FTP host address** The address of your server space. For example, the Creation Guide site's host address is *ftp.creationguide.com.*

■ **FTP site username** The username you use to access your server space. An FTP site username is generally the same as your e-mail address, such as *admin@creationguide.com.* Some providers allow you to enter your username without the *@domain.com* portion, in which case only *admin* would be necessary in the preceding example.

■ **FTP site password** A password associated with your username that enables you to access your server space.

Try This! Visit *www.tucows.com or www.download.com* to find listings of available FTP programs. Download and install an FTP program of your choice, and then put the application through its paces. You can always uninstall the FTP program you downloaded and try some others if the one you chose doesn't suit your working style. If you do find a shareware program that you like, be sure to register it.

On many FTP connection forms, you'll also be asked whether you want to transfer information in ASCII, binary, or auto-detect. The default is usually auto-detect (or some variation of that term), and we recommend that you retain the default setting whenever possible.

Note You might want to write down your password and store it somewhere safe (in a place other than on your computer). When you enter your password in FTP applications and most Web publishing wizards, dots generally display in place of your password.

To create an FTP connection, you insert the proper information into the respective fields (in CuteFTP, in the Site Settings For New Site dialog box) and finalize the configuration by clicking OK, Finish, or Connect (depending on your application). After you configure an FTP connection to your server space, you can connect to the Internet, activate the FTP connection, and upload your pages. (Call your ISP or visit your ISP's help pages if you have trouble connecting.)

Note   HTML files should be transferred in ASCII, text, or DOS text mode. All other files, including images, sounds, and videos must be transferred in binary mode. Ensuring that the Auto, Auto-Detect, All Files, or Raw Data option is selected in your FTP application's options generally means that the application can differentiate between the common file types, so you won't have to worry about specifying between images and HTML files. By default, CuteFTP (as well as most other FTP applications) is configured to auto-detect common file types.

At this point we want to mention a couple uploading rules you need to follow religiously when you copy your Web page files to a server. You can't copy files and folders willy-nilly—you have to keep the process orderly; otherwise, you'll risk creating broken links and erroneously overwriting files that have the same name. (For example, most subfolders contain a file named index.html—if you don't upload your files into the proper folders, you might inadvertently replace one index.html file with another, unrelated index.html file.) Here's the key point to remember when you're actively uploading Web pages: *Retain the file and folder structure of your Web pages.*

In other words, if your Web page consists of one index.html document and a folder named *images*, make sure that you upload the index.html file and then copy or re-create the images folder in your server space and copy the graphics stored in your local images folder into the online images folder. As mentioned, retaining your site's structure is crucial to avoiding broken links on your pages.

Here's another extremely important point: *Name your online folders with exactly the same names as your local folders.* Don't rename any folders or files when you're uploading—especially don't rename any folders that contain Web page images. (By the way, accidentally creating a folder named *image* when it should be *images* constitutes renaming a folder; furthermore, altering capitalization and adding or removing spaces within file and folder names also qualifies as an unacceptable renaming practice.) The reason for retaining your existing naming structure is simple—your HTML document probably contains HTML commands that tell browsers where to look for graphics. Image instructions (contained within the <IMG> tag, if you worked through the HTML project in Chapter 8) specifically point to images stored in a particularly named folder. If you change a folder's name without changing the HTML commands, browsers won't know where to find your Web page's graphics and the graphics won't display on your Web page. To reiterate, uploading is *not* the time to rename your Web page folders and files. In fact, the opposite is true: *Uploading is the time to replicate your local Web page file setup onto a server in as exact a manner as possible.*

After you've successfully copied your Web page files onto a server, terminate your FTP connection, open your browser, and enter your Web page's Uniform Resource Locator (URL) in your browser's Address bar. Your Web page's

URL is similar to the FTP address we mentioned earlier except that *www* appears in place of *ftp* (for example, the FTP address for the Creation Guide site is *ftp.creationguide.com* and the Web address is *www.creationguide.com*). If you've uploaded an index.htm or index.html HTML document into your domain's root directory, you should be able to access your new home page by entering your URL in your browser's Address bar without having to type a filename. For example, you can simply type *www.creationguide.com* instead of *www.creationguide.com/index.html* to view the Creation Guide home page.

As you can see, most FTP applications serve the sole purpose of providing a means to transfer and manipulate (rename, delete, move, and so forth) files across a network. If you're looking for other file transfer options or a more automated approach, you'll find that more than a few applications have built-in FTP capabilities, as you'll discover in the next section.

Tip   ISPs generally tell you where you should store your Web page files within your server space. On our server space for the Creation Guide site, we copy all our information into the ISP-generated folder named *web*. Check with your ISP to see whether you must work within similar parameters. Some ISPs simply provide you with the top-level folder that you can use to store your Web page files.

Web Folders and My Network Places

Microsoft provides another method of uploading and managing a Web site's files and folders—using My Network Places to create and manage network places that contain Web folders and files. My Network Places was introduced in Microsoft Office 2000, and it carries on in Office 2002 (prior to Office 2000, the feature was known strictly as Web Folders and it was a tad more cumbersome than My Network Places). Using My Network Places, you'll be able use the familiar Windows interface to conduct the file and folder management tasks necessary for you to create and maintain your Web site.

Caution   Before you can set up a link to your Web space in My Network Places, you must ensure that your Web server supports network places. The network places feature requires the Web Extender Client (WEC) protocol and Microsoft FrontPage extensions, or the WebDAV protocol and Internet Information Services (IIS). Call your hosting service or check the service's online FAQ pages to see if your Web space qualifies to take advantage of network places technology.

Tip   You might have to activate FrontPage extensions on your hosting service to create a network place. Although this task might sound a little daunting, most likely, it's a matter of a few mouse clicks (depending on your hosting service's support Web site). To find out how to turn on FrontPage Server Extensions on your hosting service, perform a quick search in your hosting service's Support section or call the support number.

Basically, when you use the network places feature, you can create shortcuts to network locations that contain folders stored on your Web space. After you create a link to a network place, you can manipulate the contents of Web folders stored in your Web space (typically, your *Web space* is the space you purchase on your hosting service's server) in the same manner you manipulate local files and folders. The difference is that changes made to files in a Web folder are made to the online files when you save your changes. In short, a network place serves as a shortcut to the Web folders (and the folders' contents) on your server space.

Lingo   *My Network Places* enables you to create shortcuts on your desktop to files and folders located on an Internet or intranet server.

You can access network places and Web folders in a couple ways. Specifically, you can:

■   Display your network places directly by double-clicking My Network Places on your desktop or by choosing My Network Places on the Start menu, which enables you to create new network places as well as open existing links.

■   Create a new network place or link to an existing network place from within an Office application, such as in Microsoft Word. After you set up or link to a network place, you can save files and folders directly to the network place from within the application.

Note   In views other than My Network Places, Windows also provides the options to Publish This Folder To The Web or Publish This File To The Web (depending on the type of item that's currently selected), as described later in this chapter. When you select a folder or file and click either of the preceding options, Windows enables you to copy the folder or file to a Web storage space, such as MSN or Xdrive Plus. This feature caters to people who want to share, transfer, and store non-HTML documents on the Web as well as Web pages and images.

As mentioned, you can view your network places by opening My Network Places, as shown in Figure 11-2. Notice that the My Network Places window includes a link named *Add A Network Place* in the Network Tasks section along the left side of the window. (You can probably guess the purpose of that small gem!)

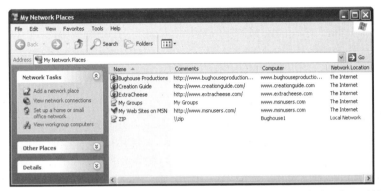

Figure 11-2   You can access and configure network places and Web folders from within the My Network Places window.

When you open a network place folder and view its contents, you'll see a list of online folders and files, along with their associated Web addresses (URLs), as shown in Figure 11-3. Within the Web folder, you can move, copy, rename, and delete folders and files as well as view folder and file properties. You can also drag files between Web servers (if you have multiple Web sites) and between a Web server and your hard disk or other storage device (such as a floppy disk). In other words, Web folders make Web site file management as straightforward as local file management.

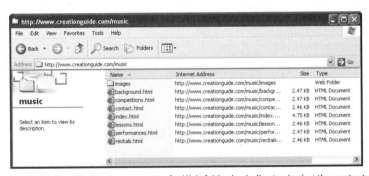

Figure 11-3   Viewing the contents of a Web folder is similar to viewing the contents of desktop folders.

Now let's take a quick look at two ways you can create network places on your system. In both instances, you'll need the following information:

- Domain information, which is your Web site's Internet address (such as *www.creationguide.com*)
- The username and password to access your server space

Creating a Network Place by Using My Network Places

To create a network place by using My Network Places, follow these steps:

1 On the Microsoft Windows XP desktop, double-click My Network Places or click My Network Places on the Start menu, and click the Add A Network Place link in the Network Tasks section.

2 In the Add Network Place wizard, click Next. The Add Network Place wizard accesses the Internet, and then provides an option to set up a network place on MSN or another network location. In most instances, you'll be setting up a network place in a location other than the MSN Web site.

3 Select the Choose Another Network Location option and click Next.

4 In the Internet Or Network Address text box, enter the Internet address of your network location (such as *www.creationguide.com*).

5 Click Next. If your Web space requires you to enter a username and password, you'll see a dialog box requesting this information, as shown in Figure 11-4.

Figure 11-4 In most cases you'll need to enter your username and password when you create a network place.

6 Enter your username and password and click OK.

7 Enter a name for the network place item in the Type A Name For This Network Place text box (for example, *Creation Guide*). The name you enter here displays in your My Network Places window, so be nice to yourself and choose a name that will make sense to you down the road.

8 Click Next, and then click Finish to complete the process.

You should now see a network place link in your My Network Places folder. You can double-click the network place icon to access the network place's Web space. If you have trouble setting up your connection, ensure that your Web server has the proper configuration to handle network places (as mentioned earlier in this chapter).

Now that you've created your Web folder, you can transfer files to your Web site by dragging them into your Web folder in your newly created network place or by saving files directly from any Office 2000 or later program. You'll find that you can use network places to modify and maintain your Web pages in a number of ways. For instance, you'll be able to open a network place and right-click filenames and folders to rename them, select and delete files and folders, replace files and folders with updated information, and otherwise modify your Web page documents and directories.

Creating a Network Place from within Word

To create a Web folder while you're working within Word, you can click the Add Network Place in the New Document task pane (click New on the File menu) or you can create a network place using the Save As dialog box. In the following steps, we show you how to create a network place using the Save As dialog box, but the steps to create a network place from the Add Network Place item in the New Document task pane are very similar:

1 In Word, click File and then click Save As. The Save As dialog box displays.

2 In the Save As dialog box, click the My Network Places icon in the Save In pane to display the contents of the My Network Places window, as shown in Figure 11-5.

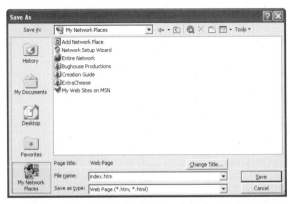

Figure 11-5 You can use the Save As dialog box to create a network place.

3 In the Save As dialog box, double-click the Add Network Place icon (shown in Figure 11-5). The Add Network Place wizard opens, as shown in Figure 11-6.

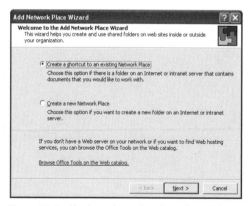

Figure 11-6 You have the option of creating a link to a network place or creating a new folder in a network place.

4 Choose the Create A Shortcut To An Existing Network Place if you want to create a link to your Web space, and then click Next.

5 In the Location text box, enter your Web site's address (such as *www.creationguide.com*), and, in the Shortcut Name text box, enter a name for the connection, as shown in Figure 11-7, and then click Finish.

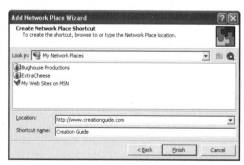

Figure 11-7 In this procedure, you enter the network place's Internet address and shortcut name in one dialog box.

> **Note** After you create a shortcut to a network location (as described in step 5), you'll be able to access the network place in the Save As dialog box and My Network Places window by double-clicking the location's icon.

6 Enter your username and password, and then click OK. The contents of the network place displays in the Save As dialog box.

At this point, you can save your Word document in a Web folder located in the network place (thereby uploading your Web page) in the same way that you save other Word documents.

7   In the Save As Type drop-down list box, specify Web Page or Web Page Filtered, specify the document's name in the File Name text box, click the Change Title button if you want to specify the Web page's title text, click the Web folder in which you want to post the HTML document, and then click Save.

Note   You'll need to establish an Internet connection before you can save a Web document in a network place.

After you save an HTML document in a Web folder in a network place, you can view the page online by entering the Web page's address in your browser's Address bar.

Other FTP Options

If you don't want to install an FTP program on your computer or if you don't want to configure My Network Places and Web folders, all hope is not lost. You can copy files to a Web server in other ways as well. Namely, you can use the FTP functions built into any of the following types of applications:

■   Web publishing wizards, such as the Web Publishing wizard that comes with Windows

■   ISP online services and HTML editors, such as FrontPage

■   Browsers, such as Microsoft Internet Explorer

Web Publishing Wizards

The Web Publishing wizard offered in Windows XP mainly serves to provide file storage and file sharing capabilities. Therefore, this tool isn't the ideal tool for publishing your Web pages (unless you're working on your MSN group site). But you can easily upload and store Web documents and other files (including images) by using the Web Publishing wizard in Windows. You might want to use this feature while you're creating documents as a backup storage medium or a means to share your working documents with others.

The Web Publishing wizard works in the same way as other wizards: It provides a series of dialog boxes that you complete to upload a folder or file to an online service provider, such as MSN or Xdrive. If you become a "serious" Web designer and you have your own Web space, you'll quickly crave the greater flexibility (and simplicity) that FTP applications and the network places tool offer.

To reiterate, the Web Publishing wizard can serve a viable purpose when it comes time to store and share files as well as possibly publish your first MSN Web site.

Note　The Web Publishing wizard is available in most versions of Windows; it was first added to Windows in the OSR2.5 release of Windows 95.

The best way to understand how the Web Publishing wizard works is to walk through the process. Because the process comes in wizard form, there's no reason for us to show you the pages you can see on your computer. To access the wizard, complete the following steps:

1　Open My Computer and select a file or folder that you want to publish to your Web space.

2　In the File And Folder Tasks section, click either Publish This Folder To The Web (if you've selected a folder) or Publish This File To The Web (if you've selected a file).

To kick off the wizard, click the Next button. Then work your way through each page, providing the proper information. When you select to publish a folder, the wizard displays a dialog box in which you can select the files you want to publish by checking or clearing check boxes, as shown in Figure 11-8. When you've completed all the wizard forms, you'll need to click Finish to upload your files. If you have the correct information on hand, the process should flow smoothly without incident, and your newly added information will display in your browser by default.

Figure 11-8　The Web Publishing wizard provides the opportunity to pick and choose the files you want to upload within a selected folder.

Try This! Select a file or folder to upload to the Web. Then work through the Web Publishing wizard to practice uploading a file or folder to an MSN personal folder.

When you place files in an MSN personal folder, the files can only be accessed with your .NET Passport. If you don't have a Passport, the .NET Passport wizard helps you to create one when you publish a file or folder to MSN. After you publish a file or folder, a link to the resource is added in your My Network Places window. Furthermore, you can access the files and folder from any Web browser in any computer, and you can add and delete files in your online folder (to access the folder's contents, double-click the link in the My Network Places window) in the same manner you add and delete files in local folders.

ISP Interfaces and HTML Editor Features

Other resources for transferring files include ISP interfaces and HTML editors. Basically, these tools are variations or hybrids of FTP applications, the network places feature, and the Web Publishing wizard. The main benefits of ISPs and HTML editor features are that the tools are often easily accessible. For example, some ISPs offer online forms you can use to upload files from your computer to the server. In fact, the Creation Guide host provides a form, but we've found it to be cumbersome, so we never use it to manage the site's files. If you're shopping for a hosting service, look into the file management services the hosting service offers. Our hosting service provides a number of quality features—such as logging statistics (including tracking the number of page hits and visitor traffic) and lots of space—so we overlooked the somewhat lame file manager feature because we knew full well that we can whip a few pages across an FTP application interface pretty quickly. In our opinion, if you're planning to use an ISP file transfer interface, make sure that the online tool is at least as intuitive as an FTP application or the Web Publishing wizard.

Similar to an ISP's online FTP forms, a number of HTML editors, including FrontPage, offer automatic file uploading features (as discussed in Chapter 10). Using an HTML editor to upload files can be extremely convenient. The main concern is that you should be keenly aware of which files are uploading and where they're going. Furthermore, know when you're replacing existing online files (which is always a good practice no matter how you're uploading files); otherwise, you might not be able to backtrack to a previous page if you decide you don't want to keep your most recent modifications. To illustrate, if you're using Internet Explorer and you have FrontPage installed, you can visit your Web site and then click the Edit button in the Internet Explorer toolbar to open a local version of your Web page in FrontPage. You can then make modifications to the page and click Save to save and upload the modified page directly to the server. When you do this, if you don't rename the newly modified page, the existing page is replaced with the updated page. Therefore, we generally reserve this feature for very simple fixes, such as correcting typos or updating dates. As you'll see in Chapter 12, you should archive your unused Web pages in case you need to revert to older pages or borrow elements from past publications. When you modify and save a page using the online access feature in FrontPage, you overwrite your existing HTML document. That's definitely something to keep in mind.

> **Tip**   You should use the FrontPage Publish Web command to initially upload Web pages you've created in FrontPage. Using FrontPage's publishing tool ensures that FrontPage features that rely on FrontPage Server Extensions are properly implemented. Even if you haven't added advanced capability to your FrontPage Web pages, we highly recommend that you use the Publish Web command to upload your Web site—at least the first time you upload the site.

To learn how to use ISP forms or an HTML editor's uploading features, refer to the application's help files or published documentation. Too many variations exist among systems to adequately provide procedural descriptions in this chapter.

Browsers as FTP Clients

Last but not least, you can use some browsers as FTP clients (depending on your Web server's setup). Most people know that you can download files from within a browser window, but few people know that you can also upload files and folders in some browser applications, Internet Explorer included. Keep in mind that your hosting service must support this feature—we've found that some sites work with browser uploads better than others. If your hosting service works well with this feature, the method is simple: You use the Address bar to display the contents of your server folder, and then you can drag files from local folders into the server folders displayed in your browser window. Furthermore, you can right-click existing online files and folders to access a shortcut menu that allows you to rename, move, and delete online files. To display your online folders, you enter the following information in the Internet Explorer Address bar: *ftp://username:password@ftp.domain.com.*

For example, an entry might look like the following: *ftp:// mmail:coffee2@ftp.microsoft.com* or *ftp://mmail:coffee2@members.ISPname.com.*

> **Tip**   To access AOL's file uploading feature, use the "myplace" or "myftpspace" keyword. If you're creating a page on AOL, your Web page's URL will be *members.aol.com/screenname/filename.*

After your server space displays, open the folder containing your Web page files and drag the files and folders into your browser window to copy the Web page components. Figure 11-9 shows FTP access to a Web folder. You can upload, delete, and rename your Web files within Internet Explorer.

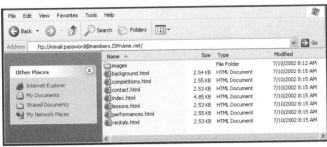

Figure 11-9 Depending on your Web server's setup, you can sometimes use Internet Explorer to transfer and manage Web files.

In this chapter we introduce a number of tools that you can use to transfer your local Web page files to a server. Try a few of the options, and see which works best for you. Because many variations exist within each category, we'd be embarking on an unrealistic task if we tried to describe every aspect of every means of transferring files to the Internet. Your best bet is to choose which uploading style you want to attempt and then give it a whirl. If you have questions, visit the application's help files or printed documentation (or e-mail us if you really get stuck). If you're uncomfortable with one process, try another approach. We're confident that if you gather the appropriate connection information and enter the information properly, you'll be able to connect to your Web space and get your pages online.

Reviewing Your Work

After you upload your Web pages, the first order of action is to surf to your pages and check your Web site's presentation. As we discussed in Part Two, you should preview your Web pages throughout the creation process—and we consider uploading part of the creation process. So check your live pages. If you've been careful, you shouldn't find too many surprises after your pages go live. Nevertheless, before you start calling all your friends and directing people to your Web site (unless you're asking them to help you review your Web site), you should view your Web pages. After you display the home page, check for the following details:

- Ensure that all images display properly. You don't want any broken image markers on your page.

- Click your links to ensure that they work, including the buttons on your navigation bar, linked logo graphics, text links, and image maps, if those appear on your page.

- Verify whether the page and its elements fit within the standard browser window. Remember—users report that having to scroll left and right to view a Web page is highly annoying.

- Complete and submit a test form to yourself if your site uses forms.

- Read each page title in the title bar for accuracy.

- Verify that text and text links are easy to read against the Web pages' backgrounds.

Basically, take the time to scrutinize your site. Click everywhere, test each interactive element, and employ your critical eye. Better to take a little extra time after uploading to check your work than to have a viewer send you an e-mail message to tell you that your Web site is lame because it doesn't display properly or respond as expected.

The last postproduction task we cover in this chapter is getting the word out that your Web site exists. The most common way to begin publicizing your site is to ensure that your Web page is readily recognizable by search engines and search directories.

Registering with Search Engines and Directories

After you upload your site and your Web pages satisfy your error-checking critical eye, you're ready to start publicizing your Web site's existence. The most popular way to start the process is to register your site with search engines and directories. You've probably used search engines, such as Yahoo!, Lycos, Google, and AltaVista, to find Web pages in the past. Now you need to approach search services from the opposite angle—instead of searching for other people's sites, you want to enable others to find your site. But first, a little background information.

The term *search engine* has come to encompass true search engines, such as HotBot, as well as directory setups, such as Yahoo!. Distinct differences exist between the two major types of information retrieval systems (although after the following brief explanation, we'll go with the crowd on this one and continue to refer to both of the following setups as search engines):

- **Search engines** Search engines create listings automatically or with a little assistance (such as a URL submission) and through spiders that crawl the Web. Whenever you post or change Web pages, search engines will eventually find your pages. Page titles, body copy, and other page elements can affect how your Web page is categorized. Generally, you don't need to supply any specific information to a search engine, although sometimes you might be required to submit your URL.

Lingo *Spiders* are automated programs that search (or *crawl*) the Internet for new Web documents. The spiders then index all the addresses they find along with content-related information in a database that search engines can use.

- **Directories** Directories rely on human input. To be listed in a directory, you must submit a short description of your site. Directory editors also write brief descriptions of the sites they review. When users run a directory search, the process looks for matches in the descriptions (not for matches within the Web pages' titles, body text, or other elements).

Popular search engines that don't require any input from you—which means they'll find your site automatically—include the following:

- All The Web (*www.alltheweb.com*)
- AltaVista (*www.altavista.com*)
- Go.com (*www.go.com*)
- Google (*www.google.com*)
- HotBot (*hotbot.lycos.com*)
- iWon (*www.iwon.com*)
- Lycos (*www.lycos.com*)
- NorthernLight (*www.northernlight.com*)
- WebCrawler (*www.webcrawler.com*)

Some search engines that require you to provide additional information or that pick and choose which sites get listed in their directories include the following:

- AOL Anywhere (*search.aol.com*) requires you to choose a category for your site to be listed and then fill out a submission form.
- Ask Jeeves (*www.askjeeves.com*) requires you to submit your URL and pay a fee.
- LookSmart (*www.looksmart.com*) requires you to choose a category for your site, write a description, provide keywords, and pay a fee, which registers you for all search engines associated with LookSmart.
- MSN (*search.msn.com*) requires you to choose a category for your site, write a description, provide keywords, and pay a fee.
- Netscape (*search.netscape.com*) requires you to choose a category for your site, write a description, provide keywords, and pay a fee.

■   Yahoo! (*www.yahoo.com*) requires you to choose a category and fill out a submission form. Yahoo! administrators decide whether and where your site gets listed.

> **Caution**   If you pay a fee to have your Web site submitted to a search engine, be sure that you note which services are included with your fee. Many fees cover registering your site with a number of services, and you don't want to inadvertently pay for registering with the same search engine twice.

> **Tip**   Some search engines query other search engines to get results from multiple sources (sometimes referred to as *metasearch engines*). A prime example is the Dogpile (*www.dogpile.com*) site.

Some sites, such as AltaVista, will list your site within a day or two after submission, but others, such as Yahoo!, can take months (many, many months) to list your site, if they choose to list your site at all.

In addition to registering your sites with search engines and directories, you can use HTML code within your HTML documents to help search engines properly classify your Web pages or ignore your Web pages altogether. The key to assisting search engines is to add META tags within your HTML document's header section.

META Tags

To some extent, you can control how search engines "see" the contents of a Web page. To do this, you can add META tags to your HTML documents that specify keywords and descriptions that should be associated with your pages. META tags are especially helpful if you want to classify a page that contains little textual content (such as a corporate splash page).

> **Tip**   Limit your META *keyword* tags to 10 to 20 keywords, with the most important keywords listed first. Likewise, some search engines will catalog only the first dozen or so words in META *description* tags, so keep your descriptions short and place the most important information up front.

To use META tags, you include them within the <HEAD></HEAD> tag set in an HTML document. (See Chapter 8 for an explanation of the <HEAD></HEAD> tag set.) You can use *keyword* or *description* META tag attributes, or both. You'll also see generator and author tags, which specify the program used to create the Web page and the Web designer's name. For instance, a simple example using all four types of META tags would look like:

```
<META NAME="generator" CONTENT="NoteTab Light 4.9">
<META NAME="author" CONTENT="Millhollon & Castrina">
<META NAME="description" CONTENT="Breakfast time!">
<META NAME="keywords" CONTENT="coffee, juice, donuts, bagels">
```

And, for comparison purposes, here's a more in-depth use of just the keywords and description META tags:

```
<HEAD>
<META NAME="keywords" CONTENT="extracheese, bughouse productions,
    web design, multimedia, Jeff Castrina, Mary Millhollon, cd-rom,
    animation, website, web, design, macromedia, director, flash,
    graphic design, illustration, writing, editing, portland,
    oregon">
<META NAME="description" CONTENT="ExtraCheese is a multimedia
    design firm specializing in Web and interactive media.
    We create Web sites, interactive CD-ROMs, Web animation,
    interactive media, and other high quality content.">
</HEAD>
```

You can also instruct search engines not to catalog your site. In other words, you can display a virtual "Do Not Enter" sign for search engines by including the following tag within your HTML document's <HEAD></HEAD> section:

```
<HEAD>
<META NAME="robots" CONTENT="noindex, nofollow">
</HEAD>
```

If you don't include META tag information in your Web pages, search engines will catalog your site according to the text information on your home page, which can work for or against your site.

Calling Attention to Your Site
Other ways you can attract attention to your site include participating in any of the following activities:

- Telling others about your site by word of mouth, e-mail messages, newsgroups, or list servers.

- Participating in reciprocal programs in which you display links on your page to other sites and vice versa (if possible).

- Displaying banner ads for other Web sites on your Web pages as well as submitting banner ads for your site on other sites.

- Getting your site publicly reviewed by a third party.

- Putting your Web site address on your printed and marketing material, including business cards, stationery, brochures, and advertisements.

After copying your Web files to a server, checking your online pages, and publicizing your site, you're ready to sit back and enjoy the fruits of your creative endeavor—at least for a little while. But don't get too comfortable. It won't be long before you're ready to update, archive, and modify your existing pages. In Chapter 12 (the final chapter in this book), we provide you with a few pointers that you can use to keep your site alive and dust-free.

Key Points

- You can use FTP applications to copy files from your computer to a server.

- You can transfer files and folders by using FTP applications, network places and Web folders, the Web Publishing wizard, ISP online forms, HTML editors, and browsers, such as Internet Explorer.

- If your server supports network places, you can use the My Network Places feature to easily upload and manipulate your Web site's files and folders in the same manner you manage local folders.

- When uploading Web files to a server, retain your Web site's file and folder structure, including using the exact naming and organizational parameters as the files and folders on your local computer.

- After you upload Web pages, always view them online to check for errors and broken links.

- To publicize your Web site, register with search engines.

- Consider adding META tags to your HTML documents to somewhat control how search engines categorize your site.

- Finally, let others know that your site is live—by word of mouth and other typical communication channels—and start the exchange of online information!

Updating, Archiving, and Moving On

By the time you've reached this point in the book, you've probably posted your Web pages online and you're enjoying a little breather. Congratulations! Soon, though, you'll want to explore ways in which you can modify and improve your site's visual appeal and content. In this chapter we give you some practical instructions for post-Web-site-production tasks as well as provide you with a few pointers for additional Web-site-creation opportunities that will arise now that you've passed the "beginner" stage of Web development.

Note   Keep in mind that even though this is the final chapter of the book and you're no longer sitting in the neophyte section among Web page developers, your Web-site-creation education is far from over. The Web-page-creation skills you've learned in this book can carry you a long way, but your skills have only just begun to blossom. In the words of Winston Churchill: "This is not the end. It is not even the beginning of the end. But it is, perhaps, the end of the beginning."

Updating Your Web Pages

One of the beauties of Web sites is that they're never really "done." Just as most self-actualized people never stop learning, effective Web pages are evolving works-in-progress. So after a few days away from your Web pages, you might want to think about ways you can update your Web site to make it more interesting and useful for visitors.

Reasons to Update

A few reasons exist that bolster the argument for updating your Web pages regularly. The following list includes some of the reasons we've run across. Pick and choose whichever seem relevant for your needs, or feel free to concoct some custom reasons for keeping your Web site fresh.

- To supply new and updated information.

- To show viewers that you're just as interested in your Web site as you want them to be. (This one's a biggie.)

- To encourage people to return to your site (not to bore them with the same old stuff).

- To provide additional features for visitors that you didn't address when you first created the site.

- To remove features that visitors find distracting or confusing.

- To promote special causes.

- To celebrate an upcoming holiday or event.

- To reflect changes in the site's parent entity (such as a company that might want to incorporate a new logo, slogan, or color scheme).

- To incorporate up-to-date technologies, such as cascading style sheets (CSS).

Keep in mind that the overriding reason you update pages should be to *benefit your viewers*. You shouldn't update your site just to provide a forum for your experimentation with Web page gimmicks. Likewise, if you have a popular item on your Web page, resist the urge to remove it just because you're tired of it. If viewers find an item useful and they voice their opinions through your feedback page, guest book, or other avenues, keep the component or upgrade it to make viewers even happier. Just as you had a reason for adding each element when you first created your Web pages, make sure you have reasons for adding and removing items when you modify your site. In other words, think before you act.

Easily Updateable Elements

Certain page elements lend themselves to being updated easily. For the most part, you'll probably want to maintain your Web site's overall structure, navigation bars, logos, color schemes, and contact information. Occasionally, though, such as when a company revamps its image or embarks on a new marketing campaign, these elements are changed intentionally. But you shouldn't make arbitrary changes just because, for example, you get tired of blue and want to try purple. Here are the four Web site elements that change most often:

■ Graphics

■ Text

■ Last-updated date

■ Recommended links

The reason the preceding elements are easy to change and are changed more frequently than others is because they generally convey a Web site's content. Most viewers can appreciate a well-styled Web site, but they return to and use sites that contain dynamic (as opposed to static) information.

Updating Tips and Tricks

Now that we've briefly outlined why you might want to update your site in the future as well as the types of elements you might want to change, let's look at some guidelines you should follow when you're updating your Web pages. Most of these guidelines are based on common sense, but they're worth noting here anyway.

> **Tip** Before an updated page goes live, consider temporarily uploading the page with a "fake" name, such as index2.html. You can then enter the path to the page in your Address bar and view the page online before enabling users to access the page directly. After you're sure the page properly reflects your changes, replace the existing file with the newly created file. Safely replacing your files is discussed in the next section.

Above all, avoid taking your perfectly good page and rendering it useless through unnecessarily complex design or coding modifications. We've actually seen clean, once-working sites "updated" with the latest and greatest Web features that were ultimately rendered unviewable by the majority of browsers. Here's a motto to keep in mind: *Aim for "better," not "deader."*

And because change is inevitable, consider the next guideline as well: *Create a regular schedule for updates.*

> **Tip**   If your site doesn't require an update or you just don't have time for revisions this month, at least take a moment to refresh the "last updated" date on your home page to indicate to viewers that you've recently checked in.

A regular schedule forces you to clearly plan how you want to update your Web site as well as provides a target date for completing future changes. For example, let's say you decide that you'll update your site every third Monday of each month. Throughout the month, you can jot down update notes to yourself or create local versions of live pages. When the third Monday rolls around, commit yourself to implementing any planned changes and uploading modified pages. Then start taking notes for the next month's update. Of course, in some instances, a quick nonscheduled update might be in order—for example, if a phone number needs to be corrected, a typo needs to be fixed, or a broken link needs to be redirected. But for more routine changes, you should try to stick to some regular schedule. Randomly updating your site can lead to slovenly or chaotic practices in which your Web page can either gather too much dust or change too frequently (which can cause regular visitors to miss some of the updates).

Here's the next rule of thumb: *Avoid directly updating a live site.*

Some HTML editors (Microsoft FrontPage included) enable you to edit live sites. This feature can be useful for emergency fixes, such as the incorrect information, typos, and broken links just mentioned. In most cases, though, you should follow these steps when beginning your update:

1 Download the most recent version of the page you want to update (this step is extremely important, because it ensures that you're working on the most up-to-date version of the page).

2 Redesign the page locally.

3 Preview the page in a browser.

4 Upload the modified page only after you've ensured that the page runs and displays properly.

> **Tip**   When you're ready to upload a new "replacement" page to your Web site, consider renaming the existing page before you copy the new page to your server. That way, you have a copy of the existing page on hand if your new page doesn't work as expected. For more information about saving information, see the next section, "Archiving Web Page Elements."

Updating a live site might result in users seeing half-completed changes as you work on the page. Furthermore, you might be hard pressed to revert to an earlier version of your site if you need to recover from disastrous or undesirable changes. (Later in the chapter we talk about archiving to avoid losing "old" data.)

Finally, as part of your routine maintenance on your site, you should follow this practice: *Regularly check the hyperlinks on your pages.*

As you know, the Web is extremely fluid; pages come and go. So check your links frequently (remember, you can use link checking software and online services to perform this task), because nothing signals a neglected Web site as clearly as hyperlinks to nonexistent pages.

Archiving Web Page Elements

Updating your Web site goes hand in hand with saving past versions of your Web pages. This practice is referred to as *archiving*. The underlying concept of archiving is this: *When you update your site, don't throw away your old Web page elements!* At least not right away.

Lingo　*Archiving* refers to copying files onto a tape or disk for long-term storage.

Best practices dictate that you let your has-been Web pages and graphics hang around for a while (at least six months in most cases and possibly a year, if you can foresee any chance that you'll need the "old" information or graphics, especially if you can't easily re-create the information). The most notable reason for archiving instead of deleting is that you never know when you might need old text, graphics, JavaScript, style settings, and so forth. Many times you can use old pages as templates or reuse old graphics in new ways. You'll find that creating an Archive folder to store past page elements is much easier than re-creating graphics and data after you've obliterated them.

Tip　When archiving HTML documents, remember to archive the associated graphics files and folders. Store the graphics in a folder with the same name as the original graphics folder so that your archived pages' links will work properly.

You can store archived information in several ways. The easiest way is to create a folder named *Archive* and copy past Web page elements into subfolders within that folder. You can store an Archive folder and its subfolders in several places:

- Local computer
- Removable storage device, such as floppy disks, Zip disks, or writable CDs

■   Web site's hosting service (You'll probably have more than enough server space for a while.)

■   Online storage space (such as the storage cabinets available on the MSN Groups site)

Another way to think of archiving is as a method to copy and store Web pages before you choose to stop displaying them for viewers. For example, let's say you created a new home page. Your updating and archiving procedures might take the following form:

1   You've named the new page *index2.html* and uploaded it to the Internet, and the page checked out. You're now ready to display the new home page in place of the existing home page.

2   Before you rename *index2.html* to *index.html* and replace the existing index.html page, you create a subfolder within the Archive folder. You give the folder an informative name, such as *Old Home Page-June-29-2002*, and then you copy the existing index.html page into the Archive folder's subfolder.

3   After copying index.html to the Archive folder, you delete the existing index.html file in your Web site's main directory.

4   You then rename *index2.html* to *index.html* and place the new index.html file into your Web site's main directory.

In the preceding steps, the old index.html file is safely stowed away for possible future use and the new page displays. Creating an organized archiving storage system and directory-naming scheme can make finding "old" information a snap.

After you master updating and archiving—and it shouldn't take you long—and you've worked your way through this book, you can safely say that you've covered all the basics of Web page creation. The next logical progression is to forge beyond the basics and into the realm of intermediate and advanced Web page development.

Moving Beyond Basic Web Pages

As we wrap up this book, we hope you've found that you've gained a strong foundation for Web page creation. Although we could go on for a few hundred more pages describing more advanced Web page creation techniques (and we really wouldn't mind doing that, either!), we realize that we've had to pick and choose what's most helpful when it comes to creating Web pages the *faster* and *smarter* way. We want to point out, though, that although we've covered quite a bit of information in this book, we haven't explained everything: Many more advanced techniques for creating Web pages are available to you. At some point you'll probably want to incorporate multimedia elements, such as video, animation, and audio (although we touch on some of these components in Chapters 9 and 10). Or maybe you'll want to add security features to your Web site by employing encryption algorithms or password protection schemes. Or possibly you'll want to link or embed custom style sheets in your Web pages to help maintain your Web site's consistency as well as conform to the most currently accepted code standards. At this point in the book, we're confident that your understanding of the Web should enable you to move on to more complex issues if you so desire. In the meantime, because you've stuck with us this long, we'll give you a couple bonus JavaScripts to play with to give you a taste of more advanced techniques.

Bonus JavaScript Components

One simple way you can add pizzazz to your sites is to incorporate JavaScript into your HTML pages. JavaScript is a lightweight programming language that enables you to add Web page functionality by inserting JavaScript code into an HTML document.

Typically, JavaScript enables effects such as fading backgrounds, button rollover effects, cursor animations, multicolored text, banner displays, stylized text, password protection, games, and other creative design elements and useful utilities. Fortunately, you don't have to be a programmer to use JavaScript. A number of sites offer free JavaScript code samples that you can copy and paste into your HTML documents. For example, check out the sites *www.usabstract.com/ cutpastejava.shtml, http://javascript-page.com,* and *http://builder.cnet.com/ webbuilding/0-7600.html* to find some clever, free-for-your-use JavaScripts. Additional links to JavaScript codes are listed on the Creation Guide Web site's Resources page at *www.creationguide.com/resources*.

Just for fun, we've included two scripts that you can play with at home and use on your Web pages—a countdown component and a background color selection feature. To use JavaScript samples, simply type the JavaScript code into a text document or an existing HTML document. Save the document as an HTML file (remember, you might have to right-click the filename and change the *.txt* extension to *.html*), and then view the document in your browser.

If you prefer not to manually enter the code necessary to create the countdown element and the background color selection feature (or if you want to see the JavaScript in action without actually creating HTML documents), visit the *www.creationguide.com/javascript/countdown* and *www.creationguide.com/ javascript/bgcolors* Web pages. Display the source code on either page, and then copy and paste the code into a locally stored HTML document.

Adding a Countdown Element to a Web Page

You can add a couple of lines of JavaScript code to create an automated count-down component on your Web page. Figure 12-1 shows the code necessary to create the countdown component. The countdown component automatically counts down to the date of your choice. You can change the *January 1, 2004* date to any date, and you can customize the countdown message by modifying the *days until the year 2004!* text. (The elements you can customize display in orange in Figure 12-1.) Figure 12-2 shows the countdown component in action.

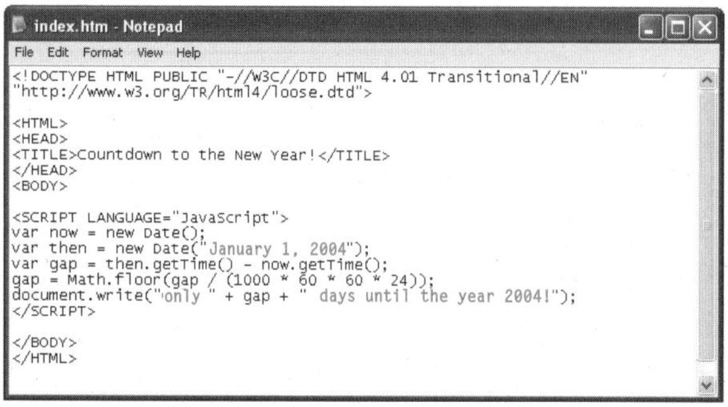

Figure 12-1   You can use JavaScript to add a countdown component to an HTML document.

```
Only 549 days until the year 2004!
```

Figure 12-2   The countdown component shows how many days remain before a specific date.

Providing the Background Color Selection Feature

Using JavaScript, you can display background color selection buttons on your Web page so that users can display your page with the background color of their choice. This feature is mostly just for fun, but it's a nice practice in inserting Java-Script and sampling the effect JavaScript can have in Web page development endeavors.

Figure 12-3 shows the code necessary to create the background color selec-tion component. You can use any color names or hexadecimal numbers (refer to *www.creationguide.com/colorchart* for color hexadecimal values and color names) when providing color selections. Remember, if you change an `onclick` value (the color you want to display after a user clicks a button), you should also

change the button's name by modifying the button's `value` parameter. In Figure
12-3, *onclick* values and *button value* parameters display in orange. Figure 12-4
shows the page that displays as a result of the code shown in Figure 12-3. To see
the color-selection buttons in action, visit *www.creationguide.com/javascript/
bgcolors*.

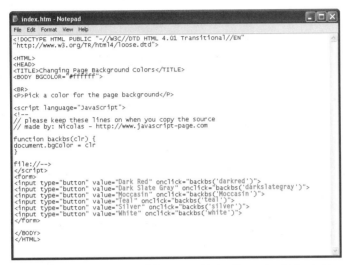

Figure 12-3   You can use JavaScript to provide background selection buttons in an HTML document.

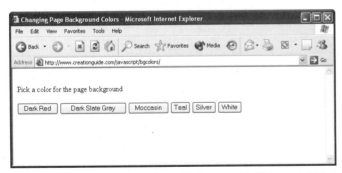

Figure 12-4   The code shown in Figure 12-3 creates this Web page, which displays color-selection buttons to
viewers; viewers can click the buttons to change the Web page's background color.

If you search the Web using the term *JavaScript*, you'll find all sorts of free
JavaScripts. When you find free JavaScript online, you can copy the code and
paste it directly into your HTML documents—no typing required! So keep those
Ctrl+C (copy) and Ctrl+V (paste) keyboard commands in mind when you want
to quickly and efficiently add JavaScript features (or other freely offered Web
code) to your Web pages.

Tip   Whenever you copy JavaScript or other freely available Web code into a document, ensure that you test your pages in various popular browsers to verify that your pages display properly for the greatest number of visitors.

Key Points

- Consider updating your Web pages regularly to keep visitors happy and Web site content fresh.

- Archive old pages and graphics (at least for a while) in case you need to reuse elements.

- Don't fear the unknown! Have fun—move beyond basic creation techniques and try your hand at various advanced procedures. You might be surprised to find how much you've learned.

- Finally—our last key point in this book. We hope you've enjoyed learning about Web page creation as much as we enjoyed creating this book and the companion site. Feel free to use all the resources incorporated into the companion site and drop us a line (mm@creationguide.com and jc@creationguide.com) if you ever have a question or want to share your Web page creation results. We'd certainly enjoy hearing from you, and we'll do our best to respond to your queries as quickly as possible. Best wishes for success on the Web!

Index